CITIES AS ENGINES OF SUSTAINABLE COMPETITIVENESS

The European Institute for Comparative Urban Research, EURICUR, was founded in 1988 and has its seat with Erasmus University Rotterdam. EURICUR is the heart and pulse of an extensive network of European cities and universities. EURICUR's principal objective is to stimulate fundamental international comparative research into matters that are of interest to cities. To that end, EURICUR coordinates, initiates and carries out studies of subjects of strategic value for urban management today and in the future. Through its network EURICUR has privileged access to crucial information regarding urban development in Europe and North America and to key persons at all levels, working in different public and private organizations active in metropolitan areas. EURICUR closely cooperates with the Eurocities Association, representing more than 100 large European cities. As a scientific institution, one of EURICUR's core activities is to respond to the increasing need for information that broadens and deepens the insight into the complex process of urban development, among others by disseminating the results of its investigations by international book publications. These publications are especially valuable for city governments, supranational, national and regional authorities, chambers of commerce, real estate developers and investors, academics and students, and others with an interest in urban affairs.

Euricur website: http://www.euricur.nl

This book is part of a series published by Ashgate under the auspices of EURICUR, Erasmus University Rotterdam.

Titles in the series include:

Sports and City Marketing in European Cities
Leo van den Berg, Erik Braun and Alexander H.J. Otgaar

The Student City
Leo van den Berg and Antonio P. Russo

The Safe City
Leo van den Berg, Peter M.J. Pol, Guiliano Mingardo and Carolien J.M. Spellier

E-Governance in European and South African Cities
Leo van den Berg, Andre van der Meer, Willem van Winden and Paulus Woets

National Policy Responses to Urban Challenges in Europe
Leo van den Berg, Erik Braun and Jan van der Meer

Empowering Metropolitan Regions Through New Forms of Cooperation
Alexander Otgaar, Leo van den Berg, Jan van der Meer, Carolien Speller

Industrial Tourism: Opportunities for City and Enterprise
Alexander H.J. Otgaar, Leo van den Berg, Christian Berger and Rachel Xiang

Toward Healthy Cities
Alexander Otgaar, Jeroen Klijs and Leo van den Berg

Cities as Engines of Sustainable Competitiveness

Competitiveness

European Urban Policy in Practice

Edited by

LEO VAN DEN BERG

JAN VAN DER MEER *and* **LUIS CARVALHO**

Euricur

EUROPEAN INSTITUTE FOR COMPARATIVE URBAN RESEARCH

European Institute for Comparative Urban Research,
Erasmus University Rotterdam,
The Netherlands
www.euricur.nl

Routledge
Taylor & Francis Group

LONDON AND NEW YORK

First published 2014 by Ashgate Publishing

Published 2016 by Routledge
2 Park Square, Milton Park, Abingdon, Oxfordshire OX14 4RN
711 Third Avenue, New York, NY 10017, USA

First issued in paperback 2016

Routledge is an imprint of the Taylor & Francis Group, an informa business

British Library Cataloguing in Publication Data
A catalogue record for this book is available from the British Library

The Library of Congress has cataloged the printed edition as follows:
Berg, Leo van den.
  Cities as engines of sustainable competitiveness : European urban policy in practice / by Leo van den Berg, Jan van der Meer and Luis Carvalho.
    pages cm. – (EURICUR series (European Institute for Comparative Urban Research))
  Includes bibliographical references and index.
  ISBN 978-1-4724-2702-1 (hardback) – ISBN 978-1-4724-2703-8 (ebook) –
  ISBN 978-1-4724-2704-5 (epub) 1. Urban policy–Europe. 2. Cities and towns –
Europe. 3. City planning – Europe. 4. Sustainable development – Europe. I. Title.

  HT151.B4197 2014
  307.76094–dc23

                                                                        2013033198

ISBN 13: 978-1-138-27983-4 (pbk)
ISBN 13: 978-1-4724-2702-1 (hbk)

Contents

Contents

List of Tables

List of Contributors

The Editors

Leo van den Berg is Director of Euricur and Professor of Urban Economics and Urban Management at Erasmus University Rotterdam.

Jan van der Meer is Associate Director of Euricur and Associate Professor of Urban Economics at Erasmus University Rotterdam.

Luis de Carvalho is Senior Researcher at Euricur and at the Department for Urban, Port and Transport Economics, Erasmus University Rotterdam.

The Contributors

Karima Azaoum is a research assistant at the City of Rotterdam.

Dave Carter is Head of the Manchester Digital Development Agency (MDDA) at Manchester City Council and Chair of the EU Connected Smart Cities Network, a joint initiative of EUROCITIES and the European Network of Living Labs (ENoLL).

Jamie Cudden is a Research Manager at the Planning and Economic Development Department, Dublin City Council.

Harriet Ellwein has a degree in geography, sociology and spatial planning from the Technical University of Munich. She has been involved in several national and international assignments in regional economic development. She is presently deputy Head of Department of Regional and Human Resources Development at the Economic Development Agency, City of Dortmund, Germany.

Eero Holstila is Senior Advisor of Futuro Consulting Helsinki Ltd, former Director of the Office of Economic Development, City of Helsinki (2006-2011) and CEO of Culminatum Innovation Ltd (2001-2005). He served as Director of the City of Helsinki Urban Facts (1985-2001).

Barbara Kovacs is an expert in urban development. She worked for many years for the Urban Building Department of the City of Budapest. She currently works for a private architecture firm.

Tanja Lahti works as project manager at City of Helsinki Urban Facts. She works with the open data service Helsinki Region Infoshare.

Chris de Lange is the coordinator of International and European Affairs at the City of Rotterdam.

Hildegard Mai has a degree in spatial planning (Technical University of Dortmund). She has been a city planner for almost 20 years and she is European Officer at the Economic Development Agency, City of Dortmund, Germany. Her main activities are in the field of EU Structural Funding, policies, projects and fund-raising.

Asta Manninen is Director of City of Helsinki Urban Facts, which is the department in charge of urban statistics, urban research, and information services as well as the city archives. She is in charge of co-operation activities with universities, research institutes and major cities in Europe. Her current attention is focused on open data development, namely the Helsinki Region Infoshare.

Oriol Nel·lo is Professor of Geography at Universitat Autònoma de Barcelona. He was the Director of the Institute of Metropolitan Studies of Barcelona (1988-1999), elected member of the parliament of Catalunya (1999-2003) and Head of Planning at the Government of Catalunya (2003-2011). He is also a visiting Professor at various universities and author of books and scientific articles in the field of urban studies and planning.

Sanna Ranto is a researcher at City of Helsinki Urban Facts.

Steven Sterkx has been European Officer for the City of Antwerp since 2010. He holds a PhD in Political Science (University of Antwerp, 2006), and is guest lecturer at the University of Leuven (KULeuven) on the history of European integration.

Anja Vallittu is Senior Advisor to the Mayor at the City of Helsinki.

Hans Verdonk is European Union representative for City of Rotterdam at the G-4 European Office, a co-operative venture between the four major Dutch cities.

Preface

By the mid-1980s, after three decades of rising prosperity, many European cities faced acute challenges such as deindustrialization, job losses, depopulation and emerging social and environmental issues. How to cope with these problems? How to turn cities into engines of broader European recovery? In 1986, the City of Rotterdam involved other European Mayors to discuss and address those issues. During the same year, Eurocities was founded to champion the interests of cities and advocate for their roles in tackling European challenges. Two years later, the Cities of Rotterdam and Barcelona – together with Erasmus University Rotterdam – created the European Institute for Comparative Urban Research (Euricur). Over the last two decades, to a lesser or greater extent, different commentators, organizations and policymakers started to pay more attention to the role of cities in national and European development.

The idea behind this book is more recent, but have the previous developments as background. How have European urban policies been developed and implemented in practice? How are cities tackling contemporary economic recovery challenges in times of heightened social and climate challenges? These are questions that this book discusses, the result of a joint reflection process launched in 2011 by the Euricur and the City of Rotterdam. Chris de Lange and Hans Verdonk were enthusiastic initiators of this process, providing valuable insight for this book and supporting the process throughout. We would also like to specially thank the persons who more closely contributed to this process, and who authored the chapters in this book: Steven Sterkx (Antwerp), Oriol Nel·lo (Barcelona), Barbara Kovacs (Budapest), Harriet Ellwein and Hildegard Mai (Dortmund), Jamie Cudden (Dublin), Eero Holstila, Anja Vallittu, Sanna Ranto, Tanja Lahti and Asta Manninen (Helsinki), Dave Carter (Manchester) and Karima Azaoum (Rotterdam).

We are also grateful to Alexander Otgaar, for the early editing of the case studies in this book, to Ankimon Vernede and Monique Valkenburg for helping with the overall administrative organization and to Jan-Jelle Witte for his support in the final editing of this book.

The Editors
Leo van den Berg
Jan van der Meer
Luis de Carvalho

Chapter 1
Cities as Engines of
Sustainable Competitiveness

Cities as "Engines": An Increasingly Acknowledged Evidence

There is nowadays plenty of evidence that cities are engines of growth and development for regions and nations. Cities are widely recognised as major sources of human, knowledge and organisational resources that support competitiveness and innovation policies. Of course, this potential is heterogeneous among cities and strongly dependent upon their dimension, economic structure and the ways they are connected nationally and internationally (e.g. OECD, 2011). Yet, whatever the group of cities considered, competitiveness and innovation-oriented policies can hardly be conceived without a strong involvement of cities as "engines" within regions and nations. Contrarily to the popular discourse, it seems that "the world is not flat". On the contrary, it is becoming more "convex" and the economic-innovation role of cities is increasing (Rodriguez-Pose and Crescenzi, 2008; McCann, 2008). Competitive countries have competitive cities, i.e. cities with the *dynamic* capacity to grow and develop over time, *nurturing* and *attracting* jobs, people and skills (e.g. Kitson et al., 2004; van Winden and Carvalho, 2008).

However, on the flip side, cities are also recognised as the main locus of acute problems in modern societies, such as ageing, unemployment, exclusion and the need for successful integration of different ethnicities (DG Regio, 2011). The same goes for environmental tensions, climate change and the need to decouple congestion, CO_2 emissions and economic growth (e.g. Mingardo et al., 2009). Therefore, a close link seems to exist between cities and the need for social innovations (Moulaert et al., 2007). Cities are places where promising and innovative governance models emerge. In the present times of global economic downturn and generalised uncertainty, it has been also advocated that European cities, metropolises and urban regions are key players in the fight against unemployment and climate change, towards a more resource efficient and inclusive society. It is also widely acknowledged that in order to sustain its competitiveness over time, a city must balance growth with social cohesion and environmental quality (e.g. van den Berg et al., 2005; Pike et al., 2010). In this sense, society and environment are not anymore a restriction to growth – they are integral components of the development "equation".

In Europe, and besides its most affluent regions and nations, the wide scope of the link between cities and innovation has also strong implications for urban policies in so-called "Convergence" regions. Cities play a key role in striking a balance between cohesion and competitiveness in these places. Moreover, they also play an active role in European spatial planning issues. When cities are seen from the perspective of their networks within wider territories (e.g. the configuration of urban systems), urban policies become a powerful instrument of spatial planning. The role of cities is crucial in order to generate spill over effects in wider territories, namely in low density areas with limited entrepreneurial capabilities.

Cities in the EU Regional Policy Agendas

Over the last decade, cities and urban development issues gained increased relevance and advocates within the European Union (EU) Cohesion Policy framework. Overall, this recognition has evolved hand-in-hand with:

- The knowledge and experience derived from successful integrative urban approaches, notably the so-called URBAN intervention ("mainstreamed" through the ERDF – European Regional Development Fund – during 2007-2013);
- New scientific evidence on the role of cities and regions for national and European development, supported by recent literatures in urban and regional studies and policy;
- The increasing relevance of knowledge, innovation and competitiveness objectives within the broader guidelines of Cohesion Policy;
- The expansion of EU city networks and forums for best practice exchange and policy circulation (e.g. supported by the URBACT programme);
- A number of ministerial and inter-governmental "urban agendas" (e.g. Leipzig charter on sustainable European cities, Toledo declaration), claiming for integrative urban approaches and for the enhanced role of cities tackling broader EU challenges.

DG Regio – the EU Directorate-General for Regional and Urban Policy – is clearly a supporter of the role played by cities in EU policy (as shown by recently adding the word "Urban" to its official designation). Recently, DG Regio launched a reflection process called "Cities of Tomorrow" (DG Regio, 2011) with a large number of urban experts and representatives of EU cities to discuss European urban futures and the role of cities tackling broader European competitiveness and development challenges. In this study, it has been clearly stated by the Regional Policy commissar Johannes Hahn that "the development of our cities will determine the future of Europe" (DG Regio, 2011, p. i).

Recently, DG Regio commissioned the study of a large number of urban development best-practices of integrated approaches supported during 2007-2013, in order to understand how cities can be "engines" in the implementation of the new EU2020 strategy across its "smart", "sustainable" and "inclusive" dimensions (EU, 2013). The relations between DG Regio and the scholarly practice that advocates the role of cities increased during the last years, as illustrated by the closer links with learned societies such as the Regional Studies Association, or the hiring of renowned urban economics scholars as permanent special advisors. The recent place-based and "smart specialization" approaches to Regional Policy also recognise that the differentiated roles and capacities of EU cities and regions should be taken seriously in policy design and support (McCann and Ortega-Argilés, 2011).

However, the recognition of cities as engines of growth, cohesion and environmental sustainability does not necessarily mean that the role of Local Authorities and Municipalities in the design and implementation of EU policy has increased in the same proportion (See Chapter 2). In EU policy spheres, many advocate that the role of Local Authorities should increase, as they are closer to the problems and in a privileged position to tackle opportunities (subsidiary principle). However, simultaneously, it is also recognised that the administrative boundaries of cities are not the right scale to tackle most of the economic, social and environmental challenges of urban and regional development (van den Berg et al., 1997; DG Regio, 2011). All in all, despite the heightened expectations attributed to cities in EU Regional policy as "engines", the most effective governance models for EU policy design and implementation are still debatable (e.g. Barca, 2009).

Looking Back

Despite the "momentum" of cities in EU policy, their role was not always recognised. Over the last decades, many EU City representatives,[1] academics and other players struggled to demonstrate the "urban added value" and the role of cities in national and regional development. For example, back in 1986 the City of Rotterdam initiated – in close cooperation with the urban economics department of Erasmus University Rotterdam – a meeting of city mayors representing large cities from the EU member states (12 at that time). The prime topic was how to re-stimulate prosperity and wellbeing in cities. At that moment the European economy was still recovering from the energy crisis of the late 1970s, sharp inflation and the beginning of a large de-industrialization process. It was the first significant slowdown after three decades of rising prosperity in Europe. Large cities were early confronted with severe problems such as depopulation, industrial decline and emerging social and environmental problems.

An important acknowledgement from that meeting (and others) was that cities should start to be paid more attention. They were not only places where problems become visible, but also cradles for solutions of regional and national problems. In 1986, a foundation was set up to position the role and defend the interests of

---

1 In this book "cities" refer to the "places" themselves; "Cities" refer to Local Authorities or Local Governments.

cities on a European level. Two years later, the Municipalities of Rotterdam and Barcelona and Erasmus University Rotterdam created the European Institute for Comparative Urban Research (EURICUR). Simultaneously, a number of lobbying organizations – such as EUROCITIES – were founded and gained considerable influence during the 1990s (e.g. EUROCITIES, 2011), contributing to position the role of cities in EU policy agendas. Since then, the EU has developed several specific initiatives and policy programmes supporting the integrated development of cities (such as the URBAN initiative). Also at the national level, and beyond sectoral approaches, many governments started to pay more attention to cities and urban development issues (van den Berg et al., 2007).

Over the last two decades, supported by local, national and EU budgets, a considerable number of investments and policy-supported initiatives have had cities as main destinations. Those investments focused in many hard and soft domains, like economic development and promotion, skills, infrastructure, quality of life, social inclusion, the environment, and many others. Those have become increasingly important as Cities increasing looked to become "competitive", differentiate themselves and, overall, attract jobs and skills (van den Berg and Braun, 1999; Pike et al., 2006; Turok, 2009).

The Aims of this Book

With the support of case studies from eight European cities, this book looks back at two decades of "competitiveness-oriented" urban policies in Europe. Moreover it looks at current challenges cities face to sustain their economic position, balancing it with social progress and environmental improvements. We thus speak about *sustainable competitiveness*, defined as "the ability of cities to keep growing and developing over time while fostering social cohesion and environmental quality". This book complements previous surveys on local and urban development and competitiveness-based strategies (e.g. Pike et al., 2006; Turok, 2009) in the sense that it provides longer term views on the evolution of such policies at the city level, from the personal perspective of City officials.

More concretely, it looks at:

- How has the urban dimension in EU policies evolved over time? What kinds of urban policy have been supported by the EU over the last two decades and how have Cities been involved?
- Which portfolios of competitiveness-oriented policies have been developed by European Cities over the last two decades? How do the Cities see the link between urban/spatial development policies and sustainable competitiveness?

Besides taking stock of former experiences and developments, the book also has a prospective character. Like in the mid-1980s, Europe seems to be facing a new "discontinuity" period, in which cities are called once again to become "engines" of growth and development. However, the playing field has changed dramatically. The links between economic growth, employment and social progress are weakening (DG Regio, 2011). Social and environmental problems in cities are heightened and imposing new ways to strike balanced growth. Therefore, this book concludes by fleshing out a number of challenges and initiatives taken by the eight European cities and their governments on the face of current challenges, namely in order to pave the way towards more competitive and sustainable urban economies. In other words, it sketches a number of policies and initiatives of cities to maintain or regain "sustainable competitiveness". Thus:

- Which new types of policies and initiatives can be currently found in European cities to steer sustainable competitiveness? What lessons and insights can be derived?

The Process behind this Book

The contents of this book are the result of a joint discussion and reflection process launched in 2011 by EURICUR, in close cooperation with the City of Rotterdam and with the participation of eight European Cities – Antwerp, Barcelona, Budapest, Dortmund, Dublin, Helsinki, Manchester and Rotterdam itself. A number of workshops were developed between EURICUR and City representatives in order to discuss, formalize and exchange knowledge on the abovementioned issues. Those meetings and workshops took place in Rotterdam during 2011-2013 and during the EUROCITIES annual meeting 2011 (AGM) in Genoa.

Each City representative – mostly City's senior staff and Heads of Department, with long experience in EU policy – was asked to prepare and present an overview of their city's socio-economic development over the last 20 years. Moreover, they were also asked to describe and explore major policy changes, developments and initiatives with impact on the competitiveness of the city. Finally, each representative was asked to describe the current situation and recently implemented (or newly intended) policies to improve the competitive position of the city in the longer term. Additionally, a report was also prepared analysing the evolution of the "urban dimension" in the EU Regional Policy over the last decade.

Each report was based on a self-assessment by the City representatives, often with the internal support of other staff members of the City; it was presented and discussed with the participants during the workshops and meetings. Its content was primarily informative, based as much as possible on facts and figures, but also on the long experience, expertise and privileged "inside knowledge" of the involved officials, bringing the resulting report's narrative more valuable and unique.

The edited reports are now published as chapters in this book. Their focus and depth of analysis vary – some focus on a specific dimension of a city's competitiveness, others are broader; some are more analytic, others more descriptive. All in all, they convey a number of valuable viewpoints that help us understanding the dynamics of urban development, the rationale of the policies and challenges involved in making sustainable competitiveness really happen. Out of these reports, a general synthesis/overview was developed and progressively discussed during the meetings, with insights directly borrowed from the narratives of local city experts themselves.

Structure and Contents of this Book

The chapters of this book – developed out of the abovementioned reflection process – can be read independently. However, they are here presented under a sequential logic.

Following this introduction, Chapter 2 presents an analysis of how the EU changed its policies and views towards cities over the last decade. It presents a well-grounded narrative based on extensive documentation since the 1960s, together with inside-knowledge from experienced City officials in Brussels. It demonstrates that the attention to urban questions has been on the European agenda for already over 50 years. Yet, there have been considerable swings and changes of position, through a process in which politics and power tended to dominate over rationality. The participation of Cities in policy making and implementation of European programmes has been still too often dependent on the willingness of Member States and regional authorities. The recent EU2020 agenda tends to imply a much stronger involvement of Cities, but whether this will happen or not remains to be seen.

Chapters 3-10 present the reports on competitiveness-related policies in each of the cities over the last two decades. Each chapter is structured along three broad sections: 1) City profile; 2) Developments and key policy changes since the early 1990s and 3) Current state of the city. The reports provide an interesting picture of the context and urban policy dynamics of the eight participating cities. This information, combined with the overviews of the recent history of urban development, is vital to understand the urban strategies that are set in motion to support future "sustainable competitiveness".

The report on Antwerp stresses the role attached by the City to improvements in the built environment as a way to increase liveability and boost the city's attractiveness, i.e. to attract and retain businesses, talent and visitors. The report shows how the City considers liveability and attractiveness as "umbrella" objectives, making other urban provisions (e.g. social housing, green areas, leisure, child and elderly care) closely linked to it. To this effect, the report describes flagship urban redevelopment projects that took place over the last decade in order to improve the City's public space and living environment (benefiting, among others, from EU funding, namely through the URBAN initiative). Yet, many urban challenges remain, of which mobility, safety and demographic shifts ("greening", "ageing" and "colouring") are among the most pressing. There are still considerable social divides in the city. Integrated spatial planning and improved community participation are seen as pivotal to tackle these challenges.

The analysis of the urban development of Barcelona skips the well-known "Olympic narrative" and focuses on the benefits and tensions provoked by the phenomena of "Metropolitanisation" since the 1990s. Metropolitanization largely increased the competitiveness and economic strengths of Barcelona, namely by creating scale and diversity, by facilitating the integration of regional markets and access to services while decreasing sub-regional development imbalances. However, on the flip side, it came together with urban sprawl and thus with mobility tensions, social segregation and many mono-functional area developments. The present and future competitive position of Barcelona is thus jeopardized: the urban agglomeration risks becoming environmentally unsustainable, functionally inefficient and lacking social solidarity. It is suggested that a deep re-thinking of urban policies is needed (housing, renewal, transport, environment). However, despite the uncertainty caused by the financial turmoil and generalized austerity policies in Southern Europe, the city is nowadays better equipped than in the past to tackle those challenges in an integrated way – namely due to the approval of a long-awaited Metropolitan Territorial Plan and a new regional governance system.

The chapter on Budapest brings to the fore the urban development challenges faced by a post-communist capital in the transition to a market economy. It describes how the values/orthodoxies of competitiveness, sustainability, liveability and quality of life permeated the local policy discourse, but also how their effective implementation was hampered by lack of integrated planning and complex administrative and governance features. Tax cuts and foreign investment inflows came associated with economic growth but also with considerable urban tensions, hardly tackled by reactive planning efforts. The report describes how the City is trying to strengthen the link between urban spatial planning and economic development objectives towards a more long-term approach. Among the priorities described – to which EU support will keep being pivotal – are the improvement of urban accessibility and the revitalization of a number of districts; among them, the planning of specific "knowledge locations" to support the city's strengths in science and R&D.

From the well-known *Ruhr* area in Germany, the City of Dortmund reports on the economic and competitive reconversion of the city following the sharp decline of its old flagship industries – coal, steel and beer. Over the last two decades, the City and its policies have been closely supporting innovation, clustering, job creation and overall competitiveness objectives. The report shows how this objective has mobilized strong coalitions of local actors – e.g. Universities, R&D institutes, the leading firm ThyssenKrupp, among others – with the active support of the Mayor's office. Since 1999, the "Dortmund project" has comprehensively integrated economic-clustering objectives with heightened urban concerns about liveability, quality of life and urban image, and has been considered transformational in that respect. The project currently inspires a new generation of urban policies to tackle unemployment and social polarization, skills improvement and new cross-clustering initiatives – which are central objectives of the coming EU policy agenda as well.

The report on Dublin describes the city's development during and after the years of the "Celtic Tiger" boom. It highlights the close relation between macroeconomic trends, national Irish policies and Dublin's development. It shows how Dublin has been the engine of Ireland's growth, but also how its developments are strongly influenced by national policy. The remarkable growth and prosperity of Dublin during the Celtic Tiger drove the city to leading positions in many city competitiveness rankings; however, it also came together with manifold urban development challenges, associated with planning and mobility. During the last decade some important urban policy investments focused on the reconversion of former run down city-centre districts towards new knowledge-related uses. The 2008 financial and economic turmoil catalysed the emergence of a new local economic governance model – the Creative Dublin Alliance – with the ambition to strengthen the long-term "smart" economy of Dublin in a more sustained manner.

The case of Helsinki highlights the city's progress over the last two decades as a "knowledge-driven" economy, with high levels of welfare and quality of life. Aging and migrations are likely to impose new challenges in the coming future, but so far the social-spatial disparities in the city are rather small – among others, a result of the long-established selective housing policy with controlled prices. The chapter reports the launching of an internationalization strategy dating from the mid-1990s, in which the City and other arm's length organizations had an important role, strengthening Helsinki's recognition and pre-eminence as an arts and science hub. The report looks into the present with an eye to the future and describes how the City and local actors are building on existing assets to pave the way to new societal breakthroughs (and EU urban policy models); examples are the championing of user-driven innovation, the release of open data and the embedding of design-thinking in society at large.

The chapter on Manchester focuses on the role played by ICTs in the economic and social reconversion of the city, following the massive industrial restructuring of the last decades. It shows how the early advent of the information society and urban ICT policies in Manchester contributed to link objectives of economic diversification with the combat of severe forms of poverty and social exclusion. Since then, the digital strategy of the City has been co-evolving with new societal needs; moreover, its status within the city's strategic framework has increased. The chapter concludes with the on-going visions, policies and ambitions of the City in order to nudge the imaginative use of digital technologies, applications and services for benefit of the public sector, business, education and community at large, an issue presently also under discussion in many EU policy forums.

Last, but not least, the case of Rotterdam describes how the city's development and competitiveness over time has been always closely linked with the development of the port. The report highlights important elements of Rotterdam's transition from a "port and industrial city" into a "city with a world port". Rotterdam is a buoyant business city, but it faces manifold social challenges, namely social-spatial polarization and "selective migration". During the 1990s, the City put strong efforts into improving the physical and living environment, championing integrated urban development approaches for different city areas. Yet, the challenge remains – and different policies are being designed in that respect – on how to make the most out of the city's youth and social diversity and how to mitigate climate change, turning it into an economic and innovation opportunity.

Chapter 12, "Back to the Future", wraps up some cross-case insights from the city reports, namely how Cities and their officials have tried (and continue to try) to give substance to sustainable competitiveness. Finally, it provides a prospective look on opportunities and challenges faced by European cities to remain "sustainably competitive", highlighting a number of polices and initiatives currently being designed and implemented in those cities, which can provide insight from EU policy design as well.

References

Barca, F. (2009). *An agenda for a reformed cohesion policy: A place based approach to meeting European Union challenges and expectations.* Brussels: DG Regio.

Berg, L. van den, and Braun, E. (1999). Urban competitiveness, marketing and the need for organising capacity. *Urban Studies,* 36(5-6), 987-999.

Berg, L. van den, Braun, E., and Meer, J. van der (1997). The organising capacity of metropolitan region. *Environment and Planning C: Government and Policy,* 15(3), 253-272.

Berg, L. van den, Braun, E., and Meer, J. van der (2007). *National policy responses to urban challenges in Europe.* Aldershot: Ashgate.

Berg, L. van den, Pol, P., Winden, W. van, and Woets, P. (2005). *European cities in the knowledge economy: The cases of Amsterdam, Dortmund, Eindhoven, Helsinki, Manchester, Munich, Münster, Rotterdam and Zaragoza.* Aldershot: Ashgate.

DG Regio. (2011). *Cities of tomorrow: Challenges, visions, ways forward.* Brussels: DG Regio.

EU-European Union. (2013). *Urban development in the EU: 50 projects supported by the European regional development fund during the 2007-13 period.* Luxembourg: Publications Office of the European Union.

EUROCITIES. (2011). *Developing Europe's urban model: 25 years of EUROCITIES.* Brussels: EUROCITIES.

Kitson, M., Martin, R., and Tyler, P. (2004). Regional competitiveness: An elusive yet key concept? *Regional Studies,* 38(9), 991-999.

McCann, P. (2008). Globalization and economic geography: The world is curved, not flat. *Cambridge Journal of Regions, Economy and Society,* 1(3), 351-370.

McCann, P., and Ortega-Argilés, R. (2011). Smart specialisation, regional growth and applications to EU cohesion policy. Economic geography working paper, 2011. Faculty of Spatial Sciences, University of Groningen.

Mingardo, G., Berg, L. Van den, and Haaren, J. van (2009). *Transport, environment and economy at urban level: The need for decoupling.* Rotterdam: Euricur, Erasmus University Rotterdam.

Moulaert, F., Martinelli, F., González, S., and Swyngedouw, E. (2007). Introduction: Social innovation and governance in European cities urban development between path dependency and radical innovation. *European Urban and Regional Studies*, 14(3), 195-209.

OECD (2011). *Regions and innovation policy.* Paris: OECD Reviews of Regional Innovation, OECD Publishing.

Pike, A., Rodriguez-Pose, A., and Tomaney, J. (2010). *Handbook of local and regional development.* Abingdon: Routledge.

Pike, A., Rodríguez-Pose, A., and Tomaney, J. (2006). *Local and regional development.* Abingdon: Routledge.

Rodríguez-Pose, A., and Crescenzi, R. (2008). Mountains in a flat world: Why proximity still matters for the location of economic activity. *Cambridge Journal of Regions, Economy and Society*, 1(3), 371-388.

Turok, I. (2009). The distinctive city: Pitfalls in the pursuit of differential advantage. *Environment and Planning A*, 41(1), 13-30.

Winden, W. van, and Carvalho, L. (2008). Urban competitiveness in the knowledge economy: Evolution paths of the Portuguese metropolises. In T. Yigitcanlar, K. Velibeyoglu and S. Baum (eds), *Knowledge-based urban development: Planning and applications in the information era.* Hershey, PA: IGI Global.

Chapter 2

Urban Policies in Europe

Hans Verdonk[1]

Introduction

In the second decade of the third millennium the focus of attention on cities and their role in European Union (EU) policies seems stronger than ever before. Smart cities, Sustainable urban transport, European green capital, and the strengthened urban dimension of cohesion policy are (some of) the examples. The recognition that without its cities the EU will never meet its Europe 2020 strategic objectives is the driving force behind it. The financial crisis and resulting budget austerity will have to result in stronger cooperation and alignment of public budgets. Cities can no longer be ignored or put aside when designing and delivering EU policies.

Will this result in the definite breakthrough of cities in the European arena? That is still too early to tell. During its history (increased) attention for cities and urban issues has been on and off the agenda. Apparent breakthroughs have been succeeded by near breakdowns. Power and politics turned out to be more important than policies and responsibilities.

Most researchers have taken the funding cycles of regional policy as a starting point in explaining how the urban dimension has developed (for instance: Tofarides, 2003, Van den Berg et al., 2004; Parkinson, 2005). This seems obvious as it can be calculated how much funding is geared (directly) towards cities. More interesting however, is to see how policies and budgets are being prepared and how the involvement of the local level has developed. This chapter will give a broad overview of these development stages of the urban dimension in Community policies.[2]

---

1 The author wishes to thank Corinne Hermant-de Callatay of the European Commission's Competence Centre for Inclusive Growth, Urban and Territorial Development; Dominic Rowles of the Local Government Association (Brussels Office) and Janneke Stalenhoef of the G-4 Europe Office for their comments and corrections. The views and opinions expressed in this chapter are solely the author's.

2 This chapter will touch upon the role of the different institutions, but it focuses primarily on the outcomes of the (negotiation) processes rather than the role of each institution in the process. This chapter will also not try to fully describe the overall developments in the various policy fields. Many books and researches have been published on this topic, but few from the point of view at the local level.

Limited Sectoral Focus (1958-1969)

In the 1950s and 1960s the focus on the European continent was on rebuilding the damage of the war. The start of the European cooperation was primarily based on Coal and Steel (ECSC – European Community on Coal and Steel), and Agriculture, Internal Market and Transport (EEC – European Economic Community). This cooperation was in the first place a cooperation between member states. As the president of the European Parliament stated when the Joint Study Group for regional and local questions was set up in 1961:

> At the outset the EEC was not clearly aware of the difficulties which might arise at regional level. On the other hand the Member States often jealously guard their prerogatives in the matter of regional and local problems. It was felt that the approach of the experts to regional problems was too technical and neglected the human aspect of the problems affecting persons living in the regions concerned. Europe cannot have regions which are systematically neglected. Therefore permanent liaison must be established with local authority organisations in order to ensure closer contact between Community bodies and those representing the regions (European Parliament, 1977).

This lack of awareness did not mean that nothing happened at the local level. Already in 1952, when it was just established, the High Authority of the ECSC discussed the necessity of low cost housing programmes in Europe. This resulted in early 1954 in the first of 13 multi-annual programmes. The first had already started by the end of 1953 (!) and ran till 1956 and was aiming to (re)develop 50-60 thousand houses annually (Leboutte, 2008). These programmes were specifically aimed at coal and steelworkers and concentrated at their regions. In December 1963 the European Commission organised a symposium on low cost housing. The need for affordable housing was much larger than the ECSC could provide for, however, the Commission lacked financial resources (Commission of the European Communities, 1963) to do anything more than commission studies and make recommendations to the Member States.

The European Investment Bank did spend some 1.9 billion units of account (approximately 1.5 billion ECU) on regional investments, 75 per cent of its total investments in the period 1958-1972 (Commission of the European Communities, 1974). Regional policy was already identified by a special Committee chaired by Paul Henri Spaak in 1956. Real progress was only made in 1964 when the Commission discussed three reports on the problems of regional development in the EEC. The second report formulated several suggestions for regional conversion including the renovation of urban structures (Commission of the European Communities, 1964). In its memorandum to the Council the Commission argued that "all concerned, including the various local bodies, must play an active part in the planning and execution of policy in each region" (Commission of the European Communities, 1965). It was stated that "Where local authorities have a high degree of autonomy they generally possess the staff and financial means to undertake certain projects. Often the practical problems are better known and can be solved at local and regional levels without the administrative delays involved in applying to the central authorities. But it can also happen that too much weight is given to local interests, with consequent ill-effects in the field of general policy." (Commission of the European Communities, 1965, p. 13). Furthermore, town planning and public utilities were identified as areas of investments. Finally, the Commission recommended to undertake a study into the costs of excessive urban concentration.

Four years later the Commission presented a regional policy for the Community (Commission of the European Communities, 1969). The proposal identified the problems of urban regions including suburbanization. Infrastructure included housing and facilities enabling urban centres to fulfil their functions. However, one of the objectives was to ensure that the urbanization trend takes place without excessive concentrations and with a suitable distribution of conurbations over the regions. Even though it was considered that "the vast majority of people in all the Community countries are turning towards an urban way of life, so this is a considerable problem of common interest" (Commission of the European Communities, 1969, p. 40), urban regions as such were not included in the proposed legal text.

Neither Cities Nor Regions (1970-1979)

Regional Policy

The 1970s started with a new European Commission that, for the first time, included a Commissioner for Competition and Regional Policy, the Luxembourger Albert Borchette. The new policy was intensively discussed and supported by the European Parliament and the Economic and Social Committee as well as the Medium-term Economic Policy Committee. Then it was the Council's turn to discuss the proposals.

These debates took place at a time when the Community was preparing to set up an Economic and Monetary Union by 1980, whilst at the same time enlargement negotiations with the United Kingdom, Denmark and Ireland were taking place. During the Paris enlargement Council of October 1972 "the Heads of State and government invited the Commission to prepare as soon as possible a report analysing the regional problems of the enlarged Community, and offering suitable proposals" (Council of the European Communities, 1972).

Months later the 1973-1977 Commission Ortoli took office with a new Commissioner for regional policy, the Englishman George Thomson. Already on 3 May he published his report "on the regional problems in the enlarged community". It clearly stated that,

> a Community regional strategy must ensure that efforts to attract new development
> in the problem regions are accompanied by "decongestion" arrangements which

will make for the efficiency and coordination at a Community level of the present policies of member states in order to discourage excessive industrial congestion in areas where this congestion can only lessen the quality of life, and encourage decentralisation of these industries and of other activities towards regions which need them (Commission of the European Communities, 1973a, p. 5).

In the next five months a legislative regulation for the new fund and a list of eligible regions were proposed. Although there was a general agreement on the direction of the policy, the Council could not reach an agreement on the size of the fund and the regions to be supported until the Paris Council of December 1974. The European Regional Development Fund (ERDF) was finally established on 18 March 1975 and the Commission approved the first projects, that were submitted by member states, in October of that year.

The regulation laying down the provisions for the new fund did not specify exactly the definition of regions. Article 3 stated that

> Regions and areas which may benefit from the Fund shall be limited to those aided areas established by Member States in applying their systems of regional aids and in which State aids are granted which qualify for Fund assistance. When aid from the Fund is granted, priority shall be given to investments in national priority areas, taking account of the principles for the coordination at Community level of regional aids (Council of the European Communities, 1975).

The areas concerned were most often territories confronted with structural difficulties, such as dependency specific on declining industries facing restructuring (i.e. steel, textile, agriculture). Most investments were directed at new infrastructure (roads, business parks) and stimulating new industries to develop (Commission of the European Communities, 1979a). The territories concerned are either part of an administrative region (such as parts of selected German Länder) or (parts of) groups of administrative regions (such as the southern part of Italy Mezzogiorno, or the north of the Netherlands).

There is no clear link identified with regional authorities and regional policy was clearly a matter of the Member States and the European Commission. This point of view is clearly illustrated by the regional policy committee in its meeting of October 1975 where the outline of the regional development plans (RDPs) prescribed by article 6 of the ERDF were adopted. The Committee stated that RDPs "are in principle concerned with regions qualifying for ERDF contributions. Member States should prepare these programmes by regions and areas or by groups of regions taking account in particular the institutional framework and the statistics available". In the same guidelines the Committee acknowledges that "a clear distinction should be drawn between Community, national and other sources (regional, local government, etc.)" (Commission of the European Communities, 1976a, p. 2). This view was reiterated by the Council resolution on the guidelines of 6 February 1979 which stated that "Regional policy is an integral part of the economic policies of the Community and the Member States" (Council of the European Communities, 1979, pp. 10-11).

The European Parliament on the other hand, considered in its second report on regional policy of November 1973 that in establishing the ERDF "these regional programmes should be worked out and implemented with the active participation of local and regional authorities and the social partners concerned" (European Parliament, 1973). However, the situation of a centralised ERDF where regional and local authorities could only (if at all) forward projects for support to their national governments that decided whether or not to submit these to the Commission was continued throughout the 1970s.

Only towards the end of this period changes were introduced step by step. In particular the 1977 reform through an important element into regional policy: Integrated programming. In March 1979, just after the new regional policy was adopted by the Council, the Commission published guidelines for this new approach. As there was little experience, the first operations were suggested "to be carried out on an experimental basis, with the emphasis on pragmatism" (Commission of the European Communities, 1979b). Interestingly enough, the first two pilot projects being put forward were aimed at urban areas. The first addressed multiple problems in the Naples area. A second was aimed at the city centre of Belfast (Commission of the European Communities, 1980a).

In July 1980 the Commission underlined in its fifth annual report on the ERDF the importance of authorities other then the Member States. It stated that in preparing for the new programme period it developed "co-operation between its departments for the Regional Fund and national governments departments at central, regional or local level" (Commission of the European Communities, 1980a). Five months later the first report on the social and economic situation of the regions stressed as a first point the geographical unit best suited for analyses. As regions should be sufficiently large in population and data should be available, the NUTS-II level[3] was considered as most appropriate, making regional authorities the focus of regional policy.

Social Policy

The ESF that was already set up in 1958 went through a major reform in the 1970s. The European Council decided on 1 February 1971 to add new responsibilities to the fund allowing for joint policies and activities at Community level accompanying council decisions and meeting in particular unemployment problems or long-term underemployment of a specific structural nature. The ESF regulation specified the industries, firms and regions to be targeted. Applications could only be submitted by the relevant Member States.

As support to firms was expressly included in the Council decision "in so far as public authorities have a share in this operation, has prompted the Commission

---

3   Statistical unit for regions coinciding with administrative regions such as the German Länder, Belgian Gewesten, Dutch Provincies and French Departements.

to define the term 'public authority' in its proposal in a way that covers the very many sources of public financing and encourage coordination of efforts at the most suitable level" (Commission of the European Communities, 1971). A further shift was made during 1976 when "the policy of the Commission in managing the Social Fund was to stimulate and encourage new initiatives at regional and local level while maintaining assistance to training organisations operating nationally" (Commission of the European Communities, 1977).

It should also be noted that the ECSC low cost housing programmes were continued and broadened in their approach amongst others by including housing for workers in the new coastal iron and steel centres and special solutions for migrant workers. The 8th programme was adopted in 1975 with a budget of 25 million units of credit (approximately €30 million) for the first 2 year stage aiming to help finance the (re)development of 9,000 houses (Commission of the European Communities, 1975).

Environmental Policy

Where regional and social policies lacked a specific urban focus, environmental policy identified urban agglomerations as one of its target areas already in the first community action plan, published in 1972. One of the four objectives identified was "to plan land use so as to curb in particular the harmful consequences of the increasing concentration of people in the towns and to meet the need for contact with nature and the aesthetic quality of life" (Commission of the European Communities, 1972). Actions identified concerned mainly air quality and noise and anti-pollution measures.

A specific role was foreseen for town planning studies as "If properly directed and accompanied by adequate town planning, urbanization contributes towards the improvement of ecological conditions and social relations and the raising of the cultural level. In the same way, urbanization facilitates the combating of certain dangers threatening the natural environment" (Commission of the European Communities, 1972, pp. 54-55). In addition the Commission planned to specifically study urban problems and identify solutions at Community level. As a reason for action, the detailed list of April 1973 indicated that "efforts to improve living conditions in densely populated areas would be in vain unless the very process of concentration were brought under control and reversed" (Commission of the European Communities, 1973b). As a specific example the development of what was called a "megapolis in North-West Europe" was put forward.

As a first major piece of environmental legislation to improve the urban environment the Commission submitted its proposal for a Council Directive concerning health protection standards for sulphur dioxide and suspended particulate matter[4] in urban atmospheres on 25 February 1976 (Commission of

---

4   Also referred to as Black smoke.

the European Communities, 1976b). This directive required the member states to comply to the protection standards set by 1982. Even though the directive was only adopted four years later, the compliance date was only delayed till 1 April 1983. The final text was not too different from the original, but interestingly enough, where the original focused on the protection of human health only, the protection of the environment was added as a reason in the final text. Furthermore, the identified maximum concentrations were labelled as "limit values" that had to be met "as soon as possible and by 1 April 1993 at the latest" (Council of the European Communities, 1980a).

Already a month after the proposal of the Council Directive on sulphur dioxide was published, the Commission presented its proposal on a new action programme on the environment. In this second programme, preventative actions, regional planning, the production of wastes and a study on the potential contribution of an "Environmental Impact Assessment" were introduced as elements of a more comprehensive policy (Commission of the European Communities, 1976c). As part of this approach the Commission proposed a two year research project on the growth of large urban concentrations. Elements included the location of economic activities, migration, an evaluation of urban planning and policies, and other relevant aspects (Council of the European Communities, 1978). Later that year a proposal for a research project in the field of recycling of urban and industrial waste for the period 1979-1982 was submitted to the council and adopted on 12 November 1979. The research areas included, among others, recovery of materials and energy from urban waste and thermal treatment of waste.

Regions Dominate the Agenda (1980-1988)

The 1980s were confronted with two enlargements and a further deepening of policies, that seriously changed the Community. The enlargement to the South with Greece (1 January 1981) and Spain and Portugal (1 January 1986) added countries that were seriously behind in development. This had in particular effects on cohesion policy both in focus and in size.

After a long deadlock in negotiations on the Community's budget, the Solemn declaration on European Union, signed at the June 1983 Stuttgart Council was the necessary step forward. The Intergovernmental Conference concluded a new Treaty extending qualified majority voting in the Council, working together with the Parliament rather than just consulting it, aiming at completing the Internal Market by 31 December 1992 and by bringing foreign policy cooperation under the Institutional cooperation (Council of the European Communities, 1985a). Also new titles on economic and social cohesion, research and technological development, and the environment were added to the EEC Treaty. This new Treaty known as the Single European Act was signed on 28 February 1986 and went officially into force on 1 July 1987.

Regional Policy: Integrated Development Programmes

The two urban pilots to test the preferred integrated approach were gradually expanded to wider regional programmes often with a strong agricultural background. In June 1981 integrated development programmes were adopted for the Western Isles of Scotland, the French department of Lozère, and the South-East of Belgium. The year after a series of feasibility studies were initiated. During the Stuttgart Council of June 1983 it was agreed that the integrated approach was the way forward to make structural Funds operations more effective. However, the Commission's proposal to apply the new approach to the Mediterranean basin, the so-called integrated Mediterranean Programmes (IMPs), was much delayed by the Council. The first draft that already originated from 1979, had the intention "to provide a comprehensive answer to the variety of development problems encountered by the Mediterranean regions" (Commission of the European Communities, 1986a).

At the same time progress in the Naples and Belfast programmes was far from ideal. The Naples operation was executed by forwarding project proposals three to four times a year. Despite the multi-level governance structure put in place, investment decisions were practically decided upon by the specific government body entirely autonomously. The various projects carried out lacked the necessary coordination. As stated:

> [t]he existence of the operation has resulted in more ERDF aid being granted
> to the area in question. Nevertheless, enquiries carried out on different
> occasions by the Court have not made it possible to ascertain whether
> national, regional or local financings have been similarly increased (Court of
> Auditors, 1988).

The Belfast operation was submitted for approval in 1981. The programme aimed to invest almost 900 million ECU of which about 60 per cent in housing and social infrastructure. The Council did not agree that housing should be part of the operation. Instead, in addition to support from the regular instruments, the Council adopted a specific regulation for 100 million ECU to promote urban renewal. The Court of Auditors was very sceptical about the results as the additional 100 million "has been managed more as a supplementary measure attached to the ERDF than as a component part of an integrated operation" and "[i]n practice, the appropriations have therefore been used to increase the finance available for investment in housing" (Council of the European Communities, 1983a, points 3.15 and 3.19).

Reform of the Policy

In 1980 the first programmes after the Reform of 1979 were adopted. In particular, the new 'non quota' section offered possibilities for Community wide actions

outside the regions under the quota section.[5] Almost immediately after the adoption
of the first programmes, discussions started for more coordinated action and
effective spending.[6] The Stuttgart Council of June 1983 made an explicit call to the
Commission to deliver their report by 1 August of that year. This work resulted in
a new proposal for an ERDF regulation by November 1983 which was adopted by
the Council on 19 June 1984 and was applicable from 1 January 1985 (Commission
of the European Communities, 1985). The most important reform however, took
place in 1988 when the provisions of the Single European Act were translated into
the new Structural Funds regulations. Until then "the Community's regional policy
has largely been limited to reimbursing Member States for national programmes"
(Commission of the European Communities, 1989a). Council regulation 2052/88/
EEC of 24 June 1988 on the tasks of the Structural Funds and their effectiveness
introduced the new architecture with five Objectives, multi-annual programmes,
partnership principles and a substantial budget increase. The budget for 1988 was
set at 7,700 million ECU and was to be doubled in real terms by 1992.

On 19 December 1988 three additional Council Regulations were published of
which the coordination regulation (Council of the European Communities, 1988a)
introduced articles on the until then tested integrated approach and Community
initiatives as the successor of the non-quota section in the previous period. The
ERDF and ESF regulations (see Council of the European Communities, 1988b,
article 10, and Council of the European Communities, 1988c, article 1 (2)a) further
introduced articles on innovative actions to be initiated by the Commission. In its
first periodic report on the social and economic situation of the regions of the
Community, published in 1980, the urban question was identified:

> The agglomeration problem is very different, involving urban congestion notably
> in respect of transportation and housing and increasing difficulties of urban
> administration and management. Account must also be taken of the dynamics
> of urbanisation – the process of suburbanisation involving movement of people
> from city cores to the surrounding suburban rings. Very often this is associated
> with the replacement in the cores of relatively well-off skilled people and their
> families by poorer and often minority, immigrant populations. Frequently there
> is also a large proportion of old people in the urban cores (Commission of the
> European Communities, 1980b, p. 17).

It was concluded that an analysis below the NUTS-II level was needed to gain
insight in these problems. The second report, published in 1984, indicated a long

---

5   From the start of the ERDF, the distribution of resources to each Member State
was based on national quotas. The introduction of the "non-quota section" gave the
Commission 5 per cent of the funding to support areas outside the traditional nationally
allocated budgets. These were primarily implemented through specific programmes (rather
than projects) such as these for steel, shipbuilding and cross border areas.

6   The Commission delivered its proposals on 21 October 1981.

list of problems associated with the decline of many major cities ranging from deteriorating housing stock and infrastructure, loss of jobs and skilled persons, to high rates of unemployment and high incidences of crime (Commission of the European Communities, 1984a).

Research into Urban Problems

To improve the insight in the problems of Europe's cities, the Commission ordered a study into urban problems and regional policy, better known as the Cheshire report after its main author. The first results were already published in November 1985 but to include Spanish and Portuguese cities after the accession of both countries, the report was finalised only in 1987. The report clearly identified the development of Europe's largest cities, but also made the case for an Urban policy at Community level:

> The Community already has responsibility for policy in a number of areas such as environmental problems, industrial decline and spatial disparities, which have specific urban manifestations. At present, however, these policies are not co-ordinated at the urban level. One of the distinguishing features of urban problems is the complexity of policy objectives and the need to co-ordinate a wide range of policy instruments to secure the objectives of urban policy (Cheshire et al., 1988, p. 12).

In the same period the European Foundation for the Improvement of Living and Working Conditions[7] conducted two studies into the Living conditions in Urban areas and Living conditions in Urban Europe (Eurofound, 1987). These studies provided further insight into issues such as Housing and living conditions, segregation in cities, specific marginal groups, families and households and neighbourhood and community. The main aim of this research was to provide policy makers with the necessary information to achieve improved quality of life for people living in urban areas.

The Place of Cities in Regional Policy Programmes

Recognition of the role of cities was a very slow process. In fact, regional policy was something of the Commission and the Member States, as was indicated in the previous paragraph. The updated ERDF resolution of 6 February 1979 (Council of the European Communities, 1979, pp. 10-11) still focussed mostly at regions and areas aided by Member States. The new 'non-quota' section on the other hand opened the ERDF for other areas. In particular the programmes aimed at the zones adversely affected by restructuring of the steel and shipbuilding industry

---

7   The Foundation was established by the Council in 1975 as one of the first bodies of the Community to work in a specialized area.

introduced operations aiming at the "improvement of run-down areas whose character is either industrial, or industrial-and-urban to the extent that these two aspects cannot be dissociated" (Council of the European Communities, 1980b, pp. 9-15, and Council of the European Communities, 1980c, pp. 16-22 article 4). These original programmes were aimed at a limited number of regions, but in the next years several regions were added (Court of Auditors, 1986).

Even though the specific focus was not on cities, several managed to secure substantial investment support over the years. Besides the funds for Naples and Belfast, projects were supported for instance in Liverpool (Maritime Museum and Maritime Complex, Waste disposal plant, Docks and Airport; see Commission of the European Communities, 1983a, point 33), Berlin (refuse incinerator, fair and exhibition complex in the TV tower area) and Manchester (conversion of Central Station into exhibition centre, and Manchester airport; see Commission of the European Communities, 1983a, points 106 and 142).

In preparing for the reform after the entry into force of the Single European Act, the Commission published an information note on procedures and content for the implementation of an integrated approach in 1986. The objectives identified, were to be achieved by "providing or reinforcing the basis for partnership between the Commission and national, regional and local authorities in the development process;" and "reinforcing the complementarity of Community structural interventions with national, regional and local sources of financing and thus increasing their efficiency and impact;" (Commission of the European Communities, 1983a, pp. 2-3). This didn't mean that cities were automatically included in the programmes. For instance the IMPs specifically excluded the large French and Italian cities of Bordeaux, Toulouse, Marseille, Genoa, Florence, Rome, Naples and Palermo (Commission of the European Communities, 1986b).

Although the Single European Act's provisions on economic and social cohesion were mainly aimed at reducing disparities between regions (article 130A) and supporting the reconversion of areas seriously affected by industrial decline (article 130C), the Structural Funds regulation 2052/88/EEC added employment areas and urban communities within the Objective 2 (industrial regions facing decline). The coordination regulation 4253/88/EC furthermore stated that where Objective-1 areas should cover NUTS II level, Objective 2 and 5b regions should normally cover one or more Nuts III regions (article 5(1)).[8]

---

8 Article 9 of the Regulation added the category "urban communities with an unemployment rate of at least 50 per cent above the Community average which have recorded a substantial fall in industrial employment" (see Council of the European Communities, 1988, p. 14). Furthermore Berlin was specifically mentioned as eligible for aid. The ERDF regulation 4254/88/EEC included under article 1b "investment relating to the regeneration of areas suffering from industrial decline, including inner cities". NUTS-III regions are ambtskommune (DK), Départments (F), Kreise (DE), provinces (BE and IT) Corop-regio's (NL), counties (UK) and Luxemburg as a whole.

The partnership article (article 4(1)) stated that Community operations "shall be established through close consultations between the Commission, the Member State concerned and the competent authorities designated by the latter at national, regional, local or other level". This partnership was covering all parts of the operation from preparation to financing, monitoring and assessing the results. To better involve regional and local authorities in the process, the Commission set up a 42 member strong Consultative Council on 24 June 1988. This Council chose the mayor of Mainz as its president (Commission of the European Communities, 1989b). The Council was dissolved when the Committee of the Regions was established by the Maastricht Treaty in March 1994 (Commission of the European Communities, 1994a, p. 28).

Social Policy

In the social domain too, the focus continued to move slowly from national to other authorities. In the ESF this was realised in the 1980 reform when the Council concluded that guidelines were needed to reinforce, amongst others "the role of undertakings and of local authorities and services" (Council of the European Communities, 1980-1981, point 97). On 8 October 1982 the Commission presented its proposals to reform the ESF to the Council. These proposals aimed to provide greater focus on specific target groups (in particular young people and disadvantaged workers such as the disabled and migrants) and a simplification in the number and types of actions. Furthermore, a stronger focus of resources was proposed, taking the NUTS-III rather than the NUTS-II level as basis for analysis and selection. As a result of the application of these indicators the areas eligible for ESF support accounted for 63 per cent of the Community's labour force in 1986. To ensure stronger focus this percentage was further reduced, as a first step to 57 per cent in 1987 (Commission of the European Communities, 1987a, pp. 71-72).

As indicated in the paragraph on Regional policy, the major overhaul of Structural funds policies included multi-annual programming and five specific objectives. Whereas the ESF could be applied in integrated programmes of particular Objective 1 and to a lesser extent also objectives 2 and 5b, most of the ESF was made available through national or multi-regional programmes. Two objectives were specifically designed to deliver the ESF goals. Objective 3 was aimed at long-term (longer than 12 months) unemployed persons older than 25. Objective 4 ensured support for (vocational) training for persons under 25 seeking employment. For these two Objectives a total of over 6.5 billion ECU was available for the period 1989-1993. The focus of the ESF was once again on target groups, both of which were clearly concentrated in Europe's urban areas. However, this did not result in specific urban recognition.

Faced with increasing unemployment levels the European Council called in its Resolution of 12 July 1982 for Community action to combat unemployment. The Council stressed "its interest in the job creation process which is also applied in local initiatives and co-operatives" (Commission of the European Communities, 1984d, point 2) and requested the Commission to assess the contribution of these initiatives to employment creation. In November 1983 the Commission published its first document on local employment initiatives (LEIs; Commission of the European Communities, 1983c). It was proposed that both the ESF and the ERDF could offer support to local employment creation. In addition Community exchange of information and research to improve future actions were put forward as main areas for action. In June 1984 the Council adopted a Resolution calling upon the Member States to include the LEIs in their policies (General Secretariat of the Council of the European Communities, 1985, point 116). In its stock taking document of February 1987 the Commission noted that although progress was made, there was clear evidence that Member States had not fully exploited the LEI potential. In particular LEIs should be developed within an overall strategy aiming at employment growth. Furthermore, greater sensibilization efforts were needed and a more favourable environment for LEIs required. Also access to finance was seen as crucial for the development of LEIs (Commission of the European Communities, 1987b, p. 5-6). The role of LEIs was also specifically included in the new ESF guidelines in the 1988 reform, in particular in relation to the long-term unemployment Objective 3 (Commission of the European Communities, 1989c, pp. 6-9).

Finally, it should be noted that the ECSC's low cost housing scheme was continued. The 9th programme was approved in 1980 with 30 million units of credit (approximately €40 million) for the first stage aiming at 10,000 dwellings (Commission of the European Communities, 1980c) and succeeded by the 10th covering the period until 31 December 1988. In 1988 a new 11th programme for the period 1989-1993 was prepared.

Environmental Policy

With the second action plan for the environment (1977-1981) ending, the Commission published its proposals for the third plan (1982-1986) in November 1981. The new programme was first of all a continuation of the activities started by the second programme. But it also anchored principles as "prevention rather than cure", the need for a general framework and the need to seek "the level of action – local, regional, national, community or international – best suited to the problems in question" (Commission of the European Communities, 1981, point 9). Fields of action included:

- Prevention and reduction of pollution and nuisances (water, air, chemicals, noise and waste);
- Protection and rational management of land, the environment and natural resources.

The Council adopted the action programme while including certain elements such as developing an environmental impact assessment procedure and provided a budget of 13 million ECU a year later (Council of the European Communities, 1983c, p. 1, and Council of the European Communities, 1984, pp. 1-5). In 1987 the Council agreed to extend the budget by three years for a total amount of 24 million ECU.

During this period environmental policy was formally included in the European Treaties. The Single European Act includes several articles on the environment, of which article 130R is particularly worth mentioning as it defines the contribution to protecting human health as one of the key principles for action. Unfortunately it is limited to taking into account the identified regions of the Community, which do not specifically include urban areas. However, this did not mean that the urban dimension was overlooked.

The fourth action programme on the environment (1987-1992) that was adopted by the Council in 1987, the European year of the Environment, included several points on urban areas. "Urban environmental problems must now assume an increased priority in Community environmental policy". However, the scale was foreseen to be too substantial for the programme to deal with as

> the Commission indicates that resources of the order of 1,000 million ECU per annum, for a 12 year period are required from public and private sectors to 'clean up' the land contaminated by former industrial activities before it can be re-used. Other urban improvements may also involve important expenditures. Moreover, in disadvantaged areas such as described above, lack of resources may mean that even the implementation of Community environmental legislation can pose problems (Council of the European Communities, 1987, p. 34).

The solution had to be found by gearing structural funds to these types of investments as these were the only Community Funds substantial enough.

Emergence of the Urban Agenda (1989-1998)

In the 1980s the Community was reformed into a Union and enlarged with 3 Member States; Austria, Finland and Sweden. The Maastricht Treaty, which was signed on 7 February 1992 and entered into force on 1 November 1993, created the building of a Union with three pillars. This Treaty change added the economic and monetary Union, and "sustainable and non-inflationary growth respecting the environment, a high degree of convergence of economic performance, a high level of employment and of social protection, the raising of the standard of living and quality of life, and economic and social cohesion and solidarity among Member States" to the Community's tasks (Commission of the European Communities, 1992a). In 1997, the Treaty of Amsterdam (entry into force 1 May 1999) introduced a Community employment strategy and transferred several policy fields that were the domain of the intergovernmental cooperation between the Member States, under the umbrella of the Commission. Most important however, were the institutional changes such as qualified majority voting instead of veto rights and co-decision with the European Parliament in several policy fields. The Council also called upon the European Investment Bank (EIB) to set up the Amsterdam Special Action Programme (ASAP) to provide for an impulse for growth and employment creation. The enlargement with three well developed Member States had only a limited effect on the Union's policies.

Regional Policy

The Delors II Commission that started in 1989 installed Commissioner Bruce Millan with the responsibility for Regional Policy. One of his first tasks was started to implement the new programmes. As the population living in Objective 2 areas should be limited to 15 per cent of the overall population in the Community, most of Europe's larger cities could only partly (if at all) participate in these programmes. Only the few cities within Objective 1 regions[9] were automatically fully covered. Commissioner Millan was very much aware of this. During the international congress on regional policy in May 1989 in Madrid he "referred to the special problem of inner cities, especially those not covered by the lists of eligible areas, which had to be limited in view of the need to concentrate resources" (Commission of the European Communities, 1989d). He made clear his intentions to make use of the new established article 10 of the ERDF regulation to undertake pilot schemes. According to the Financial Times the cities of London, Marseille and Rotterdam were specifically mentioned (Van Veelen, 1991). The Urban Pilot Projects were born.

Reform of the Policy

The next major policy reform was foreseen for 1994 but the unification of Germany and the entry of the new Länder into regional policy in 1991 had already shifted the balance in the policy. The new regions were all included as Objective 1 as their development was very much behind that of the rest of the Union. Originally only the Objective 1 programmes were foreseen to cover the entire five year period, but due to all the delays the three year term for Objective 2 was extended by the two remaining years. The reform process was set in motion by the December 1992 Edinburgh European Council that set the financial framework for the Union till 2000 and established an action plan by the Member States and the Community to promote growth and to combat unemployment. For regional policy a total amount of 159 billion ECU was reserved for the 1993-1999 period, starting with about 20 billion ECU in 1993 and increasing to 27.5 billion ECU in 1999 (Council of the European Communities, 1992). The architecture was slightly altered from the previous period by changes in the ESF (see paragraph 3.5), and with the accession of Austria, Finland and Sweden, the

---

9   That is, for example, Athens, Thessaloniki, Belfast, Dublin, Lisbon, Porto, Valencia, Naples and Palermo.

addition of a 6th Objective for the development and structural adjustment of regions with an extremely low population density (Commission of the European Communities, 1996a, p. 11).

Research into Urban Problems

Although the Cheshire report had already made the problems of Europe's cities very visible, the Commission required further assessments. In November 1991 the Commission published its report "Europe 2000; Outlook for the Development of the Community's Territory". The report looked to the European territory with a planning perspective, aiming to ensure that all regions can benefit the most from the single market. Without aiming to develop a masterplan, the intention was to ensure a better cooperation between the different policy fields, in particular regional development, transport, energy and environment. Under the heading "The development of the Community's urban system" the report sketched in 17 pages a picture of the state of the cities, building on the Cheshire report, scenario's for future development and strategic responses by and partnerships between cities (Commission of the European Communities, 1991). But, as the final conclusion in the chapter on policy implications was,

> there is no Community policy relating to the problems of urban areas as such, although assistance is being made available towards the development and restructuring of many of the most seriously affected areas under Objectives 1 and 2 of the Structural Funds. Urban communities are, however confronted with problems beyond the purely economic ... It may therefore seem appropriate that the Community should take more responsibility for problems of urban poverty and deprivation (Commission of the European Communities, 1991a, p. 202).

This view was further deepened by the Regional Development Study no. 4 "Urbanization and the function of cities in the European Community" better known after its leading author as the Parkinson report. The report identified the challenges of change faced by European cities and their strategic responses. The study further identified that in the 1980s in the largest member states either the regions are the strong decentralised tier of government, or the city governments are losing powers. Only in the Netherlands and Denmark was the counterbalance to national government provided for by the local level. When taking the urban challenges towards 2000 in mind, Parkinson stated that "The current eligible areas exclude a number of cities which have experienced substantial decline in their port-related or heavy manufacturing sectors and have suffered a variety of economic, social and environmental problems." And "the Commissions' goal of increasing the economic and social cohesion of the regions could lead it to greater concentration on urban problems and opportunities which shape, and are shaped by, the economic and social performance of the regions" (Commission of the European Communities, 1992b, p. 25).

Following the Europe 2000 report several specific studies have been carried out to both improve the level of understanding of specific transregional territories, and include the developments of the enlarged and deepened Union on board. The urban dimension was (just as the preservation of rural and the reducing of isolation of peripheral regions) set against the background of the different transregional territories each with different policy options. The results were published in 1994 in the report Europe 2000+; cooperation for European territorial development (Commission of the European Communities, 1994b). In the end all this knowledge should contribute to the establishment of the European Spatial Development Perspective.[10] The Noordwijk Council was also the start for the Member States' Urban exchange initiative, aiming to improve the exchange the knowledge on urban matters. The Informal Council in June 1998 in Glasgow called for an informal non-binding framework on urban policy by around the year 2000.

In 1996 the Commission published for the first time its cohesion report that was introduced by the Treaty of Maastricht as a tri-annual report on the progress made towards achieving economic and social cohesion. Throughout the report the (direct and indirect) effects of cohesion and other community policies on the European territories, including urban areas, were described. In its outlook for the future, the report stated that

> Many of the problems of adjusting to change appear to have fallen on some of the Union's major urban areas. There is a very real danger of a further fragmentation within European cities, rising unemployment and social exclusion being accompanied by a deepening of social divide between haves and havenots. In some Member States, the urban problem is already regarded as the major challenge to national cohesion and they have designed and implemented new integrated urban policies. A more focused approach may also be necessary at Union level (Commission of the European Communities, 1996b, p. 124).

Building on these perspectives and in the running up to the Noordwijk informal Council of June 1997, the Dutch presidency had prepared a discussion note on the role of cities in Community policies. In the same manner the Commission published a month in advance its communication "Towards an urban agenda in the European Union". This communication "examines possibilities for improving urban development and for increasing the effectiveness of existing Community intervention in urban areas. The intention is not to develop Europe wide urban policies for matters which are best dealt with at local or regional scale. However, since it is clear that cities in the European Union are facing a number of common problems, there are also opportunities at the European scale to share and facilitate

10 The first official draft of this intergovernmental work was discussed by the ministers responsible for spatial planning and urban policies during their informal Council meeting in Noordwijk in June 1997 (Commission of the European Communities, 1997a).

potential solutions. This would not require additional powers at the European level. Rather, much can be achieved through a more focused approach using existing instruments at national and Community level and enhanced co-operation and co-ordination at all levels" (Commission of the European Communities, 1997b, p. 3). The communication formed a starting point for dialogue that culminated in the first Urban Forum in November 1998.

The Place of Cities in Regional Policy Programmes

During the Intergovernmental Conference preparing the Maastricht Treaty the Commission proposed an amendment in the articles on economic and social cohesion to include support to urban areas in decline. As Commissioner Millan said in his speech at the Eurocities conference in Lisbon in 1993: "For the history books, I should mention that the Commission proposed in the context of the revision of the Treaties in 1991, the inclusion of 'urban decline' in the definition of the objectives of the European Regional Development Fund, but this was not accepted by the European Council in Maastricht" (Commission of the European Communities, 1993a). This was very unfortunate in particular when considering that rural areas were added to article 130A on economic and social cohesion. As the Amsterdam treaty did not change the main heading of cohesion policy, urban issues stayed out of the Treaty despite the increased attention for urban issues in European policies in the years after the signing of the Maastricht Treaty.

In the regional programmes that were being adopted as of 1989, several of Europe's larger cities were (partly) covered by the new objective 2 programmes[11] and as indicated in the introduction of this paragraph, several cities in objective 1 areas. For the specific category of urban communities created within Objective 2, only the Dutch city of Groningen and communities in the Madrid region were put forward (Commission of the European Communities, 1989e). The limited involvement of local partners is also reflected in the partnerships. "The weight of the three partners (Commission, national government and the regions) often seems out of proportion to that of local partners, who are nevertheless involved both in part-financing and management" (Commission of the European Communities, 1991b, p. 8). Although regional and local authorities had taken responsibility to implement the programmes, "it is to be regretted that little use has been made of global grants, which were specifically designed as an effective means of involving local partners in the implementation of Community assistance" (Commission of the European Communities, 1992c, p. 23).

---

11 Liège, Charleroi, Bremen, Dortmund and other cities in the Ruhr area, Berlin, Zaragoza, Barcelona, Lille, St Etienne, Genova, Glasgow, Liverpool, Birmingham and Manchester. According to Commissioner Millan 22 out of the 58 cities in the Community with over 200,000 inhabitants benefitted from Objectives 1 and 2 (Commission of the European Communities, 1993a).

In its annual report on the implementation of the Structural Funds over 1993 the Commission concluded that

> The practices adopted were not in all cases equal to the ambitions of the reform. The economic actors at local level should have been more involved in Community structural operations, especially in those areas of particular interest to them. There remains, in fact, much administrative inflexibility and reluctance to share powers. ... While the involvement of the regional authorities has become gradually more generalized, participation by the local authorities and other local actors has proved less common (Commission of the European Communities, 1994c, pp. 6-7).

The new programming period (1993-1999) did not bring much change to this practice. The general and the ERDF regulations were hardly changed in this respect, mainly by including the economic and social partners and by including that "The partnership will be conducted in full compliance with the respective institutional, legal and financial powers of each of the partners" (Council of the European Union, 1993a, pp. 5-19). In practice it turned out, this meant very little. As the Commission reflected in its 1995 annual report, partnership in the active phase "with the regional authorities is now widespread and accepted practice and functions satisfactorily on the whole, however, partnership with other geographically-based authorities, particularly at local level, is less well-developed" (Commission of the European Communities, 1996c, p. 23). Year after year the outcome was the same, and in its annual report over 1997 (Commission of the European Communities, 1998a) the Commission no longer included a heading on regional partnerships.

The original 'urban communities with an unemployment rate at least 50 per cent above the Community average which have recorded a substantial fall in industrial employment' was left unchanged. In the end the main result was that cities and towns were moved to the Commission's initial list of areas eligible for Objective 2 (Commission of the European Communities, 1994d). Notable exceptions were (parts of) Bordeaux, Marseille and Greater London being added to this list. More cities were added through the increased amount of Objective 1 regions. Examples are Liverpool, cities in the new German Länder, including East-Berlin and the Valencia urban area.

A major step forward was realised when the Commission, prior to the 1998 Urban Forum, published its communication on "Sustainable Urban Development in the European Union: A Framework for Action". As a result of a year long discussion on their earlier report on "Towards an urban agenda" there was an urgent need to make a step forward at the Urban Forum instead of repeating what was said during the year and a half since the Noordwijk informal council. The focus of the new communication was to provide for a better coordination of polices. "In this Framework for Action the Commission is taking a step towards increasing the effectiveness of EU policies provided for by the Treaty by making them more 'urban sensitive' and ensuring that they facilitate integrated development. There is no attempt to attain new responsibilities for urban matters or to design specific urban definitions or solutions on the European level." (Commission of the European Communities, 1998b). In realizing this goal it combined a total of 24 actions under the following four headings:

- Strengthening economic prosperity and employment in towns and cities.
- Promoting equality, social inclusion and regeneration in urban areas.
- Protecting and improving the urban environment: towards local and global sustainability.
- Contributing to good urban governance and local empowerment.

Almost in parallel the Commission launched an Urban Audit to collect comparable information on a range of economic, social, environmental and civil society indicators linked to the "Quality of Life" for 58 EU cities. The results of the "pilot phase" were published in 1999.

Specific Urban Programmes

After the announcement of Commissioner Millan in Madrid of his intentions to finance Urban Pilot Projects (UPPs) under article 10 (see paragraph 5.1.1) bids from London and Marseille were received. London's bid for Objective 2 was not supported by central government and as a result a London delegation went to the Commissioner directly (Tofarides, 2003, p. 56). Another city that did not receive support from Objective 2 and that the Commissioner had visited in January 1989 during the 7th conference of the Mediterranean regions was Marseille (Commission of the European Communities, 1989). "A major consideration in the choice of Marseille was that the Commission could not be seen to be making an exception only for the case of London, particularly when the Commissioner for Regional Policy was British!" (Commission of the European Communities, 1989f, p. 58). In February 1990 both Pilots were approved and as the Commissioner stated "We shall be considering extending the pilot schemes to the other cities, some which have already presented proposals to the Commission" (Commission of the European Communities, 1990a). Among these proposals was the pilot of the city of Rotterdam that was launched in September that year (Commission of the European Communities, 1990b), and six more, amongst which, Athens, Brussels and Dublin (Commission of the European Communities, 1990c). In both 1991 and 1992 eight new UPPs were approved and by the end of 1993, a total of 101 million ECU was awarded for 32 UPPs (Commission of the European Communities, 1994e). In June 1995 the Commission adopted the guidelines for a second series of UPPs for the period till 1999. In November a call for proposals was launched that resulted in 503 applications. In the end 26 proposals were awarded with an ERDF budget of 64 million ECU.

At the end of 1989, when most of the Objective 1 programmes were adopted, the Commission started to put serious work in the Community Initiatives (CIs) that were newly introduced into the Structural Funds regulations. First of all five non-quota programmes already approved were earmarked as CIs. In May 1990 a second set of seven CIs was approved, and in 1993 two new CIs. In preparing for the 1994-1999 period the Commission published a communication on the future of Community Initiatives (Commission of the European Communities, 1993b). The proposal was to bring the CIs into a framework of five headings so as to improve synergies between the initiatives. The need for urban issues was underlined, however, "it remains to be entirely convinced that such cooperation should be a priority for INTERREG" (Commission of the European Communities, 1993b, p. 16). This resulted in a lobby from urban networks such as Eurocities to include a CI on urban issues. Of crucial importance was also the Resolution of the European Parliament on the Community Initiatives of 28 October 1993 where it stated it

> believes that, apart from the measures envisaged under the 'Employment and
> the development of human resource' heading, which are aimed at countering
> the high levels of unemployment and social exclusion generally, there is a need
> for a specific integrated urban development programme aimed at those parts
> of the Community's major urban areas where unemployment, and particularly
> long-term unemployment is abnormally high; the object of such an initiative
> would be to stimulate local economic development by facilitating the emergence
> and harnessing the efforts of the local actors whose experience, expertise and
> commitment are essential to the regeneration of neglected and run-down areas
> and to provide ready access to the type of services and systems necessary to
> support local entrepreneurial activity (European Parliament, 1993).

In March 1994 the Commission answered these calls by proposing a Community Initiative concerning Urban Areas (URBAN) (Commission of the European Communities, 1994f) with an initial total budget of 600 million ECU. In July 1994 the Commission presented the guidelines and invited member states "to present operational programmes or where appropriate, applications for global grants for urban areas ... . Local and other authorities and the social partners should be involved in the preparation and implementation of operational programmes in the manner appropriate to each Member State" (Commission of the European Communities, 1994g, p. 9). Where this involvement largely failed in the mainstream programmes of Objective 1 and 2, it became an enormous success with URBAN. "In roughly one third of cases local authorities constitute the managing authority and in a further third, they de facto perform many of these functions. Similarly, in over 80 per cent of cases, local community groups participated in the formulation of the programme" (Commission of the European Communities, 2002, p. 3). A second call was published in July 1996 (Commission of the European Communities, 1996d), bringing in another 157 million ECU. In total 118 cities were investing some €1.8 billion with structural funds contributions of almost €900 million (ERDF and ESF; see Court of Auditors, 2001).

Social Policy

The early 1990s were characterised by high and rising levels of unemployment, with increasing numbers of long-term unemployed. This was in fact so serious that the ESF budgets were shifted from the integration of young people (Objective 4) to that of long-term unemployment (Objective 3), raising the latter's share from 45 per cent to 51 per cent in 1993 (Commission of the European Communities, 1993c, pp. 33-34). This development was further strengthened by the Treaty of Maastricht that added "adaptation to industrial changes and to changes in production systems" to the ESF (Commission of the European Communities, 1992, article 123). This new field became the new Objective 4 in the 1993 policy reform, whereas the old Objective 4 was integrated into the wider new Objective 3. The new ESF Regulation thus saw a major overhaul, strengthened by an increased focus on policy priorities and target groups, as the 1988 reform had put too much emphasis on eligibility criteria (Commission of the European Communities, 1993d). "In general the local and regional authorities increased their participation in measures financed" under the ESF (Commission of the European Communities, 1993d, p. 81). Something what the Commission felt should be strengthened in the future.

As was the case in the previous period, specific attention to local partnerships was introduced in the implementing provisions, as it was seen as "particularly suitable in the two new areas of assistance of the ESF, combating exclusion and promoting adaptation to industrial changes" (Commission of the European Communities, 1994, p. 125). In the following years the importance of Local Employment Initiatives (LEIs), or Local Development and Employment Initiatives as they were sometimes also called, started to grow further:

> The White Paper on Growth, Competitiveness and employment, published in December 1993, set out a medium-term strategy for creating more jobs and adopting a more vigorous approach to tackling unemployment. At its last meeting in Essen, the European Council decided on five priority fields of action under this strategy. Against this background, local development and employment initiatives have come to be seen as a means of boosting the employment intensity of growth. The Commission's macroeconomic outlook for 1995 and 1996 confirms the need to improve the employment intensity of growth in Europe. Hence the importance now being placed on local development and employment initiatives. (Commission of the European Communities, 1995a, p. 2).

As a first step the Commission identified 17 fields where LEIs could bring an important contribution ranging from home help services and childcare to local shops and tourism, and environmental services (Commission of the European Communities, 1995b).

As unemployment remained a serious problem, the Commission under the lead of its new President Santer, published in 1996 its communication "Action for Employment in Europe: a confidence Pact" in which it proposed to create Territorial Employment Pacts as a way to mobilise all the actors in one comprehensive strategy. The proposal included 46 actions amongst which the decentralisation of employment systems and the promotion of local initiatives for development and employment. It was mentioned that

> [t]he diversity of unemployment situations, the specific needs that arise and the potential that is available in one place or another and the complexity of the instruments with which employment systems operate all combine to make the local level more and more the appropriate level for activating employment policies (Commission of the European Communities, 1996, p. 25).

It was also concluded later in the first report on LEIs in 1997 that "[t]he experience of the Local Development and Employment Initiatives highlights certain desirable components of the territorial and local employment pacts, inspired by the European confidence pact, the key parameters are duration, territorial scope and partnership between the sectors involved" (Commission of the European Communities (1997c, p. 4). The Amsterdam Treaty further strengthened this approach by widening the sphere of social and employment policies considerably. A long list of fields had been added including a specific title on employment to allow for a European Employment Strategy, and action on combating social exclusion.

Finally, it should be noted that the ECSC low-cost housing scheme was continued. The 11th programme brought 48 million ECU for the period 1989-1993. The unification of Germany brought an additional 10 million ECU to the programme to support schemes in the new Länder (Commission of the European Communities, 1994h). The following years two more programmes were approved, but in 1997 the programme was discontinued. In 43 years 13 low-cost housing programmes brought together some 400 million ECU to support the building, purchasing and renovating of about 220.000 houses (Feantsa, 2002). In 1997 the European Investment Bank set up its Amsterdam Special Action Programme (ASAP) to support the Union's employment and growth initiative, with actions in the fields of education, health, urban environment and environmental protection, large infrastructure projects and networks and SMEs. As it was indicated "urban environment financing could include housing investment components on a prudent basis when they are integrated in well defined urban renewal and development schemes" (European Investment Bank, 2007). The ASAP was a success after which the EIB decided to include these fields as permanent elements of EIB interventions.

Environmental Policy

Although the fourth Environmental Action Programme highlighted the need for an urban focus, the actual support, in particular in comparison to that available to rural areas, was limited. After a meeting with several cities, Member of the European Parliament Ken Collins tabled a Resolution asking for a green paper on the urban environment that was approved by the Parliament in December 1988. After six preparatory conferences the Commission published its green paper in June 1990. The green paper opened by stating that "Dealing with the problem of the urban environment requires going beyond sectoral approaches. However, useful and necessary the setting of targets for air quality, water quality, maximum noise levels, etc. in Directives and Recommendations, finding lasting solutions to the environmental problems facing our cities requires a wider view of their origins" (Commission of the European Communities, 1980d, p. 1). Numerous actions were suggested ranging from planning and transport to energy and waste. The Council when welcoming the green paper and the debate the Commission had started, decided to establish an expert group on the urban environment consisting of national representatives and independent experts (Council of the European Communities, 1991, pp. 4-5). In the years that followed, the expert group delivered some important pieces of work to further the policy. In particular the "Sustainable Cities Project" consisting of the Sustainable Cities report giving a broad policy overview and examples of good practices, and the European Sustainable Cities and Towns Campaign should be mentioned (Commission of the European Communities, 1997d).

With the entry into force of the Maastricht Treaty that made sustainable development a fundamental goal, environmental policy became more important than ever before. The fifth Environmental Action Programme that was adopted in February 1993 clearly included this more horizontal approach. In addition to the traditional target sectors[12] tourism was added, but more importantly seven cross cutting fields were identified, including the urban environment. Also the recently approved financial instrument to support environmental action LIFE was detrimental in delivering results. For the period 1992-1995 LIFE had been awarded 400 million ECU. For 1996-1999 another 450 million ECU.

Other Policy Fields

The Commission's action framework, Sustainable Urban Development, identified numerous other policy fields where urban issues in recent years had been taken explicitly into consideration. The following initiatives should be mentioned:

* Research: The City of Tomorrow and Cultural Heritage Key Action within the 5th Framework programme proposals.
* Education and Training: European knowledge centres for human capital and knowledge development in urban centres, and second chance education and training arrangements in urban areas.

12　That is, industry, agriculture, transport and energy.

- Transport: Urban transport included in the Commission's views of transport policy.
- Energy: Sustainable energy management through subsidy schemes such as Altener (use of renewables) and SAVE (Energy efficiency)

Clearly, the effects and means of these policies were still moderate in comparison to the policies in the previous paragraphs.

Mainstreaming Makes the Urban Agenda Less Visible (1999-2009)

The third millennium started with yet another Treaty change, this time signed in February 2001 in Nice and entered into force on 1 February 2003. This Treaty change had no real effect on the role of cities but was crucial in preparing for the enlargement with ten new Eastern European countries on 1 May 2004 and Rumania and Bulgaria on 1 January 2007. Directly after these accessions another new Treaty was signed, the Treaty of Lisbon in December 2007, which went into force after a long ratification process on 1 December 2009.[13] The Lisbon Treaty added one crucial element to the tasks of the European Union, namely territorial cohesion (in relation to economic and social cohesion; see Commission of the European Communities, 2010a, p. 17). The more detailed article 174 had territorial cohesion added, as well as the list of regions requiring particular attention widened. The Lisbon Treaty mentions the following ones:

- Rural areas,
- Areas affected by industrial transition;
- Regions which suffer from severe and permanent natural or demographic handicaps such as the northernmost regions with very low population density and islands, cross-border and mountain regions.

In other words almost all types of regions are included except for the urbanised and metropolitan regions.

Other major developments at the European level were of course the introduction of the Euro and the start of the Lisbon strategy decided upon by the Lisbon European Council of March 2000. Here the heads of State and Government agreed on a "new strategic goal for the Union in order to strengthen the employment, economic reform and social cohesion as part of a knowledge-based economy" formulated as "to become the most competitive and dynamic knowledge based economy in the world capable of sustainable economic growth with more and better jobs and greater social cohesion" (Council of the European Union, 2000a, point 5).

---

13   The road to this new Treaty was very difficult with failed referenda in France and the Netherlands, but it falls out of the scope of this chapter to include a more in-depth analysis.

The broadening of the Lisbon Strategy with an environmental dimension as decided by the Gothenburg Council of June 2001 was another major step forward. Following the international climate negotiations after the Kyoto agreement, a strategy for sustainable development was agreed upon (Council of the European Union, 2001). This made combating climate change, sustainable transport, public health and more responsible use of natural resources an EU priority of growing importance, and cities both a part of the problem and the solutions.

Against the background of this steady move ahead of the Union and its actions, there also was a growing unease about the lack of involvement of a wide variety of actors in European policy making and delivery. In adapting the Treaties and Institutions the Commission published in 2001 their White Paper on European Governance with 14 concrete proposals, including those for stronger interaction with local and regional authorities and civil society (Commission of the European Communities, 2001a). This was a first step of what would become a key principle in strengthening partnerships and increasingly including regional and local level representatives and considerations into EU policy design.

Regional Policy: The Reform of 1999

When the Berlin Council of March 1999 finally decided on the new financial framework for 2000-2006 with a budget of €213 billion, the time was there to adopt the new regulations. The proposals were tabled by Commissioner Wulf-Mathies who had already announced a stronger attention for cities during the Cohesion Forum in April 1997.[14] The final texts were negotiated with the Council by her successor Michel Barnier. The new general regulation was already adopted on 21 June 1999. The specific fund regulations the next month on 12 July.

The result was a rather far reaching reform reducing the Objectives from six to three, one for regions lagging behind (Objective 1), one for areas facing structural difficulties (Objective 2) and one for adaptation and modernisation of the employment sector in regions outside Objective 1 (Objective 3). Within Objective 2 "urban areas in difficulty" were added as a specific strand (Council of the European Union, 1999, article 4-1) and special indicators for this category were set. Where in the previous period unemployment 50 per cent above the Community average was the criterion, now at least one of the following five criteria should be met (Council of the European Union, 1999a, article 7):

- A rate of long-term unemployment higher than the Community average;
- A high level of poverty, including precarious housing conditions;
- A particularly damaged environment;
- A high crime and delinquency rate;
- A low level of education among the population.

---

14   Forum organised in relation to the publishing of the Cohesion report.

The partnership text now included explicitly "regional, local and other public authorities" next to economic and social partners and "any other relevant organisation". They should be involved[15] in the preparation, financing, monitoring and evaluation of the programmes. Finally, in the operational arrangements such as the managing authority and the global grants, local authorities were explicitly added as a possible body.[16] The new ERDF regulation added in its scope "renewal of depressed urban areas" as well as Local Development and Economic Initiatives and SMEs. The Community Initiatives were continued, including URBAN.[17]

The Reform of 2006

The new programmes had barely started or the debate on the new reform took off. Under the lead of the new Commissioner Danuta Hübner. And again without knowing what the future budget (2007-2013) would bring. This time six member states were opposing the continuation of Objective 2 in order to reduce the Union's budget. The proposals of the Commission however, brought cohesion policy more in line with the Lisbon strategy, making the entire EU territory eligible for structural funds support. The new policy focus would consist of three objectives being:

- Convergence; the old Objective 1;
- Regional competitiveness and Employment; combining the former Objectives 2 and 3 and applying them to the EU territory outside the convergence Objective;
- European Territorial Cooperation; a strengthened INTERREG initiative.

The rest of the Community Initiatives were discontinued, or as it was called, mainstreamed into the three Objectives. That had to be covered by a more strategic approach to the programming. For that reason the Commission would have to draw up Community Strategic Guidelines linking the Union's strategic priorities to the funds operations. At national level a National Strategic Reference Framework (NSRF) would provide the link between the Commission's priorities and the national reform programmes in the light of the Lisbon strategy. The NSRF would provide for the umbrella for the national and regional programmes. Of particular

---

15 The text of previous period said "consulted".

16 In the previous period the ERDF regulation mentioned that for the implementation of global grants, appropriate bodies, including regional development bodies should be selected to assist local development initiatives (Council of the European Union, 1993b, pp. 34-38).

17 The original proposal of the Commission included only Community Initiatives for cross-border, transnational and interregional cooperation (INTERREG), rural development (Leader) and transnational cooperation on new means of combating discrimination and inequalities (EQUAL) (Commission of the European Communities, 1998c, p. 63). However, the European Parliament successfully pushed for the continuation of the URBAN initiative.

interest is the specific article on sustainable urban development within the ERDF regulation, stating that in addition to the regular ERDF activities, support can be awarded to

> the development of participative, integrated and sustainable strategies to tackle the high concentration of economic, environmental and social problems affecting urban areas. These strategies shall promote sustainable urban development through activities such as: strengthening economic growth, the rehabilitation of the physical environment, brownfield redevelopment, the preservation and development of natural and cultural heritage, the promotion of entrepreneurship, local employment and community development, and the provision of services to the population taking account of changing demographic structures (Council of the European Union, 2006a, p. 6).

These local programmes are to be included in the operational programmes as "(a) information on the approach to the sustainable urban development where appropriate;" and "At the initiative of the Member State, the operational programmes financed by the ERDF may also contain for the Convergence and Regional competitiveness and employment objectives: (a) the list of cities chosen for addressing urban issues and the procedures for sub-delegation to urban authorities, possibly by means of a global grant;" (Council of the European Union, 2006b, p. 47).

Simultaneously the so-called cross-financing option was introduced. Programme budgets could be used to invest up to 10 per cent of their Community funding for each of the programmes' priorities in actions falling within the scope of the other fund.[18] The only condition was that these actions are necessary for the satisfactory implementation of the operation. Within the ERDF article 8 sustainable urban development operations this cross-financing can even be raised to 15 per cent.

This clearly indicates the potentially crucial role for cities in the new architecture.[19] In this way the discontinuation of the URBAN initiative was compensated by the sub-delegation clause. As it was explained when introducing this possibility: "Building on the strengths of the URBAN initiative, the Commission intends to reinforce the place of urban issues by fully integrating actions in this field into the programmes. To carry this out, at the beginning of the next programming period, each Member State would propose a list of urban areas which would benefit from specific action within the programmes. The extent of the problems facing the cities and their role in promoting regional development would

---

18 That is, up to 10 per cent of ERDF funding within a priority can be spent on ESF activities.

19 The proposed text of the Commission was stronger as it did not include terms such as "where appropriate". It was phrased as follows "b) information on the approach to the urban issue, including the list of cities chosen and the procedures for sub-delegation to urban authorities, possibly by means of a global grant;" (Commission of the European Communities, 2004a, p. 42).

suggest that the number of cities concerned should be greater than the 70 today covered by the URBAN initiative in the EU15. Critical to the success of urban actions is the involvement of the city authorities both in the design of programmes and in the management. It is therefore envisaged that an arrangement involving a sub-delegation of responsibilities to these authorities would be necessary within the regional programmes. The scale of interventions organised in this way would be decided when the programmes are drawn up, but it is worth noting that today more than 10 per cent of the total EU contribution to Objectives 1 and 2 is devoted directly or indirectly to financing urban-related measures" (Commission of the European Communities, 2004b).

Analysis of the Urban Situation

During the Potsdam informal Council in May 1999, ministers responsible for regional policy and spatial planning adopted the final version of the European Spatial Development Perspective (ESDP), that identified as its main aims:

- Polycentric urban development and a new relationship between urban and rural areas;
- Access for all regions to infrastructure and know-how;
- Management of natural and cultural heritage.

These aims should provide for a stronger territorial cohesion in the European territory. The ESDP's point of view was included in the second cohesion report, which was already long overdue when it was published in 2001. Both the "growth centres" as the "significant disparities" side of urban areas were highlighted, alongside the characteristics of all other types of regions, such as mountains and islands, all under the heading of territorial cohesion (Commission of the European Communities, 2001b).

Three years later the third cohesion report provided for a general analysis of the developments of cohesion in the territories. It furthermore described the impact of Member States and Community policies on cohesion and the added value of the programmes. But its most important focus was on the newly proposed architecture for the 2007-2013 period. As such it was clearly a document to provide for a EU-wide debate on the role and the future of cohesion policy. The fourth report on the other hand included several pages on territorial trends at local level. These had become available due to an updated Urban Audit that also covered a much larger group of cities, including very large cities as London and Paris. Particular attention was being given to suburbanization processes and the concentration of problems in urban neighbourhoods.

At the same time the European Spatial Planning Observation Network (ESPON) that was established in 2002 as a result of the ESDP process, started to produce several insightful studies, some of them particularly dedicated to the performance of cities in their territories and the EU as a whole. In 2005 the Commission put out a call for tender to develop the statistical data of the urban audit into a genuine State of the European cities report. The report was published in 2007 and it

> acknowledges the role of cities as laboratories: the places where economic and societal changes are often experienced first and most profoundly and aims to provide a lens through which contemporary urban Europe can be observed. When cities seek to understand the changes around them and look for strategic re-orientation, this report provides a reference point, which can help them to identify their unique characteristics, as well as their commonalities with other European urban areas (Commission of the European Communities, 2007a, p. II).

In doing so, it not only pointed out the wide variety of characteristics under the types of European cities, it also identified some of the (future) challenges that are on the urban agenda, such as competitiveness, quality of life and governance. As such it provided insight and helped to put cities much stronger on the EU agenda.

By the end of 2008 the Commission published its Staff working document Regions 2020, identifying the "grand challenges" for Europe's future and the possible role for the Community's policies. For regional policy the following four were identified: Globalization, Demographic Change, Impact of Climate Change, and Secure, Sustainable and Competitive Energy. Although the document primarily identified how these challenges could affect the different European regions, and potentially increase regional disparities, there was also attention for the urbanised areas:

> At the sub-national level, the analysis reveals that, in many Member States, regions with major urban centres and metropolitan areas should be relatively well placed to respond to the challenges linked to globalisation. These areas tend to benefit from a large share of highly educated residents, highly dynamic sectors and leading-edge economic activities. Yet, the concentration of economic activities in agglomerations may also create negative externalities (such as congestion, urban sprawl, drain on natural resources and ecosystem services) and may also lead to under-utilised economic potential elsewhere. (Commission of the European Communities, 2008a, p. 6).

Invited by the Leipzig Informal Council of Ministers responsible for spatial planning and regional development, and the explicit inclusion of territorial cohesion in the Lisbon Treaty, the Commission launched a debate among stakeholders to deepen the understanding of the concept and identify its policy implications in 2008. As the accompanying green paper indicated, territorial cohesion was already explicitly highlighted in the 2006 Community Strategic Guidelines, and long before that always at the heart of cohesion policy, albeit more implicit. However, the Commission noted that "at the same time, there has been increasing recognition of the need to promote cooperation, dialogue and partnership between different levels of government and between these and organisations and people on the ground directly involved in the development process" (Commission of the European Communities, 2008b, p. 4). In other words, as has been discovered time and again, partnership often ends at the regional level.

Cities play a prominent role in the thinking laid down in the green paper. Whether it is on the question of concentration that leads to a high level of GDP per head or diseconomies from congestion and problems of urban decay and exclusion that leads to lower GDP, the connections of cities and towns, or cross border urban networks. As is stated in the green paper, "to tackle these and other problems effectively requires a policy response on a variable geographical scale, involving in some cases cooperation between neighbouring local authorities, in others between countries, and in yet others between the European Union and neighbouring countries" (Commission of the European Communities, 2008b, p. 7). The green paper furthermore highlights the development of metropolitan bodies bringing together several authorities to tackle joint issues. Finally, the approach taken was not limited to regional policy. It was also identified that sectoral policies had to be identified and their coordination with territorial policies improved.

The Place of Cities in Regional Programming

The addition of "urban areas in difficulty" as a new category qualifying for ERDF support in the 2000-2006 programming period and the even further reaching reform of 2006 opened up several possibilities for cities in the new programmes. According to the ESDP, 30-40 per cent of Objective 1 programme budgets are spent in urban areas and measures in Objective 2 programmes are often urban in nature (Commission of the European Communities, 1999a, p. 16). As said

> despite the assertions of the ESDP, gaining an appreciation of the urban dimension of the Structural Funds is complicated by the simple fact that few programmes focus solely on urban areas, and, equally, few measures take an explicit urban focus. The exception to this is the Urban Community Initiative. However in comparison to Objectives 1, 2 and 3 of the Structural Funds the Urban Community Initiative is extremely modest in the number of urban areas covered and the scale of funding involved. It also takes a very specific focus on tackling problems at the urban neighbourhood level, focusing particularly on issues of economic and social exclusion (ECOTEC, 2004).

This analysis is underlined by the ex-post evaluation that identified that 31 per cent of Objective-1 and 35 per cent of Objective-2 funding was spent in Urban regions (Commission of the European Communities, 2010b). However, as these regions are based on the OECD NUTS-III classification[20] it does not provide sufficient

---

20   "The basis of the OECD classification of regions is the 'local unit', a small area for which there are at least some data for all EU Member States and which corresponds to

insight into the investments in urban challenges. There are numerous examples of such urban regions where the majority of the funding is not aimed at specific urban development actions in those regions.

By fully integrating the urban dimension into the 2007-13 regulations and including specific, or strengthening existing instruments, it was the intention to ensure a better involvement of local authorities in the programmes. A first analysis of the 316 Operational Programme's for this period however, showed "few signs of direct local involvement in the design and implementation of European Regional Development Funds operational programmes. It remains to be seen if this can be improved throughout the implementation of the programmes" (Commission of the European Communities, 2008c, p. 5). In particular:

- Many of the options for improved governance of urban development programmes have not been used or reflected upon in programme documents;[21]
- Most cities have a limited role to play in programme-related decision making process and in managing budgets for investments in their territory;
- Only in few cases a delegation of responsibilities has been applied.

Fortunately, there were also some positive signs:

- More than half of the Operational Programmes include the JESSICA initiative[22] (as a plan);
- A substantial amount of money is being spent on urban operations. Of the 316 Operational Programmes, 178 contain an urban dimension, albeit that direct funding aiming at urban development totals only 3.2 per cent of the total amounts available for the Convergence Objective, and 8.9 per cent within the Regional Competitiveness and employment Objective.

---

a commune or district. NUTS 3 regions are divided in the following way between types of area:
- Rural areas, if more than half of the population of the region live in local units with population density below 150 per square km;
- Predominantly urban areas, if 85 per cent or more people live in local units with a population density of over 150 per square km;
- Intermediate areas, if 50-85 per cent or more live in local units with population density of over 150 per square km.

21   The possibility to sub-delegate responsibilities to the local level as was one of the successful features of the Urban Initiative has only been applied to the Dutch Operational Programme "Opportunities for West" and sub-delegation by global grants in general only in 12 cases (Commission of the European Communities, 2008c, pp. 34-35).

22   Jessica is the Joint European Support for Sustainable Investment in City Areas initiative aiming at financial engineering through revolving funds supporting urban renewal and development.

But probably most important is the attention given to the urban dimension in these programmes by the Commission and the systematic overviews on urban operations being presented in the evaluation reports.

Specific Urban Programmes

With the limited use of the new urban category within Objective 2 and partnerships still not fully including local authorities, the continuation of URBAN turned out to be of crucial importance. Even though its funds were just sufficient to support 70 modest programmes,[23] its results were impressive. In particular the integrated approach, focus on small areas and thus high aid intensity per head, flexible and innovative approaches, and strong local partnerships including local communities showed how effective urban programmes can contribute to local development (Commission of the European Communities, 2002).

In addition to the URBAN II programme, a specific programme for exchange of experience and support for urban networks was set up: Urbact. In its first phase from 2002 to 2006 it was focused at the cities that benefited from URBAN I, II or Urban Pilot Project support. Halfway during this first period, the programme was extended to the cities from the new Member States that due to their accession in 2004 had not been able to participate in any of the three programmes. With an ERDF support of almost €16 million, a total of 217 cities were able to participate in 38 projects. For the second period (2007-13) the programme was opened up to all cities in the EU. The budget of over €50 million was anticipated to finance a total of 46 thematic networks and 14 working groups and as such several hundred cities (Commission of the European Communities, 2009a). One of the key features of Urbact II is the aim to include the management authorities of the regional cohesion programmes in the networks, to ensure that the results will be included in the future mainstream programmes.

The complete mainstreaming of Community Initiatives into the Objectives in the 2007-13 programming period, ended the direct link between the Commission and local partners in integrated programmes. The 2006 reform offered strong possibilities to create urban type programmes within the mainstream Operational Programmes by sub-delegating powers for "small" programmes to the cities or through global grants. As the previous paragraph described, this possibility was hardly applied. Similarly the newly created JESSICA instrument was barely visible in the 2008 initial evaluation of the new programmes, but that was partly due to uncertainties in its application.

In a Memorandum of Understanding between the Commission, the European Investment Bank (EIB) and the Council of Europe Development Bank (CEB) of May 2006, the three agreed to coordinate their approach to urban renewal and development in Structural Funds developments. They were particular aiming to

---

23 The total ERDF contribution was €730 million generating a total investment of €1.6 billion.

facilitate the authorities to make more effective use of public resources and encourage greater use of firm engineering measures and revolving funds (Commission of the European Communities, 2006a). In setting up the initiative the EIB conducted a study to review the applicability and evaluate its potential. Between September and December 2006 the possibilities and difficulties were investigated in six member states. The study identified (European Investment Bank, 2007):

- The need for flexibility of the approach;
- Consistency of approach and clarity of purpose;
- Complement other public delivery approaches;
- Tailor made support (in type and scale of financial support);
- The need for sufficient and appropriate profession expertise.

After these and several other issues (in particular state aid and procurement) were cleared, more and more JESSICA initiatives were started.

Intergovernmental Progress

As noted before, the June 1998 Glasgow informal Council of ministers responsible for urban affairs called to develop the member states' urban exchange initiative into an informal non-binding framework on urban policy by around the year 2000. The result of that work was presented at the informal meeting of ministers of November 2000 in Lille. In the meeting's conclusions the ministers reaffirmed "the necessity to promote a global and integrated approach in urban planning, be it national or within the EU with reference to sustainable development, that encompasses particularly spatial, social and economic domains, emphasising employment, education, transport, environment, crime prevention and security" (Presidency of the European Union, 2000, point 2). The result was the so-called Lille-agenda that included the following nine priorities (Presidency of the European Union, 2000, p. 3):

- "Better recognition of the role of cities in spatial planning.
- New approach of urban policy at national and EU level.
- Support of the community life in disadvantaged neighbourhoods.
- Measures to eradicate social, ethnic and discriminating segregation in disadvantaged neighbourhoods.
- Work on different spatial scales.
- Partnership between private and public sectors.
- Dissemination of best practices and networking.
- Use of new technologies of communication and information.
- Deepening of the work on urban indicators."

Unfortunately, after a promising start, a few presidencies later the Lille-agenda lost its drive and actuality. However, in 2004 the Dutch presidency gave the process new focus in concluding their informal ministerial meeting on urban policy with the Rotterdam Urban Acquis aiming to promote the urban agenda on a national level,[24] strengthening cooperation between Member States and strengthening the EU urban agenda (Presidency of the European Union, 2004). From then on, the work was seriously brought forward and resulted in December 2005 in the Bristol Accord on Sustainable communities in Europe and in May 2007 in the Leipzig Charter on the European Sustainable City:

> With the Leipzig Charter, the ministers responsible for urban development agreed on guidelines for an integrated urban development policy which covers economical, social and environmental dimensions, represents a fundamental element of a national urban policy and develops strategies for action on socially and economically deprived urban areas as well as on cities as a whole. Through the political impetus which it provided, the Leipzig Charter is offering the member states an opportunity to make a valuable contribution to the work of the European Commission, in particular to the Commission's report on the follow-up process of cohesion policy due by 2010, by reporting on their experience made in this application of integrated urban development strategies (Presidency of the European Union, 2007).

Building on the Leipzig Charter, the French presidency during the second half of 2008 called on the Commission and other relevant authorities to take account of climate change in line with urban development, and promote the use of cohesion policy in support of urban integrated development. It furthermore initiated the Reference Framework for European Sustainable Cities (RFSC). The RFSC "is a tool for local debate and dialogue between different levels of governance. It should not be a tool for third parties to evaluate urban policies. On the other hand, this tool should facilitate access to knowledge of good practice and existing methods for developing locally produced indicators and could support measures to follow-up the implementation of integrated, sustainable and cohesive urban development approaches or the absence of this" (Presidency of the European Union, 2008, Annex point 2.4).

Institutional Changes

Although the role of the institutions and the processes between them is not a specific point of attention in this overview, two developments should be mentioned. First of all, the focus on integrated approaches in turn required a more integrated approach by the Commission. This was answered in December 2005 by establishing an Interservice group on urban development. This group being

---

24   This action was supported by the Euricur study into National Urban Policies (see van den Berg et al., 2004).

chaired by DG Regional Policy brings together policy officers working on urban issues from the different Directorate Generals with the following objectives:

- Promoting integrated sustainable urban development within structural funds assistance.
- Identifying initiatives under other policies aiming to support sustainable development of urban areas and ensuring the necessary interservice cooperation.
- Ensuring partnership between the various institutions and associations of cities establishing regular dialogue and exchange of views on the urban dimension. To this end a guide providing an overview of the urban dimension of EU programmes and initiatives had been produced in 2006 and been updated in 2010 (European Commission, 2010, p. 5).

Secondly, in 2005 the European Parliament created the intergroup Urban-Housing, bringing together Members from different parliamentary committees and groups with an interest on urban issues. Besides the legislative work and exchanging views on the development of EU policies in the urban practice, with practitioners and experts, the group also hosts numerous events of urban platforms. Under its first president Jean Marie Beaupuy, the partnership was build and a strong basis for continuation was established. Under its current president Jan Olbrycht, the intergroup was renamed Urban and has further developed in the political platform on urban issues within the EU institutions.

Social Policy

After the substantial changes to the ESF during the 1993 reform, the proposed changes for the 2000-06 programming period were rather modest. The main change was the introduction of alignment with Member States' actions undertaken in pursuance of the European Employment Strategy (EES) and the annual Guidelines on Employment. These were already launched in 1997 but were only fully taking shape after their inclusion into the Amsterdam Treaty. Every year the Member States present their National Action Plans and the Commission draws up the employment guidelines. In the guidelines for the year 2000 the Commission proposed that

> the Member States will promote measures to exploit fully the possibilities offered by job creation at local level and in the social economy, especially in new activities linked to needs not yet satisfied by the market, and examine, with the aim of reducing, any obstacles in the way of such measures. In this respect, the special role and responsibility of local and regional authorities, other partners at the regional and local levels, as well as of the social partners, needs to be more fully recognised and supported. In addition, the role of the public employment services in identifying local employment opportunities and

improving the functioning of local labour markets, should be fully exploited (Council of the European Union, 2000b).

To that end the ESF regulations had local development and employment initiatives fully incorporated as one of the ESF's tasks (Council of the European Union, 1999b) building on the first experiences of the Territorial Employment Pacts. And even though the Member States had shown their commitment to the EES process during the ESF negotiations, the use of local initiatives has been varying. In the evaluation of the use of the Territorial Employment Pacts it was concluded that "their reception ranges from enthusiastic acceptance through relative indifference to a degree of resistance" (ECOTEC, 2002, p.VIII). And on a broader scale "the urban focus of Objective 3 is largely coincidental – a consequence of where target groups reside rather than positive planning" (ECOTEC, 2004, p. 71).

The reform of 2006 brought the ESF, as was the case with the ERDF, further in line with the Lisbon Strategy that includes the EES. From then on the ESF had the following priorities:

- Increasing adaptability of workers, enterprises and entrepreneurs;
- Enhancing access to employment and the sustainable inclusion in the labour market of job seekers and inactive people;
- Reinforcing the social inclusion of disadvantages people (including involvement of local communities and promotion of LEIs);
- Enhancing human capital;
- "Promoting partnerships, pacts and initiatives through networking of relevant stakeholders, such as the social partners and non-governmental organisations, at the transnational, national, regional and local levels in order to mobilise for reforms in the field of employment and labour market inclusiveness" (Council of the European Union, 2006c, article 3-1e).

For the Convergence objective two priorities concerning human capital in relation to improve the educational system necessary for creating a knowledge based society, and building institutional capacity were added. To ensure concentration it was prescribed that Operational Programmes should direct their resources

> towards the most important needs and focus on those policy areas where ESF
> support can have a significant effect in attaining the objectives of the programme.
> To maximise the efficiency of ESF support, operational programmes shall,
> where appropriate, take particular account of the regions and localities facing
> the most serious problems, such as deprived urban and outermost regions,
> declining rural and fisheries-dependent areas, and areas particularly adversely
> affected by business relocations (Council of the European Union, 2006c,
> article 4-2).

With respect to good governance and partnership the provisions of the general regulation were reiterated in the ESF text. Whether this has actually resulted in a stronger involvement of the local level still has to be proven.

In parallel to the ERDF regulation, ESF actions can be spend up to 10 per cent on ERDF actions when meetings specific conditions. This percentage can be raised to 15 per cent on actions in the field of social inclusion, in particular promoting pathways to integration and re-entry into employment for disadvantages people.

Special attention has to be given to the aspect of housing. With the ECSC low-cost housing scheme and later the EIB action programme (see paragraph 3.5) housing had always been excluded from structural funds support. In the proposed ERDF regulations for the 2007-13 programming period it was still considered as non-eligible expenditure (Commission of the European Communities, 2004c, article 7). However, the specific housing situation in the new Member States made it necessary to make an exception. Therefore the adopted general regulation included provisions to support housing for the new Member States if the actions were part of an integrated urban development operation, or part of a priority aiming at areas threatened by physical deterioration and social exclusion. The maximum support was limited to 3 per cent of the ERDF and aiming at multi-family housing or houses, owned by public authorities or non-profit operators, designated for low-income families or people with special needs (Commission of the European Communities, 2004c, article 7).

Another step was made as part of the crisis recovery package of May 2009. As one of the many actions to accelerate programme implementation, co-financing of energy-efficiency improvements and renewable energy measures in housing was agreed upon. Every Member State could spend up to 4 per cent of their ERDF allocations on these measures in the remainder of the programming period (Council of the European Union and European Parliament, 2009a, p. 3).

Environmental Policy

With the ending of the fifth environmental action programme in the year 2000, the Commission published a global assessment as a preparation for a new phase. The most crucial point was, that despite the progress made, the state of the environment remained a cause for concern. To make improvements under the sixth programme, it was proposed to reinforce the integration of environmental concerns into the Community's sectoral policies and ensure a stronger involvement of citizens and stakeholders. It was suggested to develop a strategic approach to sustainable development consisting "of a set of guiding principles and objectives backed up by action plans that address the different economic, social and environmental aspects" (Commission of the European Communities, 1999b, p. 25). The sixth environmental action programme introduced this approach as 'Thematic Strategies' (Council of the European Union and European Parliament, 2002, p. 6).

Already in May 2001 the Commission presented its views on a thematic strategy for air quality under the name Clean Air for Europe (CAFE). In its introduction the main focus was on air quality in cities taking account of the new priorities Particulate

Matter (PM$_{10}$) reduction and ozone protection. The proposal for the strategy on air pollution of September 2005 established interim objectives for air pollution reduction in the EU and proposed measures for achieving, in particular through a revision of the ambient air quality legislation (Commission of the European Communities, 2005a). Whereas the strategy focused on the EU wide territory, the accompanying proposal for a Directive on ambient air quality and cleaner air for Europe focused mainly on agglomerations with more than 250,000 inhabitants, or smaller zones with a given population density to be established by the Member State (Commission of the European Communities (2005b, p. 16). The Directive was finally adopted in May 2008. Despite strong efforts to tighten the legislation by setting stricter limit values, these were in the end unchanged from the original proposal.

In February 2004 the Commission presented its Green Paper on the Urban Environment as a first step to a thematic strategy. It set as the overall aim "to improve the environmental performance and quality of urban areas and to secure a healthy living environment for Europe's urban citizens, reinforcing the environmental contribution to sustainable urban development while taking into account the related economic and social issues" (Commission of the European Communities, 2004d, p. 4). A rather broad definition resulting in a wide variety of actions proposed under the headings of sustainable urban management, sustainable urban transport, sustainable construction (i.e. buildings), sustainable urban design, as well as horizontal actions linking in with other Community policies including the other thematic strategies, and administrative integration and capacity building. Almost two years later the Thematic strategy was published, identifying an integrated approach to environmental management at the local level, and transport in particular, as its most important elements. Whereas the Green Paper suggested mandatory approaches, the final text of the Strategy itself indicated that "The Commission strongly recommends local authorities to take the necessary steps to achieve greater use of integrated management at the local level and encourages national and regional authorities to support this process" (Commission of the European Communities, 2006b, p. 5). Furthermore, the Commission would provide technical support in 2006. The same approach was taken for the development and implementation of sustainable urban transport plans. All other proposals from the Green Paper were modestly addressed under the heading "synergies with other policies".

In 2007 the LIFE instrument was extended till 2013 under the name LIFE+, aiming to support the implementation of the sixth environmental action programme, including the thematic strategies. The programme was allocated €2.1 billion for the seven year period to be focused at three priorities:

- Nature and biodiversity;
- Environment Policy and Governance;[25]
- Information and Communication.

---

25 The objectives under this heading are: Climate Change, Water, Air, Soil, Urban environment, Noise, Chemicals, Environment and Health, Natural resources and Waste,

Specifically for local authorities a framework for cooperation promoting sustainable urban development was created in 2001. EU-wide networks covering at least four Member States could be supported in the fields of:

- Implementation of EU environmental legislation at local level;
- Sustainable urban development;
- Local Agenda 21.

Based on calls for proposals, projects could be submitted for up to €350,000. For the period 2001-2004 a total of €14 million was available (Council of the European Union and European Parliament, 2001).

Transport Policy

Even though urban public transport was already identified in 1995 as important, it took till the 2001 White Paper on Transport and the Union's Strategy for sustainable development, to identify that there was a strong need to rationalise urban transport. The White Paper indicated that "even if the subsidiarity principle dictates that responsibility for urban transport lies mainly with the national and local authorities, the ills besetting transport in urban areas and spoiling the quality of life cannot be ignored" (Commission of the European Communities, 2001c, p. 85). It put forward a large number of proposals. With regard to urban transport amongst others Urban and land-use planning, Urban transport policy in major conurbations, and Developing high quality urban networks. The proposed Strategy for sustainable development primarily focused on realising a model shift, in particular in the field of the Trans European Networks and through better pricing the different modes of transport (Council of the European Union, 2001).

Despite these ambitions, it took until 2007 before a Green Paper on Urban mobility was presented. As several other policies (i.e. environment, enterprise, energy) had developed legislative initiatives in the field of urban transport, the Commission felt it necessary to develop a more integrated approach. The Green Paper furthermore included 25 questions around these challenges and other issues, as part of a consultation with stakeholders (Commission of the European Communities, 2007b).

The action plan for urban mobility that was proposed in September 2009 included 20 actions grouped under six themes that were following a different approach then the Green Paper (Commission of the European Communities, 2009b), namely:

- Promoting integrated plans;
- Focusing on citizens;
- Greening urban transport;

Forests, Innovation, Strategic approaches, Governance, and NGOs (Council of the European Union and European Parliament, 2007).

- Strengthening funding;
- Sharing experience and knowledge;
- Optimizing urban mobility.

Following the Thematic Strategy on the Urban Environment, substantial progress had been made on the guidelines for sustainable urban transport plans that were published in September 2007. As the document stated "compliance with air and noise EU legislation requires that plans addressing urban transport are drawn up in many conurbations" (Commission of the European Communities, 2007c, p. 10). In particular the 122 page annex with thorough explanations and many good practices gave good insight into how these mandatory plans could be developed.

More concrete results were realised through initiatives such as Civitas that is aiming at cleaner and better transport in cities. Launched in 2002, it supported between 2002 and 2009 in total 36 cities in eight research and demonstration projects aiming to achieve a shift towards sustainable mobility. A final element is the inclusion of clean and energy efficient road transport vehicles in public procurement legislation. This states that "Member States shall ensure that, from 4 December 2010, all contracting authorities, ... when purchasing road transport vehicles take into account the operational lifetime energy and environmental impacts" (Council of the European Union and European Parliament, 2009b, p. 9).

Energy

The focus on combating climate change shifted the attention of the Union's energy policy more and more from energy security to efficiency. In March 2000 the Commission published its ideas to reduce greenhouse gas emissions under the heading "European Climate Change Programme" (ECCP). It identified that greenhouse emissions had been increasing rather than decreasing, bringing the Kyoto commitments further away. Measures proposed to overcome this situation were related with energy supply, energy consumption, transport, waste, among others (Commission of the European Communities, 2000a).

Called upon by the Gothenburg Council, the Commission published its implementation plan for the first phase of the ECCP in October 2001. It underlined several of the measures identified before, estimated CO_2 emission reduction potential and how to realise this. In addition it identified the potential of integrating environmental considerations into public procurement, including specific guidance on energy efficiency (Commission of the European Communities, 2001d).

The Commission had already presented its draft energy efficiency action plan in April 2000, on the request of the Energy Council of December 1998. It listed a total of 69 actions in various fields such as buildings, equipment (including lighting), Combined Heating and Power, Industrial actions and transport policy and efficiency. It also underlined the crucial role of local authorities as it identified regional and urban policies as an important policy to integrate energy efficiency principles into, and the "large savings potential which can be realised by greater decentralisation of energy management and increased public involvement at the local and regional levels" (Commission of the European Communities, 2000b, p. 12). This plan was welcomed by the Energy Councils during their sessions on 30 May and 5 December 2000. The Council stressed particular actions and added a few. Specific attention was amongst others given to actions in the medium and longer-term, including measures on "procurement guidelines, including, where appropriate, guidelines on life cycle cost assessment, and best practice scheme, in particular with regard to public sector buildings" (Council of the European Union, 2000c).

As one of the first concrete measures the Council and European Parliament adopted in December 2002 the Energy Performance of Buildings Directive (EPBD). It identified that "the residential and tertiary sector, the major part of which is buildings, accounts for more than 40 per cent of final energy consumption in the Community" (Council of the European Union and European Parliament, 2003, p. 65). The EPBD set minimum requirements for the energy performance of new buildings and large existing buildings of over 1000m² floor space. Also limits were set concerning boilers, air-conditioning systems and energy certification. Half a year later the Commission made its proposal for Eco-design requirements for Energy-Use Products. This set standards for industry that needed to ensure that more energy efficient products would become available and even the norm. Under the heading 'lighting in tertiary sectors' (Council of the European Union and European Parliament, 2005, p. 41) work was being undertaken to improve office and street lighting.[26] This technical work was concluded in March 2009 aiming at a shift to more efficient lighting systems and realising a estimated energy saving of 15 per cent by 2020, compared to business as usual (Commission of the European Communities, 2009c).

In October 2006 the Commission published a second action plan for energy efficiency. This action plan focused at the development of primary energy demand and savings potential and identified where savings could be made most effective. Next to the Eco-design directive it aimed at, amongst others building performance requirements and energy efficiency in built up areas (Commission of the European Communities, 2006c).

The latter included the setting up of the Covenant of Mayors initiative, in which cities have formally committed themselves to go beyond the EU's energy objective of reducing CO_2 emissions by 20 per cent by 2020. Starting in 2008, the first official solemn ceremony brought together mayors of 350 cities who signed the covenant. In October 2009 the signatories already doubled and early 2012

---

26   Even though the original proposal already included the term tertiary sectors (Commission of the European Communities, 2003) it only became clear in 2009 that this involved public street lighting. The implementing Directive was drawn up by national experts, in consultation with the lighting industry. Local authorities as end users were neither consulted nor informed in advance, in order to adjust their investment/maintenance plans accordingly.

there were over 3000 local authorities participating, representing some 140 million citizens.

Early 2007 the Commission presented its Renewable energy roadmap. Although it focused mainly at the renewable energy sources and flanking measures to ensure their take up, it recognised the importance of local authorities. "In addition to these Commission initiatives, it should be underlined that Member States, regional and local authorities have to make significant contribution towards increasing the use of renewable" (Commission of the European Communities, 2007d, p. 13), followed by specific actions to be undertaken including the integration of renewable energies in local plans. The final Directive that was published in April 2009 went further by stating that "Member States may encourage local and regional authorities to set targets in excess of national targets and to involve local and regional authorities in drawing up national renewable energy action plans and in raising awareness of the benefits of energy from renewable sources" (Council of the European Union and European Parliament, 2009c, p. 19). Particular measures included heating and cooling from renewable energy sources, zero energy housing, information, awareness-raising, guidance and training programmes. The renewable energy roadmap and energy efficiency action plan were included in the European Council's action plan "Energy Policy for Europe" that became known by its "20-20-20" targets to be met by 2020 (Council of the European Union, 2007):

- 20 per cent greenhouse gas reduction below 1990 levels;
- 20 per cent of energy consumption from renewable;
- 20 per cent energy reduction by improved energy efficiency.

To support all these actions (limited) support for cities was made available, even though local authorities were one of the several potential beneficiaries. The Concerto initiative that was funded from the research programmes from 2005 onwards, is aiming to finance demonstrators in the building sector. Examples include innovative technologies development, use of renewable resources for cities, sustainable building and district development, energy transparency for citizens. In total 58 projects benefitted from €141 million in the period till 2007. In 2006 the Competitiveness and Innovation Framework Programme (CIP) 2007-2013 was established bringing together existing instruments such as SAVE and Altener under the heading Intelligent Energy – Europe (IEE) with a total budget of €700 million. Again this programme is not specifically targeted at local authorities, but does provide interesting opportunities for cities to participate (Council of the European Union and European Parliament, 2006).

Cities as the Driving Force for European Development (2010-2020)

Even though this final period in this overview has only just started some interesting developments are already surfacing. In institutional developments this period seems less dependent on change than the periods described before. No real Treaty change is foreseen and there are only two rather small candidates to join the Union in the short run: Croatia and Serbia. This could on the other hand change quickly if the EU will not be able to tackle the ongoing crises that are of a severe magnitude. The period started with a 4 per cent loss of GDP, a drop of industrial production to the level of the 1990s and an average unemployment of 10 per cent and youth unemployment levels up to several times higher. To tackle the crises and deal with the ongoing problems, the new Barroso Commission starting in 2010 built its Europe 2020 strategy on the building blocks of the Lisbon strategy.

Europe 2020 was presented in March 2010 and covered the following strategic focus (Commission of the European Communities, 2010c, p. 5):

- *"Smart growth*: developing an economy based on knowledge and innovation.
- *Sustainable growth*: promoting a more resource efficient, greener and more competitive economy.
- *Inclusive growth*: fostering a high-employment economy delivering social and territorial cohesion."

To realise these priorities five headline targets for member states to reach by 2020 were defined. Every year EU guidelines will be set and member states will have to put forward their (adjusted) National Reform Programmes. During the so-called European semester these will be commented upon by the Commission through country specific recommendations and overall progress will be tabled at the annual Spring Council sessions (Commission of the European Communities, 2011a). To ensure EU progress in all the defined themes, seven flagship initiatives are put forward. The EU's 20-20-20 strategy is fully incorporated both in the headline targets and the flagships. The EU's other key policies such as the Internal Market and cohesion policy are to be aligned with Europe 2020. In this respect Europe 2020 already builds on the partnership principle of cohesion policy: "All national, regional and local authorities should implement the partnership, closely associating parliaments, as well as social partners and representatives of civil society, contributing to the elaboration of national reform programmes as well as to its implementation" (Commission of the European Communities, 2010c, p. 29).

The Multi-annual Financial Framework (MFF) budget proposal for 2014-2020 of June 2011 was also fully focused at delivering the Europe 2020 goals. To answer the ambitions from this policy point of view the Commission is proposing a budget that increases by 5 per cent from the current budget to a total of €1025 billion for the seven year budget (Commission of the European Communities, 2011b). The Commission also proposes a more simple financing system moving away from VAT and non-transparent corrections. However, most interesting is the urban bonus that has been introduced within the framework of the financial allocations of the structural funds to the member states. Cities of more than 250,000 inhabitants will be awarded €4 per inhabitant per year.[27] Due to this major overhaul and strong austerity measures in member states, there is much debate on the MFF proposals making an agreement by the Council and the European Parliament a difficult process and not to be expected before 2013.

Regional Policy: The Reform of 2012

Following the MFF proposal that already included the main headings for the future regional policy, the Commission published its cohesion policy package in October 2011.[28] The proposals build on the 2007-2013 experiences and the adjustments put forward as part of the Economic Recovery Package of 2009 with a strong focus on simplification and results orientation. The new approach will cover the entire EU with three types of regions. In addition to the "Convergence" and "Competitiveness and Employment" regions of the 2007-2013 period a new category of "Transitional" regions is included. In fact this combines the regions just falling out of the first type (also known as phasing out regions) and regions still below 90 per cent of the average GDP in the EU (also known as phasing in regions) into one framework. The total budget amounts €376 billion for the seven year period, roughly one third of the MFF proposal. Over €160 billion is earmarked for the less developed convergence regions. Almost €40 billion for the transition regions and over €50 billion for the more developed regions. Furthermore, more than €10 billion is foreseen to support territorial cooperation and almost €70 billion is reserved for the Cohesion fund. In addition another €40 billion is reserved for the new Connecting Europe Facility for transport, energy and ICT.

The strategic focus of the programmes should be linked much strongly to the European objectives. The link with the indicators of the Lisbon strategy was still indicative. For the new period proposals are made to "translate" the European objectives into the Structural Funds programmes in a so-called Common Strategic Framework (to be tabled in March 2012). At Member State level, these challenges need to be further elaborated in a Partnership Contract explicitly taking into account the National Reform Programmes and the country specific recommendations. This

---

27   EU wide this totals to €2.5 billion. The largest part stems from the developed regions: €1.8 billion, 3.5 per cent of the budget proposed for these regions (calculations made by the author). That the member states allocations are calculated in this way does not mean that these monies will be automatically awarded to cities. That is something which has to be decided within the Partnership Contracts and Operational Programmes.

28   The Cohesion policy package consists of six draft regulations of which four could be of direct relevance for cities, namely the general regulation (Commission of the European Communities, 2011c), and the regulations for the ERDF (Commission of the European Communities, 2011d), ESF (Commission of the European Communities, 2011e), and Territorial cooperation (Commission of the European Communities, 2011f). The other regulations concern the cohesion fund and the European grouping of territorial cohesion.

contract will include all Operational Programmes in a member state and thus ensure coordination between the various funds.

More interesting is the role of cities in the proposals which is strengthened further compared to the previous period by including checks and balances to avoid that member states and/or regions will put the requirements to involve the local partners aside. Furthermore, the partnership is not limited to ERDF operational programmes, but includes all programmes and the overall Partnership contract.

In its proposal of April 2012 the Commission put forward suggestions for building blocks of the code of conduct to supplement the partnership contract. It intends that,

> the European Code of Conduct on Partnership (ECCP) will lay down minimum requirements which are necessary to attain a high quality partnership in the implementation of the funds while maintaining ample flexibility to Member States in ways they organise the participation of the different partners (Commission of the European Communities, 2012, p. 4).

The Commission offers proposals for all the stages of programming and includes in all cases both regional and local authorities.

Furthermore, the draft regulations contain several elements aiming to achieve a strengthened role for cities. Within the ERDF a minimum of 5 per cent of the fund is earmarked for mandatory integrated urban development. The Partnership contract should include the total amount and the beneficiary cities (Commission of the European Communities, 2011h). Many of the priority measures included in the regulation have relevance to cities, but particularly worth mentioning are low carbon strategies, brownfield regeneration, environmentally-friendly transport systems, among others. Unfortunately due to the required concentration[29] not all of these priority measures can be included in the operational programmes.

Furthermore, there are special possibilities for local groups through so-called Community Led Local Development initiatives, and the possibilities for programmes facilitated through the Jessica initiative are broadened by widening the scope for financial instruments. Also the Commission has proposed to set up an urban development platform of maximum 300 cities selected from lists provided for by the member states. Also special mention needs to be given to the reintroduction of innovative actions in the field of sustainable development under article 9 of the ERDF regulation. Finally, the regulation on territorial cooperation follows closely the general regulation in its possibilities for cities, amongst others by fully incorporating the urban dimension in the main cooperation categories (Commission of the European Communities, 2011i,

---

29   In develop and transition regions 80 per cent of ERDF funding has to be spend in three priority categories (Innovation, SME support and the shift to a low carbon economy) of which 20 per cent in low carbon economy. For the less developed regions these concentration should be 50 per cent total and 6 per cent for low carbon economy.

pp. 13-14). Whereas appropriate, integrated territorial urban development strategies and Community led local development initiatives can be included. However due to its context these focus primarily on multi-country cooperation.

Where these proposals are another important step forward in bringing cities into the core of regional policy operations, the questions remains how strong the wordings will be in the Directives finally adopted. Whereas the European Parliament has indicated it wants to closely follow the proposals "only" bringing in some necessary improvements, member states in different groupings are suggesting major changes. These include the removal of the urban bonus from the MFF, softening the partnership proposals and removing the European code of conduct, keeping out the partners accept for the Commission in the Partnership Contract, replacing referrals to urban areas by article 174 of the Treaty,[30] and altering the urban platform either by deleting it or adding member states to its members. When the MFF is adopted the Cohesion Policy Package will follow probably shortly after, so by Summer 2013 it will be clear if the "tradition" of diluting the urban dimension from the Commission proposals has been continued.

Analysis of the Urban Situation

The second state of the cities report, published in 2010, further developed the points put forward in the first report using more recent data from the 2004 Urban Audit. It furthermore identified the particular urban dimension to the EU policy measures focusing at the Europe 2020 priorities, which were still under consideration at the time of drawing up the state of the cities report. It suggested that the "Overall fulfilment of many policy goals under these priorities depends on their success in urban areas. Cities are focal points for the diffusion of knowledge and the generation of innovation, but densely populated areas also give rise to manifold social and environmental problems" (Rheinisch-Westfälisches Institut für Wirtschaftsforschung, 2010, p. 24). Just prior to the presentation of the second report, Urban Audit 2009 data were published. For the moment no third state of the European cities is foreseen. However, it is intended to annually update key statistics for 250 cities for policy development. Every third year the broad set of over 300 indicators will be collected. The internet GIS-based tool Urban Atlas will improve access and usability of the Urban Audit data.

In the same year the fifth Cohesion report was published. This was the first cohesion report after the entry into force of the Lisbon Treaty, and thus the first report to include territorial cohesion in its analysis. The main aim of the report is to support the Europe 2020 strategy and highlight the contribution of cohesion policy. It compares EU development in fields such as innovation and growth, infrastructures, environmental quality and social circumstances with other parts

---

30   The article that includes all types of regions except urban and metropolitan regions.

of the world. Furthermore, combating and adapting to climate change have been given careful consideration in the report. In its territorial analyses it uses the agree of urbanisation for comparing the different territories. The developments are indicated for densely, intermediately and thinly populated regions. The report's conclusions give pointers for the future cohesion policy. Contrary to earlier reports, urban areas are put first when identifying the territories' territorial cohesion. It identifies the need for an ambitious urban agenda with financial resources more clearly identified to address urban issues and a stronger role for local authorities in the design and programming of urban development strategies (Commission of the European Communities, 2010d). As has been described in the previous paragraph, these elements have been incorporated in the proposals for the new programming period.

Just after the proposals for the new programming period had been presented, the seventh progress report on cohesion was published. With the title "The urban and regional dimension of Europe 2020" it includes paragraphs on creative, sustainable, and inclusive cities. It concludes by stating that

> When designing regional growth strategies, cities should play an active role. Cities are uniquely placed to promote innovation by offering firms of all sizes the dynamic environments they need to succeed. They are at the forefront in the fight against climate change, creating new models of urban development with even higher resource efficiency. Last but not least, cities have a disproportionate share of social problems and poverty. As the Europe 2020 targets aims to increase employment and reduce poverty and exclusion, cities need to address urban deprivation and the disconnection from the labour market, especially in the EU-15 (Commission of the European Communities, 2011j, p. 17).

More or less in parallel to these studies, the Commission had formed a working party on the City of tomorrow. Urban experts and representatives of cities were brought together to think about the future challenges of cities. It raised awareness on possible future impacts of various trends but also on the role for cities to play in achieving EU objectives. The final report concluded that a strengthening of the European urban development model was needed aiming at cities of tomorrow having to (Commission of the European Communities, 2011k):

- Deal with challenges in an integrated holistic way;
- Match place- and people-based approaches;
- Combine formal government structures with flexible informal governance structures as a function of the scale of challenges;
- Develop governance systems capable of building shared visions reconciling competing objectives and conflicting development models;
- Strengthen city cooperation that is necessary for a coherent spatial development.

Intergovernmental Progress

Member States' cooperation in the Urban Development Group continued after the Marseille Council aiming at operationalising the Reference Framework of Sustainable Cities (RFSC). During the Spanish Presidency an informal ministerial meeting on urban development was organised in Toledo in June 2010. The resulting Toledo declaration highlighted the integrated urban approach as one of the main tools to achieve progress in the direction of the Europe 2020 strategy. They "acknowledged the role that cities can play in achieving these objectives and call for a real partnership with cities in the implementation of Europe 2020" (Presidency of the European Union, 2010). The annexed Toledo Reference Document, prepared by the Spanish Presidency, identified integrated urban regeneration as a strategic tool in realising a smart, sustainable and inclusive urban model. The ministers furthermore supported the further development and implementation of the RFSC and called for a joint future working programme or "European Urban Agenda" including mostly soft measures.

Following the Spanish presidency conclusions the RFSC was started as a large scale pilot including over eighty local authorities. Every member state put forward a small, a medium sized and a large city to test the approach taken. Even though the test results were mixed, the work was embraced by the ministers (Presidency of the European Union, 2011, point 26). The main focus of the Polish presidency in this area was to bring forward the strengthening of the urban dimension in cohesion policy as the first priority of the European Urban Agenda of the Toledo meeting. In preparing for their informal meeting of ministers responsible for EU cohesion policy, territorial and urban development in November 2011 in Poznan, the presidency prepared a background report on the urban dimension of cohesion policy post 2013.

This report underlined again the important role of cities in realising the Europe 2020 ambitions, requiring a clear involvement of the EU in urban policy making. However, it also recommended leaving the decision which areas should benefit to the discretion of "Member States in consultation with regions and cities as appropriate" (Presidency of the European Union, 2011b, p. 12). On all other issues more involvement and discretionary powers for cities were recommended ranging from their involvement in programming, to strengthening the instrument of global grants, support data collection at neighbourhood level, revitalise the URBAN experience, consider separate Operational Programmes for urban policies, and building on the proven experiences of the Urbact programme.

The presidency conclusions however, were more focused on the cohesion policy package in general and the broad view on a territorial dimension of EU policies. Nevertheless, a specific point on urban areas called for "tailored policy interventions at European, national, regional and local levels which take into account the specific characteristics of places (both the types of cities and their growth potential and needs). In the context of fighting the barriers to growth special attention should be paid to the development of deprived urban areas" (Presidency of the European Union, 2011b, point 17). The presidency conclusions did not refer to the background report and only agreed that the Commission's proposed strengthening of the urban dimension in cohesion policy could be supported. It is thus not that strange that by the end of the Polish presidency it was proposed to delete most of the referrals to cities in the cohesion policy package, or limiting their impact by adding "where appropriate".

Social Policy

For the European Social Policy the preparations for the new programming period are of crucial importance. The Commission is working towards a Comprehensive European Employment and Social Inclusion initiative for the period 2014-2020. This consists of a new integrated programme for social change and innovation[31] and the over €80 billion large European Social Fund as part of the cohesion policy package. As was the case with Regional Policy, the ESF part has been fully aligned with the Europe 2020 strategy. It aims to contribute in particular to the flagship initiatives "Agenda for new skills and jobs", "Youth on the move", "European platform against poverty and social exclusion". But it will also support the Union's Digital agenda and the Innovative Union flagship. The proposed working of the ESF has broadened compared to the previous period by including the shortfall in skill levels and low labour mobility. The new proposal includes the objectives of employment and labour mobility, education and life-long training, social inclusion and poverty combat.

Each objective includes a limited number of specific investment priorities. Each programme will have to select up to four of these priorities to focus on.[32] The ESF should however also contribute to other thematic objectives such as the shift towards low-carbon, climate resilient and resource efficient economy, enhancing the use of information and communication technologies, strengthening research, technological development and innovation and enhancing the competitiveness of small and medium-sized enterprises in particular where it involves training and education.

Specific attention is given to the involvement of a broad range of partners:

> The mobilisation of regional and local stakeholders is necessary to deliver the Europe 2020 Strategy and its headline targets. Territorial pacts, local initiatives for employment and social inclusion, community-led local development strategies and sustainable urban development strategies may be used and

---

31   This €900 million programme consist of the former EURES, PROGRESS and Progress microfinance facility. As these had and have no direct urban dimension, they will not be discussed in more detail.

32   More developed regions will have to spend at minimum 80 per cent of their budget on these four priorities. For Transition and less developed regions this minimum figures are 70 per cent and 60 per cent.

supported to involve more actively regional and local authorities, cities, social partners and non-governmental organisations in the implementation of programmes (Presidency of the European Union, 2011b, p. 9).

However, the legislative proposal on partnerships mainly focuses at social partners and other stakeholders, in particular NGOs. More attention to the urban dimension is given in the article on territorial issues. Here it is indicated that the ESF may contribute to Community-led Local Development Strategies, territorial pacts and local initiatives for employment, education and social inclusion, as well as Integrated Territorial Initiatives as indicated in article 7 of the ERDF. Complementing this last type, the ESF may also "support sustainable urban development through strategies setting out integrated actions to tackle the economic, environmental and social challenges affecting urban areas of cities which are listed in the partnership contract" (Commission of the European Communities, 2011). As is the case with regional policy, these proposals are still being discussed and negotiated by the Council and the Parliament thus the way the local dimension will be finally shaped is far from certain.

Environmental Policy

In 2010 the European Environment Agency (EEA) published its State and Outlook of the European Environment 2010. To prepare this report the EEA did research in the State of the different member states environments and delivered 13 thematic reports, including one on the urban environment. This latter report identified the developments in the different domains but also the opportunities for improving resource efficiency, and more sustainable forms of living. However,

> as a consequence of the uncertainties of the different possible development paths, the overall outlook for the future urban environment of Europe is unclear. Despite some improvements in air quality, water quality, and mitigation of and adaptation to climate change as a result of national, European and global actions, European cities will still face a number of environmental challenges. These include coping with climate change, air pollution, water stress, noise, and further urban land-take (European Environment Agency, 2010, p. 25).

The report also noted the importance of looking at the urban environment as a holistic entity as the different elements are too inter-woven to look at in isolation. Much will also depend on perception as an attractive city might be considered less polluted than an unattractive city, although pollution levels might be equal.

As indicated in the introduction of this paragraph, the EU's 20-20-20 strategy is fully incorporated in the Europe 2020 strategy and resource efficiency is one of the seven flagship initiatives. In September 2011 the Commission published its roadmap for resource efficiency towards 2050. The vision put forward in this roadmap states that "By 2050 the EU's economy has grown in a way that respects resource constraints and planetary boundaries, thus contributing to global economic transformation. Our economy is competitive, inclusive and provides a high standard of living with much lower environmental impacts. All resources are sustainably managed, from raw materials to energy, water, air, land and soil. Climate change milestones have been reached, while biodiversity and the ecosystem services it underpins have been protected, valued and substantially restored" (Commission of the European Communities, 2011m, p. 3). To realise this vision, 18 milestones that should be reached by 2020 have been defined. The ones with strong relevance for cities are air quality, zero-emission buildings and cleaner transport.

These milestones will have to be accomplished through new partnerships involving all key stakeholders and will have to be agreed upon (including the precise targets and indicators) by the end of 2013. Both the Environment Council of December 2011 and the Economic and Financial Affairs Council of February 2012 welcomed the approach taken and called for a broad consultation and impact analyses for each of the milestones set (Council of the European Union and European Parliament, 2012).

With the ending of the sixth Environmental Action Programme on 22 July 2012, the Commission started its preparations for a successor. However, first it completed its assessment of the progress made within the sixth programme to identify how to continue and potential improvements. The State and Outlook of the Environment would provide future challenges to include in the programmes orientations. As the Commission pointed out in its roadmap accompanying the 2012 work programme,

> the 7th EAP will set out an environmental strategy guided by a longer term vision and be sufficiently adaptable and flexible to respond to the increasingly inter linked nature of environmental challenges. It will also take account of those faced by economic and social policies in a globalised context and the inherent and increasingly systemic nature of the risks presented. It should put particular emphasis on better implementation of environmental legislation at all levels (Commission of the European Communities, 2011n).

Even though the Council called to forward a proposal as soon as possible to fed into the MFF discussions and allow for continuity (Council of the European Union and European Parliament, 2011a, p. 3) the Commission has foreseen the publication of the seventh Environmental Action Programme proposal only for October 2012.

To underline the important role cities play in improving the environment the Commission launched in 2010 the European Green Capital Award. Every year a city is selected, having to fulfil a number of environmental criteria. In two application rounds an expert evaluation selected three to four shortlisted cities from which the final jury selected the winner based on its vision, action plan and communication strategy. Winners thusfar were Stockholm (2010), Hamburg (2011), Vitoria-Gasteiz (2012) and Nantes (2013). In June 2012 the jury will decide on the 2014 winner and at the same time the call for 2015 will be launched.

Transport

After a year of discussions the Council reached a conclusion on the 2009 action plan on urban mobility. The Council welcomed

> the action plan and supports in particular the establishment of an urban mobility observatory in the form of a virtual platform for the voluntary exchange of information and experience. The Council underlined the fact that improvements in the field of urban mobility can be most efficiently achieved through cooperation between competent public bodies. The measures to be promoted cover areas such as environmental and health issues, clean and energy-efficient technologies, infrastructure improvement, transport and town planning, goods delivery logistics, innovation and research, road safety and awareness raising (Council of the European Union and European Parliament, 2010a, p. 10).

The Council furthermore called upon the Commission to continue its research driven programmes such as Civitas and the Green Car initiative, and invited the Commission to draw up targets and policies for promoting more efficient, sustainable and safe and healthy urban mobility in the Transport White Paper (Council of the European Union and European Parliament, 2010b).

The White Paper on Transport was published in March 2011 and contained next to Trans European Transport Networks (TEN-T), focus on aviation, shipping, road and road transport also a paragraph on urban transport and commuting. The White Paper noted that a quarter of CO_2 emissions in transport originate from urban mobility and that the gradual phasing out of conventional fuels would contribute to improved air quality, less noise, reduces oil dependency and greenhouse gas emissions. However, this would also require the construction of fuelling and charging infrastructures for the new propulsion systems. The White Paper put forward ten goals for a competitive and resource efficient transport system that should act as benchmarks for achieving a 60 per cent greenhouse gas emission reduction target. The first goal being put forward is an urban one: "Halve the use of 'conventionally-fuelled' cars in urban transport by 2030; phase them out in cities by 2050; achieve essentially CO_2-free city logistics in major urban centres by 2030" (Commission of the European Communities, 2011o, p. 9). The Annex to the White Paper contains a list of 40 initiatives including urban mobility plans, a framework urban road user charging and a strategy for near-zero-emission urban logistics (Commission of the European Communities, 2011p, pp. 26-27).

So, after the long delays in tabling the action plan on urban mobility, the White Paper put forward some very ambitious targets. The Environment Council of June 2011 considered the goals as highly ambitious and suggested the 60 per cent target of reducing greenhouse gas emissions should be indicative rather than binding. It also stressed the need carefully assess the economic impact and the financial consequences of the proposed initiatives (Council of the European Union and European Parliament, 2011b, p. 10). The European Parliament approved by its resolution of December 2011 the

> [ten] goals for a competitive and resource-efficient transport system and the targets set in the White Paper for 2050 and 2030, but considers that more specific provisions are required for the period to 2020 with regard to funding – in view of the economic situation of individual Member States – and the general challenges facing transport in the field of energy and the environment, and therefore calls on the Commission to draw up legal rules to achieve a 20 per cent reduction in emissions of CO_2 and other GHGs from transport (European Parliament, 2011).

Energy Policy

As part of the Europe 2020 flagship resource efficient Europe the Commission published in March 2011 its Low carbon economy roadmap. This roadmap sets out key elements that should shape the EU's climate action to become a competitive low carbon economy by 2050. It identifies that even when current policies are fully executed, the 20-20-20 targets will not all be reached. Additional efforts are needed in Energy Efficiency. In order to reach 80 per cent emission reduction by 2050 strong efforts will have to be undertaken to reach the (intermediate) targets in 2030 and 2050. In particular the power sector, residential and services, and industry will have to reduce emissions by 80-90 per cent. Transport is tabled for 54-67 per cent whilst agriculture is limited to maximum 49 per cent reductions. The residential reductions will have to be accomplished largely in the built environment by nearly zero-energy buildings and serious investments in energy-savings in buildings[33] (Commission of the European Communities, 2011).

In realising further emission reductions at cost-efficient levels, research and development is of crucial importance. The Commission's Strategic Energy Technology (SET) plan will have to be continued in the next research programmes with substantial budgets. The Commission's Energy 2020 communication of November 2010 states that in the next ten years €1 trillion is needed in energy investment.

A large number of actions have been put forward including four large scale European projects, of which one is particular relevant for cities. "The 'Smart Cities' innovation partnership to be launched early 2011 will bring together the best from the areas of renewable energies, energy efficiency, smart electricity grids, clean urban transport such as electromobility, smart heating and cooling grids, combined with highly innovative intelligence and ICT tools. EU Regional Policy can play an important role in unlocking local potentials" (Commission of the European Communities, 2010, p. 16).

After the publication of Energy 2020 an extensive debate with stakeholders (cities and industry) took place followed by an on-line consultation early 2011.

---

33   The Commission estimates additional investments of up to €200 billion.

Taking the responses into consideration the Smart Cities and Communities initiative was launched by an official conference in Brussels on 21 June 2011 and a month later by the first call for projects. As indicated in the 7th Framework working programme for 2012

> [the] Smart Cities and Communities Initiative intends to promote replication of successful solutions through clustering of cities with similar framework conditions and similar ambitions. To enhance this replication potential, to ensure an EU-wide impact of the measures and to facilitate the exchange of knowledge, cities from at least three Member States and/or Associated Countries are expected to team up for a project proposal (Commission of the European Communities, 2011a, p. 39).

In March 2012 a total of nine projects will be awarded a maximum of €75 million. At the same time the Commission is planning to publish a communication on smart cities that will identify how the initial start with limited budgets could be more substantially continued in the programming period post 2013. A second call for proposals is foreseen for June 2012.

Research and Development

Since the city of Tomorrow and cultural heritage key action within the 5th Framework programme proposals (see section 5), the Smart Cities programme is the first research programme specifically focusing at cities. Cities have benefited from other research programmes but these were not specifically aiming at cities.

In 2011 a Joint Programming Initiative (JPI) Urban Europe was launched. A JPI is a joint programme of member states aiming to coordinate research and make better use of Europe's public funds. JPI Urban Europe focuses on transforming urban areas to centres of innovation and technology, developing eco-friendly and intelligent intra- and interurban transport and logistics systems, ensuring social cohesion and integration and reducing the ecological footprint and enhancing climate neutrality. In November 2011 the Commission put forward its proposals for the future programme for Research and Development 2014-2020. The successor of the 7th Framework programme got the title Horizon 2020 and based on the MFF proposal a budget of €86.2 billion.

As recently stated by the Commission, "Sustainable development will be an overarching objective of Horizon 2020. The dedicated funding for climate action and resource efficiency will be complemented through the other specific objectives of Horizon 2020 with the result that at least 60 per cent of the total Horizon 2020 budget will be related to sustainable development" (Commission of the European Communities, 2011b, p. 5). The accompanying proposal for a Council decision includes in detail the various elements of the new programme. Under the heading of Societal Challenges the following actions relevant to cities are included (Commission of the European Communities (2011c):

- Foster European Smart cities and Communities;
- Making aircraft, vehicles and vessels cleaner and quieter will improve environmental performance and reduce perceived noise and vibration;
- Improving transport and mobility in urban areas;
- Further our understanding of the functioning of ecosystems, their interactions with social systems and their role in sustaining the economy and human well-being (including urban ecosystems);
- Improve the knowledge base on the availability of raw materials, including urban mines (landfills and mining waste as raw materials).

Conclusions

The attention to urban questions has been on the European agenda for over 50 years. In the beginning they were not so much recognised as urban questions as the focus was limited and primarily sectoral. In the 1960s attention was given to low-cost housing in steel making and coalmining areas and therefore relevant to only a few cities. At the same time discussions started on the problems of regional development, where the role of local authorities was identified from the start. In the periods that followed, urban questions appeared more prominently on the table, resulting in the current period that puts cities at the core of EU policies as the driving force of economic, social and sustainable development.

This development has also taken place in the development of the partnerships in EU regional policy. In the 1970s regional policy was primarily considered a national matter. In the 1980s the concept of regions became synonym for regional authorities. Proposals to include regional and local governments in the partnerships were watered down and in the end regional authorities were the only ones playing a relevant role in the programmes. In the 1990s economic and social partners were added and, with the start of the new millennium, local and other public authorities were specifically mentioned. It was prescribed to include these partners in the programming and evaluation of programmes, but in practice this was only accomplished in city specific programmes such as the URBAN community initiative. The urban dimension in the ESF was even less visible. Evaluations concluded that the involvement of cities within the ESF was only coincidental as the policy was mainly aimed at target groups that in majority lived in urban agglomerations. In the proposals for the future, the role of local authorities in partnerships has been strongly improved, and the Commission has indicated to monitor progress based on their Code of Conduct.

Within the Structural Funds urban areas have received stronger recognition over time. Whereas in the beginning the agglomeration problem was recognised, involvement of cities was coincidental at best. By the end of the 1970s and in the early 1980s cities were testing grounds for the new integrated approach and industrial-urban zones appeared in the Commission initiated non-quota programmes. At the end of the 1980s urban communities were added to the "industrial restructuring objective" of regional policy. As only a few cities were selected and many were left out, the Commission started its innovative urban pilot projects. In the early 1990s this approach was added to the main programmes by including the category "urban areas with severe problems linked to the regeneration of derelict industrial sites" and at the same time the community initiative URBAN was launched. The next reform for the post 2000 period widened the approach by including "urban areas in difficulty" to the target groups. As of 2007 the entire EU territory is covered by regional policy allowing all cities to participate, but not including specific, mandatory urban categories. For the new programming period starting in 2014 a mandatory percentage for cities as a sort of URBAN programme in the mainstream, is being proposed, complementing ESF support is being made possible, the innovative actions for sustainable urban development are reintroduced and specific urban instruments including an EU urban platform are being put forward.

In other policy fields where fewer budgets are available, the urban dimension has developed over time. In the field of environment already in the 1970s there was an urgent need to tackle air quality and noise in cities. During the 1980s this focus shifted towards prevention policies and urban environmental problems were considered as a priority of increasing importance, however without the necessary specific budgets. In the 1990s a more horizontal approach was taken and specific attention was given to the urban environment resulting in a green paper, an expert group, sustainable projects financed through the newly set up LIFE instrument, and a sustainable cities and towns campaign. The decade after, further steps were taken by the directive on ambient air quality focusing on agglomerations of over 250,000 inhabitants, a special programme supporting international cooperation in the field of promoting sustainable urban development was set up, and a specific thematic strategy for the urban environment was agreed upon. Also the European Green Capital Award scheme underlines the importance given to the role of cities in ensuring environmental quality. Finally, the 2011 resource efficiency Europe 2050 roadmap defines several actions with direct and strong relevance for cities as crucial part of reaching its objectives.

With the stronger focus on combating climate change, attention for cities is also growing in energy and transport policies. From 2000 onwards the energy performance of new (zero-energy) and renovated buildings are high on the European agenda. In the years to come this attention was broadened by renewable energy and energy efficiency in general with specific attention for public lighting and energy efficiency in built up areas, which formed the basis for the Covenant of Mayors initiative. In parallel the available budgets were raised, and specific programmes such as the Smart Cities and Communities Initiative specifically aiming at cities were set up. Specific funding for urban transport initiatives originated from 2002 and by 2007 the subsidiarity objections were finally dropped when the green paper for urban transport was published. In the 2011 transport white paper proposal, urban mobility actions are crucial elements in realising the Union's ambitions.

In conclusion it must be said that the development of the urban dimension within European policies has not been a straightforward process. Most often the Commission has taken two steps forward, followed by the member states taking at least one step back by watering down the proposals. Or when the proposals survived the negotiations with the Council, their non-compulsory nature have kept the cities effectively out of the partnerships. Cities' participation in EU policy making and implementation of European programmes is, still too often, dependent on the willingness of Member States and later on regional authorities, to allow the cities to participate. With the introduction of the Europe 2020 agenda it seems inescapable to better involve the cities. In particular the proposals for regional, environmental, energy and transport policy reflect this. However, as these proposals are either still being debated with the Council and the European Parliament or, their proposed size and focus highly dependent on the budgets made available in the negotiations on the future EU budget, is still too early to conclude a breakthrough.

Epilogue

Seven months after completing this chapter on urban policies in Europe much has happened. Although the Council did not reach a compromise on the Multi-annual Financial Framework 2014-2020, there seems to be an overall agreement to strike the urban bonus from the proposal. The mandatory focus of 5 per cent of ERDF on sustainable urban development strategies is supported by both the Council and the Parliament. However, as there is doubt whether cities have the experience to manage these relatively small programmes, the possibility for regions to manage them on behalf of the cities has been added. And as could be expected it is not up to the Cities to decide. The maximum the Council will agree on is that Cities should at least be consulted in the choice of projects run in sustainable urban development strategies. Equally, the code of conduct faces strong opposition by the Member States who argue that this code is far too prescriptive and bureaucratic. At the same time the partnership contract has been renamed in partnership agreement and Member States argue that it concerns an agreement between Member State and Commission, whereas the Commission intended it to be an agreement between the different partners involved in the programmes in the Member State.

On the other hand the proposal of the Parliament to add the possibility for a specific urban Operational Programme, or an urban priority axis to the Integrated Territorial Investments for sustainable urban development seems to be acceptable for most Member States. Whether these new instruments are going to be used remains still to be seen.

The breakthrough seems further away than ever before. When the negotiations will be concluded along the lines indicated, it will be ultimately up to the Member States and regions whether they will allow their Cities a substantial place in the new programmes. The renaming of DG Regional Policy into Regional and Urban Policy, and the 'mainstreaming' of the urban unit into the

"Competence Centre for Inclusive Growth, Urban and Territorial Development" as of 1 October 2012 are clear indications that the Commission wants to ensure that cities can indeed take their place within the programmes and are put on the EU agenda permanently.

References

Cheshire, P., Hay, D., Carbonaro, G. and Bevan, N. (1988). *Urban problems and regional policy in the European Community*. Luxemburg: Commission of the European Community.

Commission of the European Communities (1963). *Low cost housing requirements*, Press Release P/53/63 of December 1963.

Commission of the European Communities (1964). *Trois rapports sur les problèmes de developpement regional dans la CEE*. Note d'Information P/41 of 9-7-1964.

Commission of the European Communities (1965). *Regional Policy in the European Community*, 1st Memorandum by the Common Market Commission to the Council of Ministers on regional policy in the EEC, SEC(65)1170 of 11 May 1965, Brussels.

Commission of the European Communities (1969). *A regional Policy for the Community*, COM(69)950 of 15 October 1969, Brussels.

Commission of the European Communities (1971). *Reform of the European Social Fund: the Commission proposes the implementing regulation*, Press Release P/12/71 of March 1971.

Commission of the European Communities (1972). *Communication from the Commission to the Council on a European Communities' programme concerning the environment*, SEC(72)666 of 22 March 1972, Brussels.

Commission of the European Communities (1973a). *Communication on the regional problems in the enlarged Community*, COM(73)550 of 3 May 1973, Brussels.

Commission of the European Communities (1973b). *Programme of Environmental Action of the European Communities Part II; detailed description of the actions to be undertaken at Community level over the next two years*, COM(73)550 final C of 10 April 1973, Brussels.

Commission of the European Communities (1974). *Present situation in Regional Policy*, Press Release P/80/74 of December 1974.

Commission of the European Communities (1975). *Allocation of credits for new housing programme decided*, Press Release P/38/75 of July 1975.

Commission of the European Communities (1976a). Outline for Regional Development Programmes, *Official Journal of the European Communities* C69 of 24-3-1976.

Commission of the European Communities (1976b). Proposal for a Council Directive concerning health protection standards for sulphur dioxide and suspended particulate matter in urban atmospheres, *Official Journal of the European Communities* C63 of 19-3-1976, pp. 5-9.

Commission of the European Communities (1976c). *Commission proposal on a new action programme on the environment*, Press Release P/22/76 of March 1976.

Commission of the European Communities (1977). *Fifth report on the activities of the European Social Fund.* 1976 Financial Year, COM(77)398 of 28 July 1977, Brussels, point 58.

Commission of the European Communities (1979a). De regionale ontwikkelingsprogramma's, *Serie Regionaal Beleid* Nr. 17, 1979, Brussels.

Commission of the European Communities (1979b). *The Commission unveils plans for integrated regional development operations*, Press Release P/34/79 of March 1979.

Commission of the European Communities (1980a). *European Regional Development Fund*, Fifth annual report, COM(80)460 of 29 July 1980, Brussels-Luxemburg.

Commission of the European Communities (1980b). The regions of Europe, *First periodic report on the social and economic situation of the regions of the Community*, COM(80)816 of 22 December 1980, Brussels.

Commission of the European Communities (1980c). *Distribution of Appropriations for the new aid programme for low cost housing*, Press Release P/73/80 of July 1980.

Commission of the European Communities (1980d). *Green Paper on the Urban Environment*, COM(90)218 final of 27 June 1980, Brussels.

Commission of the European Communities (1981). *Mediterranean Programmes: lines of action*, COM(81)637 of 23 October 1981, Brussels.

Commission of the European Communities (1983a). *European Regional Development Fund*, Ninth annual report (1983). COM(84)522 of 27 September 1984, Luxemburg.

Commission of the European Communities (1983b). *Eleventh report on the activities of the European Social Fund*, Financial Year 1982, COM(83)434 of 30 June 1983, Luxemburg.

Commission of the European Communities (1983c). *Community action to combat unemployment – the contribution of local employment initiatives*, Press Release P/105/83 of November 1983.

Commission of the European Communities (1984a). *The regions of Europe*. Second periodic report on the social and economic situation of the regions of the Community, COM(84)40 of 7 March 1984, Brussels.

Commission of the European Communities (1984b). *Statistical Machinery for defining social fund priority regions*, Press Release P-54 of July 1984, Brussels.

Commission of the European Communities (1984c). *Twelfth report on the activities of the European Social Fund.* Financial Year 1983, COM(84)396 of 26 July 1984, Brussels.

Commission of the European Communities (1984d). *Community action to combat unemployment – the contribution of local employment initiatives,* COM(83)662/2 of 17 January 1984.

Commission of the European Communities (1986a). *Information note from the Commission to the Council and the Parliament on Procedures and Content for the implementation of an integrated approach,* COM(86)401 final/2 of 2 September 1986, Brussels.

Commission of the European Communities (1986b). *The integrated Mediterranean Programmes,* European File 1/86 of January 1986.

Commission of the European Communities (1987a). *The regions of the enlarged Community,* third periodic report on the social and economic situation and development of the regions of the Community, 1987, Brussels-Luxemburg.

Commission of the European Communities (1987b). *Follow-up to Council Resolution of 7 June 1984 on the contribution of local employment initiatives to combating unemployment,* COM(86)784 final /2 of 9 February 1987, Brussels.

Commission of the European Communities (1988). Council Regulation 2052/88/ EEC of 24 June 1988 on the tasks of the Structural Funds and their effectiveness and on coordination of their activities between themselves and with the operations of the European Investment Bank and the other existing financial instruments, *Official Journal of the European Communities* L185 of 15-7-1988.

Commission of the European Communities (1989a). *Commission takes first decision on regional policy,* Press Release IP/89/25 of 25-1-1989.

Commission of the European Communities (1989b). *Local Authorities: Privileged interlocutors for the implementation of the reform of the Structural Funds,* Press Release IP/89/353 of 19-5-1989.

Commission of the European Communities (1989c). Guidelines concerning European Social Fund intervention in respect of action against long-term unemployment and occupational integration of young people, *Official Journal of the European Communities* C45 of 24-2-1989.

Commission of the European Communities (1989d). *Mr Bruce Millan in Madrid: "Regional Policy in the 1990s: More important than ever",* Press Release IP/89/385 of 30-5-1989.

Commission of the European Communities (1989e). *Good news for the Regions,* Press Release P/89/8 of 8-3-1989 on Council Decision 89/288/EEC.

Commission of the European Communities (1989f). *The experience of integrated Mediterranean programmes and its implications for future programmes following the reform of the Structural Funds,* SPEECH/89/7 of 26 January 1989.

Commission of the European Communities (1990a). *Urban Pilot Projects: European Community Inventory actions in London and Marseille,* Press Release IP/90/133 of 15-2-1990.

Commission of the European Communities (1990b). *Politique regionale: Commission launches an urban project in Rotterdam,* Press Release IP/90/771 of 27-9-1990.

Commission of the European Communities (1990c). *Regional Policy: 18MECU for city and regional networks*, Press Release IP/90/1075 of 21-12-1990.

Commission of the European Communities (1991a). *Europe 2000 Outlook for the development of the Community's Territory*, COM(91)452 final of 7 November 1991, Brussels, pp. 133-149.

Commission of the European Communities (1991b). *Annual report on the implementation of the reform of the Structural Funds 1990*, COM(91)400 of 4 December 1991, Brussels.

Commission of the European Communities (1992a). Treaty of the European Union, *Official Journal of the European Communities* C191 of 29-7-1992.

Commission of the European Communities (1992b). Urbanization and the function of cities in the European Community, *Regional Development Studies* 4, Brussels-Luxemburg.

Commission of the European Communities (1992c). *Communication on Community Structural policies; assessment and outlook*, COM(92)84 of 18 March 1992, Brussels.

Commission of the European Communities (1993a). *M. Millan at the Eurocities conference Europe: "The challenge of urban democracy'* Lisbon 30, October1993, Abstract of Speech, Press Release IP/93/933 of 3-11-1993.

Commission of the European Communities (1993b). *The future of Community Initiatives under the Structural Funds*, COM(93)282 final of 16-6-1993, Brussels.

Commission of the European Communities (1993c). *Fifth annual report from the Commission on the implementation of the reform of the Structural Funds in 1992*, COM(93)530 final of 29 October 1993, Brussels.

Commission of the European Communities (1993d). *The operation of the Community Structural Funds 1994-1999*, COM(93)124 of 7 April 1993, Brussels.

Commission of the European Communities (1994a). Commission Decision (94/209/EC) of 21 April 1994 winding up the Consultative Council of Regional and Local Authorities, *Official Journal of the European Communities* L103 of 22-4-1994.

Commission of the European Communities (1994b). *Europe 2000+ Cooperation for European territorial development*, 1994, Luxemburg.

Commission of the European Communities (1994c). *The implementation of the reform of the Structural Funds in 1993*. Fifth annual report, 1994, Luxemburg.

Commission of the European Communities (1994d). Commission Decision 94/169/EC establishing an initial list of declining industrial areas concerned by Objective 2 as defined by Council Regulation (EEC) No 2052/88, *Official Journal of the European Communities* L81 of 24-3-1994.

Commission of the European Communities (1994e). *Regional Policy: Interim Report on the progress of Urban Pilot Projects*, Press Release IP/94/156 of 24-2-1994.

Commission of the European Communities (1994f). *Community Initiative concerning Urban Areas (URBAN)*. COM(94)61 final of 2-3-1994, Brussels.

Commission of the European Communities (1994g). Notice to the Member States laying down guidelines for operational programmes which Member States are invited to establish in the framework of a Community initiative concerning urban areas, *Official Journal of the European Communities* C180 of 1-7-1994, pp. 6-9.

Commission of the European Communities (1994h). *Activity report on the 11th programme of ECSC low-cost housing loans Period 1989-1993*, COM((4)578 final of 8 December 1994.

Commission of the European Communities (1995a). *A European Strategy for encouraging local development and employment initiatives*, COM(95)273 of 13 June 1995, Brussels.

Commission of the European Communities (1995b). *Local Development and Employment Initiatives – an investigation in the European Union*, SEC(95)564 of March 1995, Luxemburg.

Commission of the European Communities (1996a). Structural Funds and Cohesion Fund 1994-1999. *Regulations and Commentary*. January 1996, Luxemburg.

Commission of the European Communities (1996b). *First Cohesion report*, COM(96)542 final of 6 November 1996, Brussels.

Commission of the European Communities (1996c). *The Structural Funds in 1995.* Seventh annual report, 1996, Luxemburg.

Commission of the European Communities (1996d). Action for Employment in Europe: a confidence Pact, *Supplement 4/96 to the Bulletin of the European Union*, pp. 11-33, 1996, Luxemburg.

Commission of the European Communities (1997a). *European Spatial Development Perspective*. First official draft, 1997 Luxemburg.

Commission of the European Communities (1997b). *Towards an Urban agenda in the European Union*, COM(97)197 of 6-5-1997, Brussels.

Commission of the European Communities (1997c). *First report on local development and employment initiatives – lessons for territorial and local employment pacts*, 1997, Luxemburg.

Commission of the European Communities (1997d). *Progress report of the European Commission's Expert Group on the Urban Environment 1993-1996*, Luxemburg.

Commission of the European Communities (1998a). *The Structural Funds in 1997.* Ninth annual report, 1998, Luxemburg.

Commission of the European Communities (1998b). *Sustainable Urban Development in the European Union: A Framework for Action*, COM(98)605 final of 28 October 1998, Brussels.

Commission of the European Communities (1998c). *Proposal for a Council Regulation (EC) laying down the general provisions on the Structural Funds*, COM(1998)131 final of 18 March 1998, Brussels.

Commission of the European Communities (1999a). *ESDP European Spatial Development Perspective Towards Balanced and Sustainable Development of the Territory of the European Union*, 1999, Luxemburg.

Commission of the European Communities (1999b). *Europe's Environment: What directions for the future? The Global Assessment of the European Community Programme of Policy and Action in relation to the environment and sustainable development, 'Towards Sustainability'*, COM(1999)543 of 24 November 1999, Brussels.

Commission of the European Communities (2000a). *Communication on EU policies and measures to reduce greenhouse gas emissions: towards a European Climate Change Programme (ECCP)*. COM(2000)88 final of 8 March 2000, Brussels.

Commission of the European Communities (2000b). *Action plan to improve Energy Efficiency in the European Community*, COM(2000)247 final of 26 April 2000, Brussels.

Commission of the European Communities (2001a). *European Governance A White Paper*, COM(2001)428 of 25 July 2001, Brussels.

Commission of the European Communities (2001b). *Unity, solidarity, diversity for Europe, its people and its territory. Second report on economic and social cohesion*, 2001, Luxemburg.

Commission of the European Communities (2001c). White Paper European transport policy for 2010: time to decide, COM(2001)370 of 12 September 2001, Brussels.

Commission of the European Communities (2001d). *Communication on the implementation of the first phase of the European Climate Change Programme*, COM(2001)580 final of 23 October 2001, Brussels.

Commission of the European Communities (2002). *The programming of the Structural Funds 2000-2006 an initial assessment of the Urban Initiative*, COM(2002)308 final of 14 June 2002, Brussels.

Commission of the European Communities (2003). *Proposal for a Directive of the European Parliament and of the Council on establishing a framework for the setting of Eco-design requirements for Energy-Using Products and amending Council Directive 92/42/EEC*, COM(2003)453 final of 1 August 2003, Brussels.

Commission of the European Communities (2004a). *Proposal for a Council Regulation laying down general provisions on the European Regional Development Fund, the European Social Fund and the Cohesion Fund*, COM(2004)492 final of 14 July 2004, Brussels.

Commission of the European Communities (2004b). *A new partnership for cohesion. Convergence, Competitiveness, Cooperation.* Third report on economic and social cohesion, 2004, Luxemburg.

Commission of the European Communities (2004c). *Proposal for a Regulation of the European Parliament and of the Council on the European Regional Development Fund*, COM(2004)495 final of 14 July 2004, Brussels.

Commission of the European Communities (2004d). *Towards a thematic strategy on the urban environment*, COM(2004)60 of 11 February 2004, Brussels.

Commission of the European Communities (2005a). *Thematic Strategy on air pollution*, COM(2005)446 of 21 September 2005, Brussels.

Commission of the European Communities (2005b). *Proposal for a Directive of the European Parliament and of the Council on ambient air quality and cleaner air for Europe*, COM(2005)447 of 21 September 2005, Brussels.

Commission of the European Communities (2006a). *European Investment Bank, Council of Europe Development Bank, Memorandum of Understanding in respect of a coordinated approach to the financing of urban renewal and development for the programming period 2007-2013 of the Community Structural Funds*, 30 May 2006, Brussels.

Commission of the European Communities (2006b). *Thematic Strategy on the Urban Environment*, COM(2005)718 of 11 January 2006, Brussels.

Commission of the European Communities (2006c). *Action plan for Energy Efficiency: Realising the Potential*, COM(2006)545 final of 19 October 2006, Brussels.

Commission of the European Communities (2007a). *State of the European Cities report. Adding value to the European Urban Audit*, May 2007, Brussels, page II.

Commission of the European Communities (2007b). *Green Paper Towards a new culture for urban mobility*, COM(2007)551 of 25 September 2007, Brussels.

Commission of the European Communities (2007c). *Sustainable Urban Transport Plans. Preparatory Document in relation to the follow-up of the Thematic Strategy on the Urban Environment, Technical Report – 2007/018 of 25 September 2007*, Luxemburg.

Commission of the European Communities (2007d). *Renewable Energy Roadmap. Renewable energies in the 21st century: building a more sustainable future*, COM(2006)848 final of 10 January 2007, Brussels.

Commission of the European Communities (2008a). *Regions 2020 An assessment of future challenges for EU regions*, SEC(2008)2868 of November 2008, Brussels.

Commission of the European Communities (2008b). *Green Paper on Territorial Cohesion. Turning Territorial Diversity into Strength*, COM(2008)616 final of 6 October 2008, Brussels.

Commission of the European Communities (2008c). *Fostering the urban dimension. Analysis of the Operational Programmes co-financed by the European Regional Development Fund (2007-2013)*. Working document of the Directorate-General for Regional Policy, 25 November 2008, Brussels.

Commission of the European Communities (2009a). *Promoting sustainable urban development in Europe – achievements and opportunities*, 2009, Brussels.

Commission of the European Communities (2009b). *Action Plan on Urban Mobility*, COM(2009)490 of 30 September 2009, Brussels.

Commission of the European Communities (2009c). Commission Regulation (EC) No 245/2009 of 18 March 2009 implementing Directive 2005/32/EC of the European Parliament and of the Council with regards to ecodesign requirements for fluorescent lamps without integrated ballast, for high intensity discharge lamps, and for ballasts and luminaires able to operate such lamps, and repealing Directive 2000/55/EC of the European Parliament and of the Council, *Official Journal of the European Union* L76 of 24-3-2009, pp. 17-44.

Commission of the European Communities (2010a). Consolidated version of the Treaty of the European Union, *Official Journal of the European Communities* C83 of 30-3-2010.

Commission of the European Communities (2010b). *Ex-Post Evaluation of Cohesion Policy programmes 2000-06 co-financed by the ERDF (Objective 1 and 2). Synthesis report*, April 2010, Brussels.

Commission of the European Communities (2010c). *EUROPE 2020 A strategy for smart, sustainable and inclusive growth*, COM(2010)2020 final of 3 March 2010, Brussels.

Commission of the European Communities (2010d). *Investing in Europe's future. Fifth report on economic, social and territorial cohesion*, November 2010, Luxemburg.

Commission of the European Communities (2010e). *Energy 2020 A strategy for competitive, sustainable and secure energy*, COM(2010)639 final of 10 November 2010, Brussels.

Commission of the European Communities (2011a). *Concluding the first European semester of economic policy coordination: Guidance for national policies in 2011-2012*, COM(2011)400 final of 7 June 2011, Brussels.

Commission of the European Communities (2011b). *A Budget for Europe Part I*, COM(2011)500 final of 29 June 2011, Brussels.

Commission of the European Communities (2011c). *Proposal for a Regulation of the European Parliament and of the Council laying down common provisions on the European Regional Development Fund, the European Social Fund, the Cohesion Fund, the European Agricultural Fund for Rural Development and the European Maritime and Fisheries Fund covered by the Common Strategic Framework and laying down general provisions on the European Regional Development Fund, the European Social Fund and the Cohesion Fund and repealing*, Regulation (EC) No 1083/2006, COM(2011)615 final of 6 October 2011, Brussels.

Commission of the European Communities (2011d). *Proposal for a Regulation of the European Parliament and of the Council on specific provisions concerning the European Regional Development Fund and the Investment for growth and jobs goal and repealing*, Regulation (EC) No 1080/2006, COM(2011)614 final of 6 October 2011.

Commission of the European Communities (2011e). *Proposal for a Regulation of the European Parliament and of the Council on the European Social Fund and repealing Regulation (EC) No 1081/2006*, COM(2011)607 final of 6 October 2011.

Commission of the European Communities (2011f). *Proposal for a Regulation of the European Parliament and of the Council on specific provisions for the support from the European Regional Development Fund to the European territorial cooperation goal*, COM(2011)611 final of 6 October 2011.

Commission of the European Communities (2011g). *The urban and regional dimension of Europe 2020 Seventh progress report on economic, social and territorial cohesion*, November 2011, Luxemburg.

Commission of the European Communities (2011h). *Cities of tomorrow Challenges, visions, ways forward*, October 2011, Luxemburg.

Commission of the European Communities (2011i). *Proposal for a Regulation of the European Parliament and of the Council on the European Social Fund and repealing Regulation (EC)* No 1081/2006, COM(2011)607 final of 6 October 2011, article 12.2.

Commission of the European Communities (2011j). *Roadmap to a Resource Efficient Europe*, COM(2011)571 final of 20 September 2011, Brussels.

Commission of the European Communities (2011k). *Roadmap 7th Environmental Action Programme*, version of November 2011, Brussels.

Commission of the European Communities (2011l). *White Paper Roadmap to a Single European Transport Area – Towards a competitive and resource efficient transport system*, COM(2011)144 final of 28 March 2011, Brussels.

Commission of the European Communities (2011m). *A Roadmap for moving to a competitive low carbon economy in 2050*, COM(2011)112 final of 8 March 2011, Brussels.

Commission of the European Communities (2011n). *Work Programme 2012 (Revised) Cooperation Theme 5 Energy*, COM(2011)9493 of 20 December 2011, Brussels.

Commission of the European Communities (2011o). *Horizon 2020 – The Framework Programme for Research and Innovation*, COM (2011)808 final of 30 November 2011, Brussels.

Commission of the European Communities (2011p). *Proposal for a Council Decision establishing the Specific Programme Implementing Horizon 2020 – The Framework Programme for Research and Innovation (2014-2020)*. COM(2011)811 final of 30 November 2011, Brussels.

Commission of the European Communities (2012). *Staff Working Document, The partnership principle in the implementation of the Common Strategic Framework Funds in elements for a European Code of Conduct on Partnership*, Brussels 24-4-2012.

Council of the European Communities (1972). Meetings of the Heads of State or Government, Conclusions of the preparatory work, *Bulletin of the European Communities* No. 10 1972, Brussels, pp. 8-26.

Council of the European Communities (1975). Council Regulation 75/185/EEC of 18 March 1975 setting up a Regional Policy Committee, *Official Journal of the European Communities* L73 of 21-3-1975, pp. 47-48.

Council of the European Communities (1978). Council Decision 78/150/EEC of 7 February 1978 adopting a European Economic Community concerted research project on the growth of large urban conurbations, *Official Journal of the European Communities* L45 of 16-2-1978, pp. 24-26.

Council of the European Communities (1979). Council Resolution of 6 February 1979 concerning the guidelines for Community regional policy, *Official Journal of the European Communities* C36 of 9-2-1979, pp. 10-11.

Council of the European Communities (1980a). Council Regulation 80/779/EEC of 15 July 1980 on air quality limit values and guide values for sulphur dioxide and suspended particulates, *Official Journal of the European Communities* L229 of 30-8-1980 pp. 30-48, article 3.

Council of the European Communities (1980b). Council Regulation (EEC) No 2616/80 of 7 October 1980 instituting a specific Community regional development measure contributing to overcoming constraints on the development of new economic activities in certain zones adversely affected by restructuring of the steel industry, *Official Journal of the European Communities* L271 of 15-10-1980, pp. 9-15.

Council of the European Communities (1980c). Council Regulation (EEC) No 2617/80 of 7 October 1980 instituting a specific Community regional development measure contributing to overcoming constraints on the development of new economic activities in certain zones adversely affected by restructuring of the shipbuilding industry, *Official Journal of the European Communities* L271 of 15-10-1980, pp. 16-22, article 4.

Council of the European Communities (1980-1981). *Twenty-eight review of the Council's work, 1 January – 31 December 1980*, 1981, Brussels.

Council of the European Communities (1983a) Council Regulation 1739/83/EEC of 21 June 1983 introducing an exceptional Community measure to promote urban renewal in Northern Ireland (Belfast). *Official Journal of the European Communities* L171 of 29-6-1983, pp. 1-3, article 4.

Council of the European Communities (1983b). Council Decision 83/516/EEC of 17 October 1983 on the tasks of the European Social Fund, *Official Journal of the European Communities* L289 of 22-10-1983.

Council of the European Communities (1983c). Council Resolution of 7 February 1983 on the continuation and implementation of a European Community policy and action programme on the environment (1982 to 1986). *Official Journal of the European Communities* C46 of 17-2-1983.

Council of the European Communities (1984) Council Regulation 1872/84/EEC of 28 June 1984 on action by the Community relating to the environment, *Official Journal of the European Communities* L176 of 3-7-1984.

Council of the European Communities (1985a). *Thirty-first review of the Council's work 1 January – 31 December 1983*, 1985, Brussels-Luxemburg.

Council of the European Communities (1985b). Council Decision 85/568/EEC of 20 December 1985 amending, on account of the accession of Spain and Portugal, Decision 83/516/EEC on the tasks of the European Social Fund, *Official Journal of the European Communities* L370 of 31-12-1985.

Council of the European Communities (1987). Resolution of the Council of the European Community and of the representatives of the Governments of the Member States, meeting within the Council of 19 October 1987 on the communication and implementation of a European Community policy and action programme on the environment (1987-1992). *Official Journal of the European Communities* C328 of 7-12-1987.

Council of the European Communities (1988a). Council Regulation 4253/88 EEC of 19 December 1988 laying down provisions for implementing Regulation (EEC) No 2052/88 as regards coordination of the activities of the different Structural Funds between themselves and with the operations of the European Investment Bank and the other existing financial instruments, *Official Journal of the European Communities* L374 of 31-12-88, pp. 1-14.

Council of the European Communities (1988b). Council Regulation 4254/88 EEC of 19 December 1988 laying down provisions for implementing Regulation (EEC) 2052/88 as regards the European Regional Development Fund, *Official Journal of the European Communities* L374 of 31-12-1988, pp. 15-20.

Council of the European Communities (1988c). Council Regulation (EEC) No 4255/88 of 19 December 1988 laying down provisions for implementing Regulation (EEC) No 2052/88 as regards the European Social Fund, *Official Journal of the European Communities* L374 of 31-12-1988, pp. 21-24.

Council of the European Communities (1991). Council Resolution of 28 January 1991 on the Green Paper on the urban environment, *Official Journal of the European Communities* C33 of 8-2-1991, pp. 4-5.

Council of the European Communities (1992). *European Council in Edinburgh 11-12 December 1992, Conclusions of the Presidency*, Brussels.

Council of the European Union (1993a). Council Regulation 2081/93/EEC of 20 July 1993 amending Regulation (EEC) No 2052/88 on the tasks of the Structural Funds and their effectiveness and on coordination of their activities between themselves and with the operations of the European Investment Bank and the other existing financial instruments, *Official Journal of the European Communities* L193 of 31-7-1993.

Council of the European Union (1993b). Council Regulation 2083/93/EEC of 20 July 1993 amending Regulation (EEC) No 4254/88 laying down provisions for implementing Regulation (EEC) No 2052/88 as regards the European Regional Development Fund, *Official Journal of the European Communities* L193 of 31-7-1993.

Council of the European Union (1999a). Council Regulation 1260/99/EC laying down general provisions on the Structural Funds, *Official Journal of the European Communities* L161 of 26-6-1999, pp. 1-42, article 4(1).

Council of the European Union (1999b). Regulation 1784/99/EC of the European Parliament and of the Council of 12 July on the European Social Fund, *Official Journal of the European Communities* L213 of 13-8-1999, pp. 5-8.

Council of the European Union (2000a). *Lisbon European Council 23 and 24 March 2000 Presidency conclusions*, 2000, Brussels.

Council of the European Union (2000b). Decision 2000/228/EC of 13 March 2000 on guidelines for Member States' employment policies for the year 2000, *Official Journal of the European Communities* L72 of 21-3-2000, pp. 15-20.

Council of the European Union (2000c). *2318th Council meeting Industry / Energy Brussels, 5 December 2000*, PRES/00/466, 2000, Brussels.

Council of the European Union (2001). *Presidency Conclusions Göteborg European Council 15 and 16 June 2001*, SN200/1/01 REV 1, 2001, Brussels.

Council of the European Union (2006a). Regulation 1080/06/EC of 5 July 2006 on the European Regional Development Fund and repealing Regulation (EC) No 1783/1999, *Official Journal of the European Communities* L210 of 31-7-2006, pp. 1-11.

Council of the European Union (2006b). Council Regulation 1083/06/EC of 11 July 2006 laying down general provisions on the European Regional Development Fund, European Social Fund and the Cohesion Fund and repealing Regulation (EC) No 1260/1999, *Official Journal of the European Communities* L210 of 31-7-2006, pp. 25-74.

Council of the European Union (2006c). Regulation 1081/06/EC of 5 July 2006 on the European Social Fund and repealing Regulation (EC) No 1784/1999, *Official Journal of the European Communities* L210 of 31-7-2006, pp. 12-18.

Council of the European Union (2007). *Presidency Conclusions Brussels European Council 8/9 March 2007*, 7224/1/07 REV 1 of 2 May 2007, Brussels.

Council of the European Union and European Parliament (2001). Decision No 1411/2001/EC of the European Parliament and the Council of 27 June 2001 on a Community Framework for cooperation to promote sustainable urban development, *Official Journal of the European Communities* L191 of 13-7-2001, pp. 1-5.

Council of the European Union and European Parliament (2002). Decision No 1600/2002/EC of 22 July 2002 laying down the Sixth Community Environment Action Programme, *Official Journal of the European Communities* L242 of 10-9-2002, pp. 1-15.

Council of the European Union and European Parliament (2003). Directive 2002/91/EC of 16 December 2002 of the European Parliament and the Council on the energy performance of buildings, *Official Journal of the European Communities* L1 of 4-1-2003, pp. 65-71.

Council of the European Union and European Parliament (2005). Directive 2005/32/EC of the European Parliament and of the Council of 6 July 2003 establishing a framework for the setting of ecodesign requirements for energy-using products and amending Council Directive 92/42/EEC and Directives 96/57/EC and 2000/55/EC of the European Parliament and of the Council, *Official Journal of the European Union* L191 of 22-7-2005, pp. 29-58.

Council of the European Union and European Parliament (2007). Regulation (EC) No 614/2007 of the European Parliament and of the Council of 23 May 2007 concerning the Financial Instrument for the Environment (LIFE+). *Official Journal of the European Union* L149 of 9-6-2007, pp. 1-16.

Council of the European Union and European Parliament (2009a). Regulation (EC) No 397/2009 of 6 May 2009 amending Regulation (EC) No 1080/2006 on the European Regional Development Fund as regards the eligibility of energy efficiency and renewable energy investments in housing, *Official Journal of the European Union* L126 of 21-5-2009, pp. 3-4.

Council of the European Union and European Parliament (2009b). Directive 2009/33/EC of the European Parliament and of the Council of 23 April 2009 on the promotion of clean and energy-efficient road transport vehicles, *Official Journal of the European Union* L120 of 15-5-2009, pp. 5-12.

Council of the European Union and European Parliament (2009c). Directive 2009/28/EC of the European Parliament and of the Council of 23 April 2009 on the promotion of the use of energy from renewable sources and amending and subsequently repealing Directives 2001/77/EC and 2003/30/ EC, *Official Journal of the European Union* L140 of 5-6-2009, pp. 16-46.

Council of the European Union and European Parliament (2010a). *Press Release 3024th Council meeting Transport, Telecommunications and Energy*, Presse 191 of 24 June 2010, Luxemburg.

Council of the European Union and European Parliament (2010b). *Action Plan on Urban Mobility – Adoption of Council Conclusions*, 10603/10 of 10 June 2010, Brussels.

Council of the European Union and European Parliament (2011a). *Assessment of the Sixth Community Environment Action Programme and the way forward, and Towards a 7th EU Environment Action Programme – Council conclusions*, Information note 15384/11 of 11 October 2011, Brussels.

Council of the European Union and European Parliament (2011b). *Press Release 3098th Council meeting Transport, Telecommunications and Energy Transport*, Presse 175 of 16 June 2011, Luxembourg.

Council of the European Union and European Parliament (2012). *Press Release 3139th Council meeting Environment, Presse 506 of 19 December 2011, Brussels, and, Press Release 3148th Council meeting Economic and Financial Affairs*, Presse 57 of 21 February 2012, Brussels.

Court of Auditors (1986). Special Report No 2/86 on the ERDF's specific Community regional development measures (non-quota measures) accompanied by the Commission's replies, *Official Journal of the European Communities* C262 of 20-10-1986, pp. 1-19.

Court of Auditors (1988). Special Report No 2/88 on the integrated approach to Community financing of structural measures together with the Commission's responses, *Official Journal of the European Communities* C188 of 18-7-1988, pp. 1-15, point 2.25.

Court of Auditors (2001). Special report No 1/2001 concerning the URBAN Community initiative together with the Commission's replies, *Official Journal of the European Communities* C124 of 25-4-2001.

Eurofound (1987). *European Foundation for the Improvement of Living and Working Conditions, Living conditions in urban Europe*, 1987, Luxemburg.

ECOTEC (2002). *Thematic evaluation of the Territorial Employment Initiatives*, 2002, Brussels.

ECOTEC (2004). *ESPON action 2.2.3: Territorial effects of the Structural Funds in urban areas. A final report to the ESPON coordination unit*, 2004, Birmingham.

European Commission (2010). *The urban dimension in European Union policies 2010, – Introduction and Part 1*, Brussels, European Commission.

European Environment Agency (2010). *The European Environment State and Outlook 2010 – Urban Environment*, 2010, Copenhagen.

European Investment Bank (2007). *Jessica preliminary evaluation study*, 2007, Luxemburg.

European Parliament and of the Council of 24 October 2006 establishing a Competitiveness and Innovation Framework Programme (2007 to 2013). *Official Journal of the European Union* L310 of 9-11-2006, pp. 15-40.

European Parliament (2011). *Single European transport area*, P7_TA-PROV(2011)0584 provisional edition of 15 December 2011, Strasbourg.

European Regional Development Fund (1985). *Tenth annual report (1984)*. COM(85)516 of 4 October 1985, Luxemburg.

European Parliament (1973). *Second report on the proposals from the Commission of the European Communities to the Council (Doc. 152/73) for I. a decision on the creation of a Committee for Regional Policy, II. A financial regulation relating to special provisions to be applied to the European Regional Development Fund, III. A regulation establishing a Regional Development Fund*, EP PE34.405 fin of 13 November 1973, Strasburg, point 13.

European Parliament (1977). *Report on the communication from the Commission of the European Communities to the Council (Doc. 183/77) concerning guidelines for Community regional policy*, EP Document 307/77 of 10 October 1977, Strasburg.

European Parliament (1993). *Resolution on the future of Community Initiatives in the framework of structural funds*, A3-0279/93, 28-10-93.

Feantsa (2002). *Housing in EU policy making – overview of EU policies affecting the social function of housing policies*, 2002, Brussels, European Commission.

General Secretariat of the Council of the European Communities (1985). *Thirtieth review of the Council's work*, 1 January – 31 December 1984, Brussels 1985.

Leboutte, R. (2008). *Histoire économique et sociale de la construction européene*, 2008, Brussels, pp. 646-647.

Parkinson, M. (2005). Urban Policy in Europe. Where have we been and where are we going?, In: Antalovsky, E., Dangschat, J. and Parkison, M., *European Metropolitan Governance. Cities in Europe – Europe in the cities*, Vienna and Liverpool.

Presidency of the European Union (2000). *Conclusions of the French Presidency of the European Union at the end of the informal meeting of Ministers responsible for urban affairs at the Conference "Europe, spatial and urban development"*, 2 November 2000, Lille, point 2.

Presidency of the European Union (2004). *Ministerial Meeting Urban Policy "Cities empower Europe" Conclusions Dutch Presidency 2004*, Rotterdam.

Presidency of the European Union (2007). *Conclusions of the German EU Council Presidency on the Informal Ministerial Meeting on Urban Development and Territorial Cohesion*, 24 and 25 May 2007, Leipzig.

Presidency of the European Union (2008). *Final statement by the ministers in charge of urban development*, 25 November 2008, Marseille, Annex point 2.4.

Presidency of the European Union (2010). *Toledo Informal ministerial meeting on urban development*. Declaration, 22 June 2010, Toledo.

Presidency of the European Union (2011a). *Polish Presidency Conclusions on the territorial dimension of EU policies and the future of Cohesion Policy. Towards an integrated, territorially differentiated and institutionally smart response to EU challenges*, 24-25 November 2011, Poznan.

Presidency of the European Union (2011b). *Urban dimension of Cohesion Policy post 2013. Background report*, July 2011, Warsaw.

Rheinisch-Westfälisches Institut für Wirtschaftsforschung (2010). *Second State of European Cities Report*, Essen: Rheinisch-Westfälisches Institut für Wirtschaftsforschung.

Tofarides, M. (2003). *Urban policy in the European Union: a multi-level gatekeeper system*. Aldershot: Ashgate.

van den Berg, L., Braun, E. and Meer, van den (2004). *National urban policies in the European Union*. Rotterdam, Euricur.

Van Veelen, A. (1991). De Europese Gemeenschap en economische en sociale vernieuwing in Rotterdam, *Bestuurswetenschappen 1991*, 7, 508-511.

Chapter 3
Antwerp

Steven Sterkx[1]

City Profile

The city of Antwerp is the largest city of Flanders, the Flemish or Dutch-speaking part of Belgium. Flanders counts 13 so-called 'central cities', i.e. cities that perform a central function vis-à-vis their environment, in diverse areas such as employment, health care, education, culture and recreation. Of these 13 central cities, only Antwerp and Ghent can be labelled as 'metropolitan' cities. Antwerp is situated along the river Scheldt, which is connected to the North Sea by the Western Scheldt estuary. This estuary belongs to the territory of the Netherlands, and is a crucial shipping route for the port of Antwerp. The city of Antwerp is divided into 9 districts. In alphabetical order, these are Antwerpen (which comprises the historical city centre as well as a part of the left bank of the river Scheldt), Berchem, Berendrecht-Zandvliet-Lillo, Borgerhout, Deurne, Ekeren, Hoboken, Merksem and Wilrijk. The entire city has 20,426 hectares, of which more than 25 per cent or 5,462 hectares is residential area (Stad Antwerpen, 2010).

Demography

In January 2011, the population of Antwerp totalled 492,149 inhabitants, which represents close to 8 per cent of the total Flemish population (Stad Antwerpen, 2011). An important trend is the increase of the share of young children (0-9 year olds) by 23 per cent since 2000. Another group that has expanded significantly is the 80+ group. This age category featured an increase of 32 per cent since 2000. In addition, also the category of 20-29 year olds has grown: +17 per cent since 2000. In sum, the city features relatively high shares of very young ('greening') and very old people ('ageing'), and seems to be an attraction pole for young adults. At the same time, some age groups have decreased in number: the category of 60-69 year olds and in particular the category of 70-79 year olds (-17 per cent) have diminished since 2000.

1   The author would like to thank the following persons for their valuable contributions: Ine Goris, Jos Goossens, Dirk Van de Poel, Roeland Gielen, Bruno Verbergt, Tom Meeuws, Hardwin De Wever, Reinhard Stoop, Pieter Rotthier, Rebecca De Backer, Petra Heytens, Wim Blommaart and Liesbeth Wouters.

In relation to the housing situation, the city of Antwerp measures a density of 41.4 households per hectare. The various districts, however, show very diverging figures: 10.9 households/hectare in Berendrecht-Zandvliet-Lillo versus 53.6 in Antwerpen and 69.8 in Borgerhout. In January 2008, Antwerp totalled 250,385 residences, 49.1 per cent of which are apartments (in comparison with only 20 per cent in Flanders), 44.5 per cent single-family dwellings. 53.4 per cent of all residences are privately owned (in comparison with 74 per cent in Flanders). In 2010, public housing accounted for more than 10 per cent of all residences (Stad Antwerpen, 2010).

In Flanders, Antwerp is the city with the highest share of foreigners. More than 17 per cent of the city's population consists of foreigners, in comparison with a Flemish average of only 6 per cent. From a more global perspective, Antwerp currently hosts 173 different nationalities, making it one of the most 'international' cities in the world. Of these foreigners, almost 57 per cent has a non-EU nationality. The percentage of foreigners, however, does not fully reflect the ethnic diversity or composition of the city of Antwerp, as a large number of inhabitants of foreign origin has obtained Belgian nationality in the past few decades. Overall, the number of inhabitants with a migratory background – i.e. foreign nationals or Belgian nationals born with a foreign nationality – represents 32 per cent of Antwerp's population. This number mainly concerns the following ethnic origins (top-3, January 2011): Morocco (38,886 or 7.9 per cent of the total population of Antwerp), The Netherlands (16,025 or 3.3 per cent) and Turkey (13,419 or 2.7 per cent) (Stad Antwerpen, 2011).

Overall, population figures have been on the rise since the year 2000, when Antwerp had only 452,609 inhabitants (Stad Antwerpen, 2011). In ten years' time, the population has increased 40,000 inhabitants (around 9 per cent). Population growth, due to a combination of a positive migratory balance (since 2000) and a higher birth rate (since 2004), has been most visible since 2004. When controlling for ethnic background, it appears that this population growth is mainly a migratory pattern: the number of inhabitants with a migratory background – including many people originating from the new EU Member States – has increased with 39 per cent since 2004. In the same period, the number of natives has decreased by 5 per cent. This decline – in sharp contrast to the increase of non-natives – is caused by the combination of a low birth rate, a high mortality rate (due to the ageing of the native population), and – selective – emigration from the city ('urban flight').

Economy

The city of Antwerp displays a diverse picture of business activity. As in most cities, the tertiary sector has grown significantly over the last decades: in 2010, the service sector accounted for 59.1 per cent of all businesses located in Antwerp. The secondary sector remains very important, representing 15.5 per cent of businesses in Antwerp. The primary sector has a relatively marginal position with only 0.5 per cent of all businesses, while the quaternary sector continues to grow, representing 11.3 per cent of businesses in Antwerp (Stad Antwerpen, 2010b).

In 2009, the totality of Antwerp businesses accounted for a turnover of more than 118 billion EUR, which represents 21.1 per cent of total turnover in Flanders. This figure is equivalent to almost €14 billion of added value, or 14.6 per cent of total added value in Flanders. Industry generates the largest share of added value, i.e. 30.8 per cent in 2008. Also the sectors of transport and storage (21.5 per cent in 2008), wholesale and retail trade (15.3 per cent), and administrative and support services (12.3 per cent in 2008) contribute significantly to the total amount of added value. Between 1996 and 2008, the 'knowledge economy' in Antwerp experienced a growth in added value of 271 per cent, in comparison with an increase of (only) 91 per cent for the 'general economy' (Stad Antwerpen, 2010c). Since 2003, investment growth in Antwerp has been higher than in the rest of Flanders. In 2009, the sector of transport, storage and communication was responsible for 44 per cent of all investments in the Antwerp economy (Stad Antwerpen, 2010c).

In the area of employment, the city of Antwerp is faced with a paradox: Antwerp is the biggest employer in Flanders but at the same time has the highest unemployment rate (Stad Antwerpen, 2011b). In other words: although there are plenty of jobs in Antwerp, these positions are filled by people not living in Antwerp (i.e. commuters). Unemployment is particularly high among young people aged below 25 (unemployment rate of 21.6 per cent, in comparison with 11.8 per cent in Flanders) and people with a non-EU origin (49.7 per cent of all job seekers, in comparison with 24.9 per cent in Flanders). What is more, the labour market in Antwerp features a high amount of unfilled vacancies (5,360 in June 2011), of which 4 out of 10 are labelled as shortage professions (Stad Antwerpen, 2011b).

Not only for Antwerp, but for the entire Flemish economy, the port of Antwerp is extremely important. In 2009, the added value – direct and indirect – generated by port activities totalled 17.7 billion EUR (Vlaamse Havencommissie, 2011). In 2010, the port of Antwerp handled a total freight volume of 178,168,003 tonnes, an increase of 12.9 per cent in comparison with the recession year of 2009. Growth continued throughout the first six months of 2011, during which the port of Antwerp handled 95,869,516 tonnes of freight, an increase of 10.4 per cent compared with the first half of 2010 (Port of Antwerp, 2011).

Based on 2010 figures, Antwerp is ranked the second largest port in Europe for international shipping freight (second to Rotterdam and before Hamburg) and the tenth largest in the world. In the Le Havre-Hamburg range, the port of Antwerp accounts for 16.7 per cent of all maritime traffic in 2010 (Vlaamse Havencommissie, 2011) With three quarters of conventional freight carried in containers, Antwerp plays a leading role in maritime container handling. Furthermore, the port area hosts the largest and most diversified petrochemical cluster in Europe, second only to Houston in the rest of the world (Antwerp Headquarters, 2011). In 2009, direct employment in the port of Antwerp amounted to more than 62,500 FTE (of which 27,000 in the maritime cluster and almost 23,500 in industry). An important factor for the success of the port of Antwerp is its central location, closest to the largest urban agglomerations in Europe, as well as its unique location as an inland seaport.

Also the diamond sector has a leading place in the Antwerp economy. Next to port activities (logistics) and the petrochemical industry, the diamond industry is one of the three 'flagship sectors' in Antwerp. It is estimated that more than 80 per cent of the world's rough diamonds and around 50 per cent of all polished diamonds are traded through Antwerp every year (Antwerp Headquarters, 2011). Total – direct and indirect – employment in the diamond sector amounts to 30,000 FTE. Also the touristic impact of Antwerp's position as 'diamond capital of the world' cannot be underestimated.

Finally, the city of Antwerp is known for its fashion industry. Although the label of 'city of fashion' is important for the branding and image of Antwerp (and hence for tourism), the direct economic impact is rather limited: in 2008, fashion represented only 2.4 per cent of the total added value of the creative economy in Antwerp, and 2.6 per cent of the total employment created by the creative economy in Antwerp (Stad Antwerpen, 2011).

Governance

The city of Antwerp is governed by a total of 10 local authorities: one central authority for the entire city, and 9 district authorities. These authorities are each composed of a board and a council. Governance in Antwerp is the result of inner-city decentralization, with a total of 265 directly elected representatives (Stad Antwerpen, 2011c).

Starting point for strategic planning in Antwerp is the coalition agreement. An 'objectives tree' is drafted – for the first time – at the start of the legislature, and then continuously adapted in light of changing context, policy or insights (Stad Antwerpen, 2007).

The city administration is headed and directed by the secretary, the strategic coordinator and the financial manager. There are 10 departments and 26 autonomous entities. The Public Centre for Social Welfare is composed of 5 departments, and next to these, there are 6 autonomous entities. In each district, a district secretary is in charge of coordinating everyday activities. All these entities (together labelled as the 'group Antwerp') are responsible for the realization of the city's overarching objectives, as derived from the coalition agreement.

Developments and Policy Changes since Early 1990s

Governance, Communication and Policy: Fundamental Changes

In the course of the last two decades, the city of Antwerp has undergone major changes in governance, policy development and communication with its citizens.

To a certain extent, this can be seen as a gradual process (and the changing priorities of the subsequent coalition agreements bear witness to this), but the 2003 political crisis – the so-called 'Visa-crisis' – has unquestionably accelerated the on-going evolution, acting as a catalyst for change. The crisis, which emanated from an investigation into the wrongful use of credit cards (for personal expenditures) by civil servants, police staff and politicians, led to several indictments against and convictions of high-ranking officials within the city administration and police, as well as to the resignation of the entire Board of Mayor and Aldermen.

In an addendum to the 2001-2006 coalition agreement, the new Board proclaimed the need for an abrupt change in style, in order for governance in Antwerp to become 'sober, open and incorruptible' and with the ultimate aim of restoring confidence between citizens and city authorities (Stad Antwerpen, 2003). This proclamation was the harbinger to a series of fundamental and interrelated changes the city of Antwerp would go through.

First of all, in the area of governance and city organization, several steps were taken to adopt a more 'managerial' approach and to transform the city into a modern and professional organization. This involved – among other – the appointment of a strategic coordinator (in charge of coordinating the execution of policies by the entire city organization, by means of strategic planning and translation of policy into operational objectives), the establishment of strategic cells within the city organization, and the creation of autonomous entities in charge of specific competencies. Although these entities have their operational autonomy, the entire 'group Antwerp' cooperates and coordinates in order to achieve the overarching objectives as defined by the coalition agreement and the 'objectives tree'. In the realization of objectives, among other by means of projects that require a great deal of cooperation (also with private partners), it is the city administration that has a 'directing' role. In the political sphere, a shift occurred from 'old political culture' – characterized by (personal) services rendered to the public and a 'politicized' administration – to a 'new political culture', based on a more objective, strategic and managerial approach to policy-making.[2]

Secondly, as from 2004, a new and more professional communication campaign has taken off in Antwerp, of which the main elements are a new slogan, logo and the introduction of corresponding city values. The slogan '*t Stad is van iedereen* ('The city belongs to everyone') was intended to fundamentally break with the past, and to make Antwerp citizens proud of their city again. The 2003 political crisis revealed that Antwerp had evolved into a 'divided city', marked by a growing gap between different population groups on the one hand and between citizens and city authorities on the other. The city urgently needed to reconnect with its citizens. The new slogan was a first step to create a 'we-feeling' again, and was complemented with a new logo of a radiant 'A' and a set of so-called 'A-values'

2 In fact, this has been a gradual shift, spurred by the electoral success – above all in Antwerp – of the extreme-right political party Vlaams Blok ('Flemish Bloc') since the early 1990s.

(i.e. respect for diversity, integrity, customer-orientation, cost-consciousness and cooperation) by which all city personnel should abide.

Thirdly, in the area of policy development, Antwerp has witnessed a shift from sectoral approaches to integrated planning. The current coalition agreement coins the ambition to make Antwerp 'the most attractive environment' for people to live, work or visit (Stad Antwerpen, 2007). All urban policies are geared towards that ambition. Key instruments to create an attractive living environment are spatial planning, city renewal and architecture, i.e. urban development policies. Indeed, there is strong belief that interventions in the environment have a positive impact on human and social behaviour: investing in bricks ('hardware') is investing in people ('software').

This is not to say that the focus on urban development has been the only 'discourse' in Antwerp over the last two decades. Also other discourses, in particular a 'firmer' way of dealing with security issues (i.e. a policy of 'rights *and* duties'; see under 'integrated urban development') as well as a changed social discourse vis-à-vis *sans papiers*, people without a residence permit and asylum-seekers (with emphasis on how their presence 'weighs' on the city's integration policy and social welfare budgets; see 'state of the city'), have been – and still are – very present.[3] Nevertheless, the highlighting of urban development provides a perspective that best explains how the city has developed, in terms of planning and achievements. Furthermore, in the process of sketching these developments, it will become clear how these other important discourses are linked to urban development. As such, the phenomenon of uncontrolled migration is incompatible with the idea of creating attractive and liveable neighbourhoods, which are characterized by a balanced 'social mix'. The same goes for security policy: in order to guarantee the attractiveness and liveability of places, there is a need to intervene against public nuisance and to enforce respect for spatial developments and the quality of public spaces.

The ambition to boost the attractiveness of the city reflects how Antwerp wants to position itself in terms of 'sustainable competitiveness', both in relation to other cities and to rural and suburban areas. In all policy fields, ranging from economic development to housing, Antwerp aspires to acquire the assets needed to attract residents (or refrain them from moving), tourists, students, workers and businesses. Urban development and infrastructure investments – e.g. child and elderly care, social housing, mobility, green areas, leisure activities, etc. – have the capacity to increase the liveability and attractiveness of the city, and to counter the phenomenon of 'urban flight', which in Antwerp is a selective problem that manifests itself among native Belgians and young families with children.

Finally, this ambition is something the city wants to achieve in cooperation with its citizens and with relevant organizations and associations: the

---

3 Over the last few years, a 'sustainability discourse' has also made significant progress. Here, the emphasis is on energy efficiency and CO_2-reduction. The participation of the city to the Covenant of Mayors (since 2009) and the adoption of both a 'climate action plan' (2010) and a 'climate plan' (2011) for Antwerp are the pinnacles of this discourse.

attractiveness of the city is a *common* project. Therefore, in its policy planning, Antwerp has evolved towards 'co-production', with community participation being vital to the success of urban development projects. In recent years, large city projects in Antwerp – such as Park Spoor Noord ('Park Railway North'), Scheldekaaien ('Scheldt Quays') and the reorganization of the area Ruggeveld-Boterlaar-Silsburg (District of Deurne) – have all been subject to intensive participation trajectories.

Integrated Urban Development

During the last two decades, Antwerp has evolved towards integrated policy planning, with urban development obtaining a key position. The seeds for this change were already sown in the early 1990s, when the city council endorsed a Global Spatial Structure Plan for Antwerp (GSA – Globaal Structuurplan Antwerpen, 1990). For the first time, and in contrast to the 1970s and 1980s during which urban development steadily languished, this plan attempted to promote a new development strategy for the entire territory of Antwerp and was intended to halt the process of on-going suburbanization and degeneration of the city. The best-known concept of the GSA was Stad aan de Stroom ('City on the Stream'), which involved the reorientation of the city towards the river and the development of three key areas that had lost their former harbour functions, i.e. Eilandje ('the Islet'), Scheldekaaien ('Scheldt Quays') and Nieuw Zuid ('New South'). An international competition even yielded plans from renowned designers like Toyo Ito and Manuel de Solà Morales. However, the time was not yet ripe for an ambitious long-term vision and large-scale regeneration projects. The GSA and Stad aan de Stroom never achieved a big break (Stad Antwerpen, 2009).

'Stad aan de Stroom' and the international attention that went along with it, did however culminate in the awarding of Antwerp with the title of European Capital of Culture in 1993. Antwerp '93 in turn gave rise to the city festival Zomer van Antwerpen ('Summer of Antwerp'), which since 1995 has provided the citizens of Antwerp (and beyond) with a wide-ranging cultural programme during the summer months. In retrospect, these cultural successes in the early 1990s were the years of city marketing, during which Antwerp was claiming its place on the international scene. The 1995-2000 coalition agreement unequivocally refers to the crucial need for Antwerp to 'make itself known', within the city and outside (Stad Antwerpen, 1995).

In 1996, a Flemish decree on spatial planning obliged municipal governments to draw up their own spatial structure plans. This obligation is reflected in the 2001-2006 coalition agreement, which states that the elaboration of a municipal spatial structure plan is a policy priority, and that it should be the translation of a global vision on the spatial development of the city as well as an instrument for integrated policy (Stad Antwerpen, 2000). At the same time, we would have to wait until the endorsement of Antwerp's new spatial structure plan in 2006 and the new 2007-2012 coalition agreement to actually witness the *full* implementation of this global vision and the idea of integrated urban development. In the early years of the turn of the century, most attention still went out to sectoral policies and priorities (in particular the need to turn Antwerp into a safe and clean city), which were not yet linked to urban development.

Although a global vision was still lacking, major development projects had already kicked-off in strategic zones, such as the Central Station area (since 1993), the Schipperskwartier ('Sailor's Quarter', since 1998) and Park Spoor Noord ('Park Railway North', since 2000). These new dynamics were linked to financial support for urban development that was made available since 1994 at European level (Urban I, Urban II and Objective 2), after which the Flemish (by means of the Social Impulse Funds and City Renewal Fund) and federal government (by means of its Federal Urban Policy) followed suit (Stad Antwerpen, 2009).

The abovementioned changes since the early 1990s have culminated in the current 2007-2012 coalition agreement, which truly put the emphasis on infrastructure investments and city renewal as driving forces for the attractiveness and liveability of the city and specific neighbourhoods. Urban development has become the spearhead of all policies, the starting assumption being that the quality of the environment and public spaces has a positive impact on the quality of life of the citizens. Therefore, there is a need to invest in deprived neighbourhoods, quality housing, mobility and accessibility, industrial sites and brownfields, green and recreational areas, sports infrastructure, and so on. Urban development is inherently linked to other policy areas: investments in urban development will bring about positive results in the area of employment, economic activity, environment, safety, social well-being, leisure, etc. (Stad Antwerpen, 2007).

For example, in the area of culture, the last two decades have witnessed increasing links with urban development. In deprived neighbourhoods, regeneration projects have been accompanied by cultural events and programmes, ultimately with the aim of improving the attractiveness and liveability of those areas. Investments in culture have the capacity to boost urban development. Living examples include the opening of the Permeke public library in Antwerp North in 2005 – as part of the regeneration of the De Coninck Square – and of the landmark Museum aan de Stroom ('Museum by the Stream', MAS) in 2011 – as part of the development of the former port quarter Eilandje ('the Islet'). Also in the area of safety, there is an integrated vision on the quality of public spaces and security policy. Since the 1990s, the concept of security has significantly evolved: at a time when Antwerp started going through a process of re-urbanization with a range of large-scale development projects, the need emerged to explicitly call for respect for spatial developments and the quality of public spaces. In order to increase the liveability and safety in public spaces, the idea of 'citizenship' had to become stronger.

As mentioned in the previous section, the emphasis on urban development in the 2007-2012 coalition agreement goes hand in hand with the elaboration and implementation of a new spatial structure plan for Antwerp. Responding to the 1996 Flemish decree, which stated that every Flemish province and municipality would have to elaborate a spatial structure plan, the city of Antwerp commissioned Milan-based architects Bernardo Secchi and Paola Viganò to design a structure plan for its territory. In 2006, this *strategisch Ruimtelijk Structuurplan Antwerpen* (s-RSA, 'strategic Spatial Structure Plan') was approved by the city, the province and the Flemish government. From then onwards, it would provide a legal framework for the city's policy on spatial planning and city renewal. Projects that had already started (Central Station area, Park Spoor Noord, Eilandje, Scheldekaaien, Schipperskwartier, etc.) were integrated into the s-RSA (Stad Antwerpen, 2009).

Growing Challenges

The policy shift towards integrated urban development corresponds with a series of growing challenges that impact significantly on the quality of life in the city, and are to a great extent linked to the need to invest in infrastructure. Among these challenges, the mobility situation in the city, demographic changes and – last but not least – the phenomenon of (selective) 'urban flight' rank high on the list of city priorities. Although this list is by no means exhaustive, the way in which the city authorities handle these priorities, will have a great influence on the city's 'sustainable competitiveness'.

Mobility has been a priority since the early 1990s. Increasing traffic volumes coupled with reduced accessibility affect the economic viability of the city and its port and are a menace to liveability and road safety. Together with the city authorities, the Flemish region is an essential partner in formulating sustainable solutions to Antwerp's mobility situation. In 2000, the Flemish government endorsed a master plan for mobility in Antwerp (Masterplan Mobiliteit Antwerpen), which totalled a list of 16 infrastructure projects in and around Antwerp. These projects were further elaborated and refined in the so-called Masterplan 2020, which was approved by the Flemish government in 2010. In response to the problem of congestion, which has only worsened since the approval of the 2000 mobility plan, the new master plan emphasizes the need for modal shifts: it calls for an active policy to transfer freight from road to rail and inland waterways, and to encourage alternatives to car traffic (Vlaamse Overheid, 2010). This latter policy objective corresponds to the 2007-2012 coalition agreement which prioritizes mobility by foot, bicycle or public transport (in that order) over private transport (Stad Antwerpen, 2007). Next to modal shifts, the new master plan also calls for a more participatory approach, as changes in mobility structure do not stand alone, but are part of an integrated vision on mobility, spatial planning, economic development and liveability in and around Antwerp. Such an approach, as a means to obtaining societal support for infrastructure projects, corresponds to the emphasis put by the city of Antwerp on the need for participation trajectories, as part of large-scale urban development projects. A prime example of this was the 2009 referendum, in which the citizens of Antwerp were asked to give their opinion on the proposed *tracé* for the so-called Oosterweel link, i.e. the mobility project for the completion of the Antwerp ring road, needed to improve accessibility and the flow of traffic into, out of and around the city.

Demographic change in Antwerp has a major societal impact, and is a challenge for liveability in the city. Although population rise (of around 9 per cent between 2000 and 2011, in contrast to a population drop of 19 per cent between 1970 and 2000) can be seen as an indicator of the (regained) attractiveness of the city, it is also accompanied by challenges related to the growth of specific population groups. The combination of 'greening' and 'ageing' of the population has significant policy implications in the area of education, child and elderly care (Stad Antwerpen, 2007). At the same time, the city is subject to a 'colouring' of its population: whereas in 2004, inhabitants with a migratory background accounted for 24.5 per cent of the population, in 2011 this share has risen to 32.2 per cent. Furthermore, half of the 'population formation'[4] since 2001 can be attributed to non-natives, as opposed to only 25 per cent before 1990 (Stad Antwerpen, 2010). In particular the category of inhabitants with a non-EU origin, characterized by a higher unemployment rate and a higher share of persons on welfare support, is a group that presents additional challenges for social policy and community development in the city (Stad Antwerpen, 2010). In addition, it is a growing priority for the city to control the presence and influx of *sans papiers*, people without a residence permit, and asylum-seekers who have not been assigned to Antwerp (Stad Antwerpen, 2007).

In spite of the overall population growth, Antwerp is subject to the phenomenon of selective 'urban flight': every year, the number of families with – in particular very young – children is decreasing. This problem manifests itself above all among the native population. The presence of families with children is, however, extremely important for the liveability of the city and its neighbourhoods. Although the subsequent coalition agreements since the 1990s have highlighted the problem of 'urban flight' (Stad Antwerpen, 1995), it is in particular the current agreement that made it a core priority: in particular in its housing policy, the city wants to focus on one particular target group, i.e. families with children. The city not only wants to prevent them from leaving, but also has the ambition to attract new families to its territory. Among other policy measures, housing policy – aimed at quality and affordable housing – is indeed an important instrument to counter 'urban flight'. In this context, the city authorities acknowledge the necessity to invest in additional social housing in Antwerp. Current legislation, however, leaves little room for an autonomous housing policy at city level (Stad Antwerpen, 2007).

---

4   'Population formation' is defined as the share of the inflow of people that actually contributes to the population (at the time of measurement). For example, 'population formation' by 19-year olds in 2001 is the share of people who entered the city as 19-year olds and are still present in the population (at the time of measurement).

State of the City

Site of the Century

Over the last decade, Antwerp has solidly invested in an integrated urban development policy. In several city areas, new projects have been initiated. While some of them are finished, others remain work in progress. Together, these investments have rightfully turned Antwerp into the so-called *Werf van de Eeuw* ('Site of the Century'). In the process of urban development and city renewal, the s-RSA ('strategic Spatial Structure Plan') has had – and still has – a guiding role. The s-RSA contains a long-term vision for the spatial development of the city. It presents two types of policy, which are complementary to each other: a 'generic' and an 'active' policy. The execution and structure of the generic policy is based on seven 'inspiring images', which are relevant for the entire city. The active policy is executed within five concretely defined 'strategic spaces', and is therefore area-oriented (Stad Antwerpen, 2009).

The seven inspiring images all refer to the collective memory of the city, and transform known and valued qualities of the city into ambitions for the future:

1. *Water city*: reorientation towards the river Scheldt, and the use of water (including creeks, canals and docks) to improve the quality of the living environment.
2. *Eco-city*: efficient use of open spaces and the city's ecological infrastructure.
3. *Port city*: improving logistics and access to the port, and restoring a balanced relationship between city and port.
4. *Railway city*: enhancing mobility and accessibility within the city territory, mainly by improvements to the 'lower network' of local roads and public transport.
5. *Porous city*: optimizing urban space, by giving social, economic, recreational and green functions to unused building and plots.
6. *Villages and metropolis*: organization of Antwerp according to the different functions of a polycentric (various local and urban centres) and metropolitan (inner city) city.
7. *Mega-city*: exploiting Antwerp's location, centrality and economic assets within the metropolitan area of Northwest Europe.

Five strategic spaces, where investments will be concentrated, have a key role in the renewal of the city:

1. *Hard Spine*: restoration and reinforcement of the relationship between the city and the river Scheldt as the main structuring element of Antwerp as a metropolitan city. This strategic area stretches from the district of Hoboken in the south to the district of Ekeren in the north, and comprises Eilandje

('the Islet'), Scheldekaaien ('Scheldt Quays') and Nieuw Zuid ('New South') as the main project areas for city renewal.

2. *Soft Spine*: interconnection of green open spaces (in particular five important park areas in Antwerp), with waterways as a linking element.

3. *Lower network and Urban centres*: investing in a network of local roads and public transport (in particular tram lines) in order to structure the urban and metropolitan region.

4. *Groene Singel* ('green ring road area'): creating a qualitative open and green space, connecting the outer city as well as the five parks of the Soft Spine to the inner city.

5. *Lively Canal*: improving the quality of the areas alongside both banks of the Albert Canal (in the districts of Merksem and Deurne).

Infrastructure and city renewal projects in these strategic areas, combined with a policy of community development projects across the city, materialize Antwerp's evolution towards integrated urban development. The ultimate goal is to boost the city's attractiveness vis-à-vis residents (as such countering the phenomenon of 'urban flight'), tourists, students, workers and businesses.

One of the key projects in Antwerp's process of city renewal is Park Spoor Noord ('Park Railway North'). This project embodies the various spatial, social, cultural and organizational elements that are inherent to integrated planning. In 2000, the NMBS (National Belgian Railway Company) abandoned a 24 hectares railway site in the north of the city.

By means of a network of paths, the park connects three quarters – i.e. Dam, Stuivenberg and Seefhoek – that were previously cut off from each other by the railway site. These quarters are deprived neighbourhoods in the north of Antwerp, an area which ranks very low on the city's 'liveability index' (Stad Antwerpen, 2010d). The development of this area – a densely and diversely populated area where only 1 in 8 households owns any outside space – was therefore very welcome. The opening of a new park – a 'garden for locals' as well as park for the city – was correspondingly intended to give a positive incentive to the attractiveness and liveability of this part of the city (Stad Antwerpen, 2009).

From the outset, the local community had been involved in the planning process. From the conceptual to the design phase (2001-2005), several participation and communication occasions were organized. In addition, the site itself hosted a Wervend Programma ('Inspirational Programme') which involved a series of exhibitions and festivities, intended in the first place to make the neighbourhood inhabitants enthusiastic about the new park in the making (Autonoom Gemeentebedrijf Stadsplanning Antwerpen, 2011).

Finally, the entire process – ranging from the initial plans for the railway site to the actual execution of the project – was accompanied by a series of organizational adjustments, changing the way the city would deal with spatial planning and urban development *tout court*. In 2001, an autonomous municipal company AG ANN (Autonoom Gemeentebedrijf Antwerpen Nieuw Noord – 'Autonomous Municipal

Company for the Renewal of Antwerp North') was established and made responsible for the management of subsidies (Federal Urban Policy and Objective 2-funding) allocated to the new park and for the development of the project (including public procurement and commissioning). A project team within the city's planning cell was put in charge of coordinating the actual project. In 2008, the mandate of AG ANN was expanded into AG Stadsplanning ('Autonomous Municipal Company for City Planning'), a new autonomous municipal company which would be in charge of coordinating area-oriented programmes and executing strategic projects, as defined by the s-RSA. The city's planning cell was incorporated into AG Stadsplanning. Today, the city's reorganization with regard to spatial planning has yielded a division of tasks between different entities, which closely cooperate towards the realization of urban development projects:

- The Stadsbouwmeester ('Chief city architect', since 1999) has the explicit role to advise and raise awareness about spatial quality.
- Bedrijfseenheid Stadsontwikkeling ('City administration for Urban Development') is in charge of 'generic' policy related to spatial planning and the public domain, and responsible for licenses and permits.
- AG Stadsplanning (since 2008) has an 'active' role related to area-oriented programmes and strategic projects.
- AG VESPA ('Autonomous Municipal Company for Real Estate and City Projects in Antwerp', since 2003) also has an 'active' role, and is responsible for the execution of the city's land and property policy and for real-estate transactions. In addition, AG VESPA coordinates projects that specifically rely on public-private cooperation, and manages funds from supra-local governments (Stad Antwerpen, 2009).

In addition, given the city's emphasis on the integrated character of urban development, city projects require further cooperation with other departments and entities in charge of – among other – culture (e.g. cultural programmes, exhibitions and festivities), sports (e.g. organization of sports events), economy (e.g. attractiveness of shopping streets and development of business sites) and social policy (e.g. community participation).

Cooperation with External Partners

Cooperation with external partners has been an essential element for the implementation of integrated urban development projects and city renewal. Above all, relationships with external parties – in particular supra-local authorities and private investors/companies – are vital to the generation of the resources needed to execute projects. In individual projects, these resources are often a combination of public funding and private investments.

For its city projects, Antwerp obtains funding from the Flemish, federal and European level. The 'City Fund' of the Flemish government provides the so-called 'central cities' in Flanders with structural financing to implement projects aimed at increasing the liveability of the city and its neighbourhoods. Antwerp, being the largest city in Flanders, is also the largest beneficiary. In the current programming period of the City Fund, the city's 2007-2012 coalition agreement (which fully prioritizes city attractiveness and liveability) forms the basis of the 'multi-annual agreement' with the Flemish authorities. This agreement outlines how Antwerp will use the financing provided by the Fund, and which objectives it wants to realize. Special attention goes out to 'priority neighbourhoods' and 'priority groups'.

Funding from the Belgian government proceeds through the Federal Urban Policy, which is principally geared towards the largest urban centres in the country. Since 2009, funding is provided on the basis of annual 'sustainable city'-contracts. These are 'integrated' contracts, aiming for sustainable solutions to the problems cities are faced with, and which are elaborated in close consultation with the city authorities and stakeholders involved.

Since Flanders belongs to the category of Objective 2-regions, financing of city projects in Antwerp is provided through the European Regional Development Fund (ERDF). The 2007-2013 Operational Programme concluded between the Flemish government and the European Commission contains an 'urban priority', to the benefit of Flemish cities. This urban priority supports urban development projects, aimed at strengthening entrepreneurship and innovation in the city.

What these funds have in common, is that they support integrated urban development. As such, they have allowed the city of Antwerp to connect the specificities of each fund to the priorities of the current coalition agreement. The various funding channels have been used for different purposes. Whereas – generally speaking – resources of the Flemish 'City Fund' have been largely allocated to a range of social/community projects, funding through the Federal Urban Policy and the ERDF has been predominantly used for city renewal and infrastructure investments. This has certainly been the case with Park Spoor Noord, which attracted a great deal of its funding through the Federal Urban Policy and ERDF.

Next to public funding, the city of Antwerp also needs private investments and Public-Private Partnerships (PPP) to finance its urban development projects. Park Spoor Noord clearly illustrates that commercial aspects have been vital to the project's success. Key to the development of the park has been the 2001 agreement between the city, AG ANN, the National Belgian Railway Company (NMBS) and Euro-Immo-Star (i.e. an autonomous entity of the NMBS in charge of real estate): in exchange for 18 hectares of public space (which would be used by the city for the development of the park), the NMBS and Euro-Immo-Star received commercial development rights for 192,000 m² at a 6 hectares plot to the west of the park (i.e. 'kop Spoor Noord'). The NMBS was also responsible for carrying out the necessary decontamination of the soil. Other elements of public-private cooperation include the 2008 decision by Artesis University College Antwerp to co-finance the building of a sports hall in the WDT hangar (Autonoom Gemeentebedrijf Stadsplanning Antwerpen, 2011).

Finally, for its projects, Antwerp is not only in need of investments, but also looking for the right expertise. The project 'Blue Gate Antwerp', i.e. the development of a brownfield (former Petroleum South, along the river Scheldt and part of the 'hard spine') into an eco-effective business site, provides a good example. Part of the project involves the construction of a logistical zone, including a regional and urban water-related distribution centre. For the development of the concept of 'smart logistics', the University of Antwerp has been a key partner.

Impact of the Financial-Economic Crisis

The 2008-2009 financial economic crisis has produced both demographic and economic effects. The impact was substantial, but not devastating. Signs of recovery have been visible since 2010.

In demographic terms, the crisis has led to a temporary slowdown of international migration into the city. This has probably to do with the uncertainty engendered by the economic crisis, and resulted in 2010 into a decrease in the sharp population growth which Antwerp had witnessed since 2000. The year 2011, however, shows a record population growth again, caused by an acceleration of international migration, as well as by the effects of a large-scale national regularization campaign held in 2009 (Stad Antwerpen, 2011). In Antwerp, this campaign gave rise to 7,283 applications, for a total of 10.391 candidates (38 per cent of whom originating from North Africa, 17 per cent from West Africa and 11 per cent from the Middle East). The concentration of candidates is the highest in Antwerp North (31.8 per cent of all applications, which translates into 47.7 applications per 1,000 inhabitants) (Stad Antwerpen, 2010e).

After a substantial decrease between 2006 and 2008, the unemployment rate in Antwerp mounted again as a result of the crisis, peaking with 16.0 per cent in July 2010. Most 'central cities' in Flanders went through a similar evolution (Stad Antwerpen, 2010b). In 2011, the unemployment rate dropped to 14.2 per cent (Stad Antwerpen, 2011b).

The port of Antwerp endured a severe recession in 2009. That year, total added value plunged by 8.5 per cent, total employment by 4.7 per cent and the total freight volume handled by 16.7 per cent Vlaamse Havencommissie (2011). Faced with these results, and under the motto 'Never waste a good crisis', the Antwerp Port Authority and Alfaport (i.e. the association of port companies) drew up the action plan 'Total Project for a More Competitive Port'. This plan already yielded positive figures in 2010, a trend which continued in the first half of 2011 (Port of Antwerp, 2011).

Overall investments in Antwerp decreased in 2009. In comparison with 2008, the total value of investments dropped by 26.0 per cent. The year 2008, however, was a peak year in terms of investments. As such, when comparing with 2007, the decline due to the recession is much less outspoken. Looking at specific sectors, the plunge of investments is most obvious in wholesale and retail trade and – in particular – industry (Stad Antwerpen, 2010c). For large-scale urban development projects, the recession had no indelible effects: investments might have slowed down, but no projects were cancelled.

Finally, economic activity in Antwerp reduced in 2009: the number of business failures was the highest since 2004, and the number of establishments went down by 8.7 per cent (Port of Antwerp, 2011).

Accomplishments

First of all, in the last decade and in particular since the s-RSA and the current coalition agreement, the city of Antwerp has made a priority of integrated urban development, investing a great deal of time, effort and resources in spatial planning and city renewal. Various large-scale and integrated projects, many of which are still work in progress, have significantly boosted the attractiveness of the city. Due to the recent and on-going character of most projects, it is still too soon to accurately measure the results in terms of 'sustainable competitiveness' of the city. Nevertheless, some effects of the city's policy and investments will be briefly touched upon.

In each neighbourhood (but also at the level of individual housing projects), the city authorities focus on creating the appropriate 'social mix', i.e. a balanced community (in which diverse population groups and income categories are present) stimulating the liveability of the area. The 'liveability index' shows that the most 'unliveable' neighbourhoods are composed of too many 'young starters', are subject to a large influx of poor incomes, and lack the presence of (in particular native) families with children (Stad Antwerpen, 2010c). Despite the low scores of some city areas on the liveability index, Antwerp has succeeded in preventing these areas from becoming 'no-go zones', as is often the case in metropolitan cities. Investments in deprived areas, by means of integrated urban development, are vital to attaining the 'social mix' which is necessary to reach an appropriate level of liveability. With the aim of attracting (in particular two-income) families with children, these investments relate – among other – to creating green, open and recreational areas (Park Spoor Noord being a prime example), and to providing affordable and quality housing. As social housing policy by itself does not suffice, the city also has a policy of intervening in the private rental housing market. These interventions (e.g. housing benefits, attestations of conformity of rental housing) seek to guarantee rental housing quality and to control rental prices.

Statistics on 'urban flight' show signs of slight improvements since 2008: less native inhabitants are leaving the city, and also families with children – i.e. the most sensitive group – have become more inclined to stay (Stad Antwerpen, 2010f). Nonetheless, investments in urban development have also generated unwanted side-effects: 'gentrification' – which goes hand in hand with mounting property values – tends to arise in city neighbourhoods which have been subject to major investments (e.g. Eilandje). Given its distorting effect on the social balance in city neighbourhoods, the phenomenon of gentrification is perceived as an unwelcome evolution. Its progress, however, is difficult to quantify. The city of Antwerp currently does not have a method to measure gentrification, nor any data on the mobility of residents according to their socio-economic status. Furthermore, as gentrification is a long-term process, its measurement would need to rely on extended time series, which are not (yet) available.

Also for the area around Park Spoor Noord, gentrification will be a point of attention. Available data show that real estate prices have risen more than average in the period 1995-2009. In general, however, the development of the park has so far yielded mostly positive effects: the number of unoccupied dwellings has gone down, while the number of renovation permits (in various neighbourhoods around the park) has increased (Autonoom Gemeentebedrijf Stadsplanning Antwerpen, 2011). In this early stage, though, it is still too soon to measure the overall impact on poverty and deprivation.

Secondly, the relations between the city of Antwerp and the regional and federal governments in Belgium have significantly improved over the last decade. Today, the different layers of government are considered to be 'equal partners'. The way in which Antwerp has proceeded with integrated planning (and how this is reflected in the funding agreements with the Flemish and federal government) has had a 'maturing' effect on its relations with supra-local governments. Even more so, in Flanders, the city of Antwerp has acted as a 'pioneer' when it comes to integrated planning. Antwerp is explicitly asking the Flemish government to support its integrated approach, instead of 'imposing' sectoral perspectives on policy-making.

In spite of these improved relations, some 'frustrations' still persist. Mobility and migration are two policy areas which are highly challenging for the city of Antwerp, but in which it has to rely on – respectively – the Flemish and federal government to take action. The 2007-2012 coalition agreement is very clear about this. With regard to mobility, the city of Antwerp has conveyed a memorandum to the Flemish government, in which it stresses the need to safeguard and improve the accessibility and liveability of the city. Relating to migration, a memorandum to the federal government addresses the problem of *sans papiers*, people without a residence permit and asylum-seekers who have not been assigned to Antwerp. As the city feels it is not 'in control' of migration to its territory (with detrimental effects on its integration policy), it wants the federal government to take appropriate measures: actions against municipalities which do not fulfil their obligations towards asylum-seekers who have been assigned to their territory, a humane and effective return policy, an efficient immigration policy, faster procedures for refugee status determination, limitations to secondary migration, stricter rules on immigration by marriage, as well as an anticipatory approach towards the measures taken by neighbouring countries (Stad Antwerpen, 2007).

Finally, the communication campaign launched in 2004 – as part of a more professional city organization *tout court* – has borne fruit. Surveys indicate that the amount of citizens who are 'proud of their city' has significantly increased (from 62.5 per cent in 2004 to 67.1 per cent in 2010). At the same time the number of citizens who are 'not proud of their city' has decreased (from 23.4 per cent in 2004 to 17.2 per cent in 2010) (Stad Antwerpen, 2010g). The internal focus of the city of Antwerp – with the logo of the radiant 'A' being oriented toward its own citizens and organization – has been an effective way to make amends with the crisis of 2003. Today, with a reborn pride, and with all these investments in urban development boosting the attractiveness of the city, the question arises whether Antwerp should start a new phase of external orientation. Possibly, the logo of the radiant 'A' also has its external value.

References

Antwerp Headquaters (2011). [Online]. Available at http://www. antwerpheadquarters.be. [accessed: 2011].

Autonoom Gemeentebedrijf Stadsplanning Antwerpen (2011). *Park Spoor Noord*. Antwerpen: Stad Antwerpen.

Port of Antwerp (2011). [Online]. Available at http://www.portofantwerp.com [accessed: 2011].

Stad Antwerpen (1995). *Bestuursakkoord 1995-2000*. Antwerpen: Stad Antwerpen.

Stad Antwerpen (2000). *Bestuursakkoord 2001-2006*. Antwerpen: Stad Antwerpen.

Stad Antwerpen (2003). *Addendum Antwerps Bestuursakkoord*. Antwerpen: Stad Antwerpen.

Stad Antwerpen (2007). *Bestuursakkoord Antwerpen 2007-2012*. Antwerpen: Stad Antwerpen.

Stad Antwerpen (2009). *Urban development in Antwerp*. Antwerpen: Stad Antwerpen.

Stad Antwerpen (2010). *Monitor Wonen 2010*. [Online]. Available at http:// www.antwerpen.be/docs/Stad/Bedrijven/Sociale_zaken/SZ_Woon/ Woonmonitor_2010.pdf [accessed: 2012].

Stad Antwerpen (2010b). *Kerncijfers stad Antwerpen 2010*. [Online]. Available at http://www.antwerpen.be/eCache/ABE/80/36/867.html [accessed: 2012].

Stad Antwerpen (2010c). *Indicatorenmonitor 2010: Economie in Antwerpen uit de doeken*. [Online]. Available at http://www.antwerpen.be/eCache/ABE/4/088. Y29udGV4dD04MDM2ODY3.html [accessed: 2012].

Stad Antwerpen (2010d). *De leefbaarheidsindex: kaartmateriaal*. Antwerpen: Stad Antwerpen.

Stad Antwerpen (2010e). *Tabellenrapport regularisatie 2009*. Antwerpen: Stad Antwerpen.

Stad Antwerpen (2010f). *Verhuisbewegingen in Antwerpen 2009*. Antwerpen: Stad Antwerpen.

Stad Antwerpen (2010g). *Antwerpse Monitor, April 2010, surveys of city of Antwerp in cooperation with Made4it and TNS Dimarso*. Antwerpen: Stad Antwerpen.

Stad Antwerpen (2011). *Bevolkingsoverzicht 2011*. Antwerp: Stad Antwerpen.

Stad Antwerpen (2011b). *De arbeidsmarkt in juni 2011.* [Online]. Available at http://www.antwerpen.be/eCache/ABE/4/088.Y29udGV4dD04MDM2ODY3.html [accessed: 2012].

Stad Antwerpen (2011c). *Themastuk Strategische Organisatie, Stedenfonds – Visitatiecommissie 2010-2011.* Antwerpen: Stad Antwerpen.

Vlaamse Havencommissie (2011). *De Vlaamse havens. Feiten, statistieken en indicatoren 2010.* [Online]. Available at http://www.vlaamsehavencommissie.be [accessed: 2011].

Vlaamse Overheid (2010). *Masterplan 2020. Bouwstenen voor de uitbreiding van het Masterplan Mobiliteit Antwerpen.* [Online]. Available at http://www.antwerken.be/masterplan/wat-is-het-masterplan.aspx [accessed: 2012].

Chapter 4
Barcelona

Oriol Nel·lo

City Profile[1]

Four major forces are said to be shaping the future of our societies and regions (Smith, 2010): the new demographic transition that has led to an increase in world population from 3 to 7 billion inhabitants in less than half a century; the use of dwindling natural resources (water, minerals, energy, land) under conditions of extraordinary pressure and very unfair distribution; climate change, which is largely due to human actions and involves global warming to which human society will invariably have to adapt; and, finally, economic globalization as a result of the expansion of capitalist production on the planet as a whole, which has led to the integration of the world economy and made it highly interdependent, thus radically altering power relations between capital and labour.

In this context, which is so problematic in so many ways, the region of Catalonia shows great potential in certain areas (Nel·lo, 2005; 2007a). This potential is derived primarily from its geographic location, which has allowed Catalonia to play the role of gateway and hinge between the Iberian Peninsula and the rest of Europe. Though Catalonia only has an area of 32,113 km² (6.3 per cent of the area of Spain), two of the main corridors of activity on the Iberian Peninsula pass through it (the River Ebro valley and the Mediterranean Arc) and the region also boasts two of the leading ports on the Mediterranean Sea (Barcelona and Tarragona). Though it is true that the region lacks natural resources, the pleasant physical conditions (mild climate, varied geography) have historically favoured long-term settlement in the region.[2]

The existence of this potential and the structure of Catalonia society led to the creation in Catalonia of one of the main focal points of industrialization on the Iberian Peninsula and in Southern Europe in the nineteenth century: the first steam-powered factory in Spain opened in Barcelona in 1832; the first railway on the Iberian Peninsula, which ran between Barcelona and Mataró, was inaugurated in 1848; and Catalonia boasted the largest working class in Spain and a dynamic, enterprising bourgeoisie. The evolution of this economic activity and associated

---

1 Previous versions of this chapter appeared in Nel·lo (2012a and 2012b).

2 See for example Vila (1937) and Vilar (1964), two classical interpretations of the Catalan spatial structure and how its geographical potential is linked to the historical evolution.

social relations, which were nearly always conflictive, decisively marked the historical development of the city and Catalonia as a whole until the last quarter of the 20th century, when, pushed by the integration of the world economy and the fragmentation of production processes, the relative weight of industrial activity began to decline and give way to an increasingly services-based economy.

Demography

Within the context of this economic evolution, the population has experienced irregular, but very notable growth in the last fifty years, as is clear from the fact that the 2010 population of 7.5 million virtually doubled the 1960 population of 3.9 million. Catalonia is therefore the second most populated autonomous community in Spain and has a considerably denser population (233 inhabitants km²) than the mean for Spain (92.4 inhabitants/km²). Also of note is that this growth has been not so much due to the natural movement of people, limited by persistently low birth rates, as to the result of different episodes of major waves of immigration that were particularly intense in the 1959-1975 and 1996-2007 periods (Cabre, 1999).

From the spatial perspective, the most notable consequence of this historical evolution has been the process of urban development, which is to be considered both the driving force and the result of industrialization, economic modernization and population growth. This process has resulted in the configuration of a powerful urban structure headed by the Barcelona metropolitan area. In 1960, the greater Barcelona metropolitan area had a population of 2.6 million. After five decades of growth, it reached 5 million inhabitants in 2010, to become one of the ten leading metropolitan areas in Europe in terms of population and one of the leaders of the Iberian urban system, along with Madrid and Lisbon (Serra, 2002; Nel·lo, 2004). Moreover, Barcelona is a complex metropolitan area in which a very dense centre of no more than 500 km² that is home to 3.1 million people is surrounded by a string of medium-sized cities (Mataró, Granollers, Sabadell, Terrassa, Vilanova, Vilafranca) with populations in most cases of more than 100,000 inhabitants. The metropolitan consolidation of Barcelona has driven the functional and economic integration of the region as a whole without rendering the rest of the regional urban system insignificant. Quite the contrary: the rest of Catalonia has a number of small and medium-sized cities (including Figueres, Girona, Vic, Manresa, Igualada, Tarragona, Reus, Tortosa and Lleida) that provide their respective areas with activity and services.

Economic Structure

In the same period, the Catalan economy also experienced a very notable structural transformation. Industrial jobs accounted for 40.3 per cent of total employment in 1977, but had dropped to 19.2 per cent by 2010, whereas services as a percentage of total employment grew from 41.6 per cent to 69.7 per cent in the same period. This process of economic modernization and tertiarization of the economy has been accompanied by a sharp increase in income. After Spain joined the European Union in 1986, average per capita income (based on purchasing power parity) in Catalonia went from a figure equivalent to 86 per cent of the EU average (EU-15 = 100) to one that surpassed the EU average by 20 percentage points (EU-27 = 100) and surpassed the eurozone average by 12 percentage points (eurozone = 100) in 2009. Today, Catalonia's 7,512,381 inhabitants represent 16 per cent of the Spanish population, but the weight of Catalonia's GDP (€207 billion in 2009) accounted for 19.7 per cent of the Spanish total and Catalonia's exports in 2010 represented 26.2 per cent of the total for Spain as a whole (IDESCAT, 2011; see Trullén (2011) for an analysis of the economic structure of metropolitan Barcelona).

Public Administration

Finally, since the end of the 1970s, the return to democracy and the reinstatement of the *Generalitat*, Catalonia's own regional government, have resulted in a very notable increase in the legitimacy, quality and effectiveness of the public administration. Thus, despite the persistence of major problems of fit between the aspirations of the Catalan Parliament and the Spanish institutional framework (which became very clear in the controversial debate in 2006 on the redrafting of Catalonia's Statute of Autonomy[3]), the Catalan government now has resources[4] and levels of self-government that are unprecedented in recent history. From the perspective of urban planning and spatial planning, this means that the Catalan government now has exclusive competencies in this area, whereas the Spanish government is responsible for regulating only basic matters affecting constitutional rights, as well as planning and executing general-interest infrastructure projects. Also particularly important here is the action taken by municipal councils, which have made major contributions to improving public facilities and services in urban centres. In particular, the evolution of the city of Barcelona has attracted international attention as an example of a city that has experienced major improvements in its physical structure, foreign projection and the population's average living conditions at the same time that its economic base has been transformed. In general terms, it is unquestionable that Catalan

---

3 The attempt to enlarge the powers of Catalan institutions through a new Statute of Autonomy was approved in referendum by the Catalan citizens but was heavily restricted by the Spanish Constitutional Court in 2010. This entailed a major political crisis which led to the formation of a pro-independence majority in the Catalan Parliament after 2012 elections. The results of these far reaching political events are yet uncertain.

4 The 2010 budget of the Catalan government amounted to €32.52 million, equivalent to 15.7 per cent of Catalan GDP in 2009 (see IDESCAT – National Statistics Institute of Catalonia, 2011).

cities have improved considerably since the end of Franco's dictatorship nearly four decades ago (Nel·lo, 1999; Ferrer and Sabaté, 1999; Ferrer, 2005).[5]

It can therefore be stated that, despite problems and insufficiencies, which have been aggravated since 2008 by the international financial crisis, Catalonia, with a per capita GDP among the top ten countries in the European Union and a life expectancy at birth of 81.7 years in 2008 (78.7 for men, 84.6 for women, 2.5 years above the EU average), could be counted at the beginning of the twenty-first century among the societies with the highest level of wellbeing on the planet.

However, after 2008 the Catalan society, together with the rest of Spain and most of the Southern European countries, has been heavily hit by the effects of the financial economic crisis and the so-called austerity policies. This has resulted in a drastic reduction of the economic growth rate, including periods of recession, and an alarming raise of unemployment up to the scandalous figure of 0.9 million people in Catalonia, 26.3 per cent of the total economically active population (as in March 2013; for Spain as a whole unemployment affects 6 million people, 27 per cent of the total). Salaries have dropped significantly and the Catalan population living below the poverty line is getting dangerously close to 30 per cent (26.3 per cent in Catalonia, 29 per cent for Spain as a whole). In this context, the ability of the Spanish State and the Catalan regional or local administrations to develop urban, environmental and infrastructural policies has been severely curtailed (Sarasa, 2013).

Developments and Policy Changes since Early 1990s

The Metropolitanization Process

In the last half century, the potential and evolution of Catalonia's spatial structure have been at once the driving force and the result of this notable social transformation. As stated above, the most relevant expression of this evolution can be found in the urbanization process, which has led to increased metropolitanization and integration of the region. Let's take a closer look at the main features and phases of this process by focusing in particular on the Barcelona metropolitan area, the keystone of Catalonia's urban system. However, as discussed below, the main features of the process affect the Catalan region as a whole.

The integration of the Catalan region around its system of cities has remote historical precedents (Garcia Espuche, 1998; Nel·lo, 2001; 2002; 2004). However, it was only after the agricultural and commercial modernization of the 18th century and through subsequent industrialization in the 19th century and the first three quarters of the 20th century that this integration led to the

---

5   The bibliography on urban planning intervention in Barcelona is very extensive; among others, see Indovina (1999) and Marshall (2004). For critical perspectives, see Capel (2005) and Borja (2009).

prodigious increase in the urban population, configuring Barcelona as a great city that tended to expand physically and to join together the whole region in functional, economic and political terms. Throughout this long period, the development of Barcelona and its immediate vicinity was largely characterized by the city's ability to first attract people and activities from all over Catalonia and then those of the other regions of Spain. This attraction led to a powerful trend of concentration of the population, which resulted in the growth of the city and the municipalities around it due to their own endogenous development and the incoming flow of people and resources from the rest of Catalonia and Spain. This concentration phase reached its peak in the 1959-1975 period, i.e. the period of accelerated economic growth in the second half of the Franco dictatorship, at the end of which, in 1975, the city of Barcelona (whose city limits, it should be remembered, cover an area of only 100 km^2) would reach its all-time maximum population of 1,751,136 inhabitants. This concentration also led to metropolitan growth characterized by the physical expansion of the urban fabric, whereby the city of Barcelona became conurbated with the urbanized area of the municipalities immediately surrounding it (Hospitalet de Llobregat, Badalona, Santa Coloma de Gramenet, etc.), thus giving rise to a functionally integrated metropolitan area made up of about thirty municipalities covering an area of only 500 km^2 (not more than 2 per cent of the area of Catalonia) and containing more than 50 per cent of the population of Catalonia in 1975. Similar processes took place in the other main urban areas of Catalonia between 1960 and 1975: besides the city of Barcelona, the rest of the cities with more than 100,000 inhabitants went from accounting for 5.9 per cent of the population in 1960 to 20.7 per cent in 1975; the city of Lleida grew by 60.7 per cent, whereas the population of the rest of the municipalities in the counties around Lleida dropped by 3.9 per cent; the city of Tarragona grew by 124.5 per cent, whereas its surrounding area grew by only 37.4 per cent; Girona grew by 97 per cent and the rest of the municipalities in its area grew by barely 17.3 per cent.

The concentration phase ended in the mid-1970s, not only in Catalonia but in the rest of major Spanish metropolitan regions as well. At this point, the progressive move to a more services-based economy, the fragmentation of production processes, improvements in infrastructure, the increase in motorization rates, and differences in land and housing prices led to the onset of a new urban development phase. This phase was chiefly characterized by two features (Nel·lo, 2001; Burns, 2008): on the one hand, there was a substantial extension of metropolitan dynamics which expanded to encompass more than a hundred municipalities in the counties surrounding Barcelona; and, on the other, a rapid process of decentralization of the population took place. As shown in Table 4.1, there was an extraordinary drop in the population of the city of Barcelona, which lost one quarter million people, going down to 1,508,805 residents in 1996. The municipalities in the immediately outlying area of Barcelona went through a similar process and tended to lose population to the rest of the metropolitan region.

Table 4.1   Evolution of the population of Catalonia (inhabitants), 1960-2010

Area	1960	1975	1996	2010
Barcelona	1,557,863	1,751,136	1,508,805	1,619,337
First ring	449,085	1,228,853	1,339,830	1,497,653
Total metropolitan area (27 mun.)	2,006,948	2,979,989	2,848,635	3,116,990
Second ring	559,785	1,039,724	1,379,413	1,895,971
Total metropolitan region	2,566,733	4,019,713	4,228,048	5,012,961
Other parts of Catalonia	1,298,497	1,640,680	1,861,992	2,499,420
Total Catalonia	3,865,230	5,660,393	6,090,040	7,512,381

Source: IDESCAT (2011)

Conversely, the areas with the highest growth were located primarily in the second metropolitan ring, in counties such as Maresme, Vallès Oriental, Vallès Occidental and Garraf. However, in these areas of strong absolute and relative growth, the swell of the population did not tend to concentrate in the densest and most populated centres (the string of cities with an industrial tradition mentioned above: Mataró, Granollers, Sabadell, Terrassa, etc.), which in many cases also had problems maintaining their population and even experienced net losses. Rather, the areas that grew the most were smaller towns with more scattered populations. The push for decentralization that emptied out the densest and most populated city centres was thus accompanied by the dispersal of people and activities in the rest of the metropolitan area.

More or less similar processes took place on a different scale in the urban areas of the counties around Tarragona and Girona, to such an extent that Catalan cities with more than 100,000 inhabitants went from accounting for 51.6 per cent of the population in 1975 to 45.6 per cent in 1996, whereas cities with fewer than 20,000 people increased their relative weight in the same period from 27.6 per cent to 31.2 per cent. Therefore, while the evolution of the population in Catalonia in the 1960-1975 period was primarily characterized by a trend towards concentration due to interregional migration associated with the job market, in the following two decades, from 1975 to 1996, the transformation of settlement was largely driven by a trend towards decentralization and dispersal due mainly to intra-metropolitan migration associated with the housing market.

The shift from the first to the second phase in the metropolitanization process was perceived incompletely and belatedly by the public administration and professionals. There is a chance that something similar has happened in that Catalonia and Spain in the last 15 years, in such a way that we have actually covered a new phase of urban development and we are still not aware of it (Nel·lo, 2004; Nel·lo, 2007b).

Indeed, according to the data in Table 4.1, it is clear that from 1996 to 2010 the population of the city of Barcelona grew once again. The city's population, which had dropped to 1,503,884 inhabitants in 2001, surged to 1,619,337 in 2010. This was a common feature of the central cities in the seven largest metropolitan areas in Spain and also affected, to different extents, the main towns in the rest of Catalonia. Therefore, the main cities in the metropolitan area of Barcelona that, as discussed, lost inhabitants or had very limited growth in the previous period, grew once again, as occurred in Lleida, Tarragona and Girona. As a whole, the population of Catalan towns with more than 100,000 inhabitants that had increased by only 95,517 in the two decades between 1975 and 1996 grew by 259,647 in the fifteen years from 1996 to 2010.

Given this development, one might think that a recentralization movement was in progress, as predicted by the urban life cycle theory (van den berg, 1987). Thus, part of the people who left the main cities in the 1975-1996 period would now be returning to the city centre. And yet this does not appear to be the dominant trend or the chief explanation. In fact, in the first place, the data in Table 4.2 clearly show how, despite the increased growth of the city of Barcelona and the largest municipalities, the most growth continues to occur in smaller towns, particularly municipalities with between 20,000 and 50,000 inhabitants. Thus, the metropolitanization process now combines two features: major growth in absolute terms in the city of Barcelona, the rest of the first metropolitan ring and the group of cities with more than 100,000 inhabitants; and a redoubled increase in the population of the second metropolitan ring and the municipalities with fewer than 100,000 inhabitants, where the greatest absolute and relative growth is concentrated. In other words, the drive for decentralization now coexists with growth in the central area of the metropolis and the densest and most populated municipalities.

Table 4.2   Evolution of the population of Catalonia, by municipality size, 1960-2010

Size of the municipality	1960	1975	1996	2010
Less than 2,000 inhabitants	506,309	413,516	388,762	359,397
Between 2000 and 10,000 inhabitants	711,990	774,798	852,858	1,031,019
Between 10,001 and 20,000 inhabitants	235,364	370,550	659,159	802,488
Between 20,001 and 50,000 inhabitants	325,182	668,153	756,877	1,251,110
Between 50,001 and 100,000 inhabitants	300,557	512,656	658,478	924,282
Between 100,001 and 500,000 inhabitants	227,965	1,169,584	1,265,101	1,524,748
More than 500,000 inhabitants	1,557,863	1,751,136	1,508,805	1,619,337
Total Catalonia	3,865,230	5,660,393	6,090,040	7,512,381

Source: IDESCAT (2011).

Secondly, the data in Table 4.3 help us understand the reasons behind this combination of phenomena by showing not only the evolution in the number of inhabitants, but also their nationality. Thus, if we focus on the city of Barcelona, we can see that the number of people of Spanish nationality living in the city has continued to decline notably and is now down to 1,336,543 residents. This is certainly due to the persistence of intra-metropolitan migrations whose chief aim is to leave the city and go to the outlying metropolitan area. However, a new component has not only made up for these losses, but has turned the trend around: the arrival of major waves of foreigners. The foreign population, which was very low in 1996 (29,059 people), increased tenfold to 282,794 foreigners registered in 2010 (17.4 per cent of the city's population). A similar situation has occurred in municipalities in the first metropolitan ring, where the Spanish population continues to drop and foreigners now represent 17.8 per cent of the total. In this way, from 1996 to 2010, the 27 main municipalities in the metropolitan region, including Barcelona, lost nearly 200,000 Spanish residents and gained nearly half a million foreign residents. By contrast, in the second metropolitan ring the Spanish population has increased by nearly 300,000 to clearly exceed the increase in the foreign population in such a way that the proportion of foreigners in the second ring is only 12.4 per cent. As explained on other occasions, this trend of recent immigrants who first settle in city centres of metropolitan areas is common to the seven largest metropolitan areas in Spain (Nel·lo, 2004).

Table 4.3   Evolution of the population in the Barcelona metropolitan by nationality, 1996-2010

Area	Population 1996			Population 2010		
	Spanish	Foreign	Total	Spanish	Foreign	Total
Barcelona	1,479,746	29,059	1,508,805	1,336,543	282,794	1,619,337
First ring	1,323,433	16,397	1,339,830	1,271,239	226,414	1,497,653
Total metropolitan area	2,803,179	45,456	2,848,635	2,607,782	509,208	3,116,990
Second ring	1,358,111	21,302	1,379,412	1,660,665	235,306	1,895,971
Total metropolitan region	4,161,290	66,758	4,228,048	4,268,447	744,514	5,012,961

Source: IDESCAT (2011).

We can therefore conclude that the evolution of the population in the Barcelona metropolitan area and the region of Catalonia as a whole has gone through three major phases in the last half century: the first one, 1959-1975, in which the evolution of settlement is mainly explained by the existence of interregional migrations associated with the job market; the second one, 1975-1996, which was mainly conditioned by the presence of intra-metropolitan migrations associated with the housing market; and, finally, the third phase, which started in 1996, in which there have been intra-metropolitan migrations associated with the housing market (which first affected the population of Spanish nationals) and international migrations associated with the job market.

State of the City

Opportunities and Problems

As stated above, the evolution of the urbanization process, with its alternating periods dominated by trends towards population concentration followed by de-concentration and even dispersal, has had very positive effects on the development of the economy and the welfare of the population. Regional imbalance has been reduced, there is a larger critical mass and more capacity to attract economic activity, labour markets have tended to become more unified, and services are more accessible than ever from everywhere in the region.

This evolution, however, has also led to some major problems that, if they were to last, could compromise this generally positive balance and stifle the potential of the Catalan economy and Catalan society.[6] There are essentially three trends that are of particular concern from a spatial point of view: the progressive urban sprawl in the region, the growing functional specialization of different areas, and the risks of social segregation.

Urban sprawl is a direct corollary of the aforementioned metropolitanization processes and its most obvious result is the very sharp increase in the use of urban land. This phenomenon has meant that, in the Barcelona metropolitan area, the amount of transformed land (due to urbanization or infrastructure) went from 56,000 to 77,000 ha between 1977 and 2000. This is an increase of 36 per cent, at a rate of almost 900 ha per year, i.e. 2.5 ha per day for more than two decades (Font and Carrera, 2005; Font, 2007). A large part of this transformation was due to low-density residential urban development (Muñoz, 2007; 2011); in 2000 the area destined for this type of land use was almost twice that of land destined for intensive residential use (27,000 ha and 14,000 ha, respectively, in

---

6   For a compendium of the main social consequences of spatial dynamics in the region for the Barcelona metropolitan region in recent decades, see Nel·lo (2010). The effects of the ongoing economic crisis over these trends are still uncertain. Between 2006 and 2011 the rate of population growth dropped dramatically in the central municipalities of seven largest Spanish metropolitan areas (Madrid, Barcelona, Bilbao, Sevilla, Málaga, Zaragoza and Valencia). It seems as well that both foreign and intra-metropolitan migrations are losing intensity and strength. However, it is too early to assess which is the real impact and future implications of these developments.

the region as a whole). It is true that much of this development can be attributed to earlier projects, but the fact is that it became consolidated in this period.

It has sometimes been argued that low density today does not necessarily mean the disappearance of the "urban condition", as it is possible to provide the population residing in this type of settlement with services and living conditions of a quality comparable to that of densely urbanized areas (Indovina, 2009). However, the fact that the technology and resources are available does not necessarily mean that creating this urban environment is harmless in terms of sustainability, functionality and social and spatial cohesion. In fact, many studies have shown the harmful consequences of urban sprawl and rampant occupation of land: fragmentation of open spaces, occlusion of biological corridors, the increase in surface-water run-off, greater exposure to natural hazards (forest fires, soil erosion), increased water and energy consumption associated with single-family homes, increased mobility requirements and the difficulty of providing for them using public transport, increased costs of providing services, among others (Camagni et al., 2002; Rueda, 2002; Muñiz et al. 2007; Prieto et al., 2011).

The second major group of problems caused by the way in which the urbanization process has evolved is the growing functional specialization of different places. The expansion of urban areas and the dispersal of the population and activities have brought the whole metropolitan area to work as a single land market. In this context, the price of land, associated with the qualities, accessibility and amenities of the locations, ends up causing each place to specialize in certain uses, based on the ability of each activity to pay for the land occupied. This is a somewhat inevitable consequence of the urbanization process that has traditionally taken place inside each locality. But, the dynamics of metropolitanization have changed the scale of the phenomenon and, along with exacerbated market tensions, the lack of appropriate supra-municipal planning and occasionally by the application of outdated zoning principles, has led to the increasing specialization of many places exclusively in residential, production and commercial uses. As a result, some municipalities boast most of the activity and jobs, whereas many others are specialized only in residential settlements.

The increase in mobility requirements of citizens comes as a direct result of this situation. The needs that were once met within the same municipality, such as living, shopping, working, taking children to school, etc., must now be catered to over a much wider area (Nel·lo et al., 2002; López, 2003). The most evident result of the extensive use of the land deriving from this situation is municipalities' growing inability to contain the mobility they generate, known in technical terms as the capacity for self-containment. In 1990, nearly 65 per cent of the employed population residing in the Barcelona metropolitan area worked and lived in the same municipality, whereas this rate had fallen to below 48 per cent by 2006, thus indicating a drop in municipal self-containment of almost 20 percentage points in just over 15 years.[7]

The increase in the number and length of daily journeys has led to a reduction in journeys on foot as a proportion of mobility as a whole: in 1990, 26.9 per cent of people in the Barcelona metropolitan area walked or cycled to work, but the proportion had fallen to 18.4 per cent by 2006. Conversely, there was a notable absolute and relative increase in the number of journeys in motorized vehicles, which put tremendous pressure on the land-transport infrastructure used by collective transport and private vehicles. It should also be remembered that, in much of Catalonia, deficiencies in the collective-transport network, together with the proliferation of low-density residential and activity areas with no connection to pre-existing urban centres, make it very difficult for public transport to cater to these mobility requirements. Hence, the use of private vehicles for work (and other) travel increased substantially in the Barcelona metropolitan area between 1990 and 2006: it accounted for 43.6 per cent of work travel in 1990 and 52.7 per cent in 2006. Paradoxically, the Barcelona metropolitan area has the best public transport service in Catalonia. The consequences of functional specialization are therefore considerable: many towns and neighbourhoods are deprived of activity for many hours a day and many days a week, and the increase in mobility involves very high social costs in terms of energy use, pollution, accidents, public health and longer working days. Furthermore, these social costs are not distributed equally among citizens, but are borne to a greater extent by those with lower incomes, women, young people and the elderly.

Finally, the urbanization process provides a third major challenge: social segregation. Not surprisingly, functional specialization has been accompanied by growing social specialization. In a real-estate market characterized by an overwhelming predominance of ownership, where the price of a new home increased by more than 300 per cent between 1996 and 2007, and where social-housing policies have traditionally been weak or ineffective, very large segments of the population have experienced considerable difficulty gaining access to housing (Donat, 2010). This difficulty has several effects: a higher nest-leaving age, increased indebtedness of families and an increased risk of segregation of social groups in urban areas.

As known, the ability of each household to choose its place of residence is a function of its level of income, in such a way that different social groups tend to become separated in space based on their ability to bid in the real-estate market. So the most affluent sectors, which are freer to choose where to live, tend to do so among their peers, in municipalities with a high level of services and no urban-

---

7 According to data from the Survey on Habits and Living Conditions of the Population: see Nel·lo (2010) and Oliver-Frauca (2010). The same source was used for the data on mobility mentioned in the following paragraph. Again, the effects of economic crisis over these trends are still uncertain. It is possible, however, that they may entail a reduction of inter-municipal commuting.

planning deficiencies. Conversely, those with less purchasing power tend to live in neighbourhoods where prices are relatively lower (Carme Trilla, 2002). A high proportion of this second group are people who have immigrated to Catalonia in the last 15 years. Thus, urban areas run the risk of becoming divided into socially very uniform neighbourhoods, with the added twist that the enlargement of the metropolitan area now makes this mechanism occur not only between neighbourhoods in the same city, but between entire municipalities in the metropolitan area. This leads to the paradox that many of the municipalities with the greatest social demands also tend to be those with a weaker economic and tax base for catering to these demands. The effects of segregation therefore have a direct effect on the ability to provide the population with public services and a quality urban environment, while encouraging separate reproduction of social groups (particularly through the school system). Urban segregation thus increases the risk that spatial factors will become an additional barrier to equal opportunities among citizens.

Urban and Regional Policies

According to this diagnosis, only the main aspects of which are discussed here, Catalonia is a region with considerable potential due to its position, diversity, urban structure and organizing capacity. However, it also faces major challenges associated with the dynamics of urban sprawl, functional specialization and social segregation. If these challenges were to persist over time, the city and the region would face the risk of becoming environmentally unsustainable, functionally inefficient and lacking in social solidarity. The present circumstances of social and economic crisis make even more poignant these risks.

Meeting these challenges required a deep-seated rethinking of the regional management principles and instruments that have been in use in Catalonia since the return to democracy. A number of important innovations have taken place in this area in recent years, including the approval of the long-awaited Metropolitan Territorial Plan in April 2010. Therefore, although the current situation has its positive and negative sides, it seems clear that the Barcelona metropolitan area might be in a better position today than it was a decade ago in terms of management tools and urban policies. Let's take a closer look at the areas of housing, urban renewal, public transport, transportation infrastructure, the environment, spatial planning and administrative organization.[8]

Housing Starting in 2004, urban-planning legislation established a general system of compulsory quotas for social housing. Consequently, the owners of each urban-planning sector must now earmark a percentage of the total residential space for this type of housing. This percentage ranges from 20 per cent to 30 per cent, depending on the municipality's size and administrative level. As a result

---

8　For an assessment of these policies, see Nel·lo (2012a).

of these percentages, the social-housing units built in each sector may, in some cases, account for nearly half of the total, given that the average size of social-housing units is considerably smaller than free-market housing units. The goal of this measure is to mitigate the difficulty of gaining access to housing caused by the boom in the real-estate cycle (1996-2007) and the credit restrictions imposed in recent years. Social housing must be distributed as uniformly as possible throughout the municipality. However, the start of the economic crisis in 2008, closely linked in Spain to the collapse of the real-estate market, led to a drastic reduction in the number of new housing units built. Therefore, the total number of social-housing units being built is still very low. Although housing prices have fallen considerably, current credit restrictions make it impossible for many families to obtain a mortgage. Thus, access to housing in the Barcelona metropolitan area continues to be a major problem for a large proportion of the population.[9]

Urban renewal As explained above, the development of the real-estate market has led to an increased risk of urban segregation of social groups and the concentration in certain neighbourhoods of people with the greatest social needs. In order to tackle these risks, the Catalan government has developed an ambitious, innovative programme: the Act for Urban Neighbourhoods and Areas Requiring Special Attention (Llei de barris), a tool inspired by the European Union's URBAN programmes. In the first seven years since the act was passed, comprehensive renewal action has been undertaken in 141 neighbourhoods throughout Catalonia with a total population of more than one million people and involving a total committed investment of €1.33 billion to be paid in almost equal parts by the regional and municipal governments. Overall, it is the most ambitious single urban renewal project ever undertaken in Catalonia and has become a key part of the urban policies in the Barcelona metropolitan area (Nel·lo, 2011b). However, the implementation of the Law was suspended by the Catalan administration in 2011 allegedly due to lack of funding due to the economic crisis.

Public transport in the Barcelona metropolitan area is managed by the Metropolitan Transport Authority (ATM), a consortium made up of the regional government, Barcelona city council, metropolitan institutions and representatives of other municipal authorities in the metropolitan area with public-transport services. Set up in 1995, the ATM is responsible for financial management of the public-transport system, regulating fares, scheduling infrastructure investment and dealing with the public and private companies that operate transport services. In 2010, a total of 922 million journeys were made within the area of the ATM

---

9 Evictions of families unable to keep paying the mortgage or the rent are the most visible and dramatic face of present housing market conditions. In 2012 there were in Catalonia 6,960 judicial evictions due to mortgage defaults – 38,976 for Spain as a whole, according to data from the Colegio de Registradores de España (2013).

system at a total operating cost of €1.2 billion, of which €499 million came from fares. The rest was subsidized by public administrations. One of the most notable achievements of the ATM has been the implementation of the integrated fare system throughout the public-transport operators in the Barcelona metropolitan area, which has considerably increased system intermodality and efficiency.

Transportation infrastructure connecting the Barcelona metropolitan region has been considerably improved in recent years. Nevertheless, there is considerable debate regarding the deficiencies of this infrastructure and the responsibility of the Spanish government, which is administratively responsible for most of it, for failing to adequately meet the needs and expectations of the city and the region. Many of the motorways that provide access to the city of Barcelona, such as the ones from the South along the coast, from the interior along the Ebro River valley, and from the French border, are still exclusively toll roads, because the Spanish government has not provided sufficient funding to complete the high-capacity toll-free network in the region. A high-speed rail link has been in place between Barcelona and Madrid since 2008 and is very successful in terms of the number of passengers. However, the link to the French border is not completely finished yet, which means that there are difficulties transporting goods from the Port of Barcelona to France on a standard-gauge track. Furthermore, no adequate response has been given to the long-expressed demand of the communities on the Spanish Mediterranean coast for a high-performance rail corridor that runs along the Mediterranean coast. With the new terminal added to Barcelona Airport in 2009, along with other improvements still in progress, it handled more than 31 million passengers in 2011 and now has the capacity to handle a total of 55 million. Finally, the Port of Barcelona, one of the leading ports on the Mediterranean, handles 41 million tonnes of cargo and 3.4 million passengers a year, and was recently expanded by diverting the course of the Llobregat River to increase its operating capacity.

The environment and landscape In the Barcelona metropolitan area, responsibility for the environment is distributed between metropolitan institutions and the regional government. Therefore, the water cycle and waste management in the 30 municipalities in the system's central area are managed by the Barcelona Metropolitan Area. In the rest of the metropolitan area, however, the regional government is directly responsible for regulating and managing these services through the Catalan Water Agency and the Catalan Waste Management Agency. Major steps have been taken in recent years to protect undeveloped land, including the Coastal System Master Plan (approved in 2005 with the aim of stopping the urbanization process along the coast) and the classification of two-thirds of the entire metropolitan area as land under special protection or farmland through the regional planning discussed below. Furthermore, following the lead of the European Landscape Convention sponsored by the Council of Europe, approval in 2005 of the Landscape Protection, Management and Planning Act has generated policies for assessment, protection and management of the landscape in the metropolitan area.

Metropolitan planning   One of the demands of the social and economic agents of Barcelona that had gone unanswered since the mid-20th century is the need to equip the Barcelona metropolitan area with joint regional planning tools. This demand became even more intense when increasing spatial integration made the inefficiency of planning powers among a large number of municipalities more evident. However, in the second half of the 20th century, progress in this field was limited to the approval of the General Metropolitan Plan of 1976, which covered only the 27 municipalities in the centre part of the metropolitan area. Therefore, the approval of the Metropolitan Territorial Plan in 2010 should be considered a very relevant step. The plan covers almost the entire functional metropolitan area (3230 km² and 164 municipalities) and proposes structuring the area as an integrated, multinodal urban entity, thereby taking advantage of metropolitanization and addressing the negative aspects of the urbanization process discussed above. With this goal in mind, the plan establishes standards, guidelines and recommendations in three thematic fields: open spaces, where it provides protection for almost two-thirds of the metropolitan region with the aim of establishing an interconnected system of undeveloped land; settlements, where it establishes guidelines for municipal planning in order to prevent urban sprawl and encourage a multi-centre urban network; and infrastructure, for which it establishes a system aimed at increasing network connectivity and branching, and moving gradually towards collective transport.[10]

Administrative organization   Finally, significant progress has also been made in recent years in terms of improving governance of the Barcelona metropolitan system. As mentioned, this is characterized by considerable administrative fragmentation, which was further exacerbated by the fact that the Barcelona Metropolitan Corporation, the government body created in 1974 with the aim of coordinating urban-planning management and other services in the 27 municipalities in the central part of the metropolitan area, was eliminated in 1987. The lack of integrated management bodies had to be partly filled with lighter, more flexible instruments, such as voluntary associations of municipalities and the drafting of a Metropolitan Strategic Plan. Several different versions of this plan have appeared since the early 1990s and it has helped provide a joint project for the institutions and social agents of the city of Barcelona and its immediate surroundings. In July 2010, the Catalan Parliament passed an act to re-establish the Barcelona Metropolitan Area, a local government body for the centre part of the metropolitan area covering 34 municipalities. It is responsible for urban planning, the water cycle, waste management, transport, economic promotion and other areas. However, attempts to create an administrative body for the functional

---

10   For a discussion on the contents and implications of Barcelona 2010 Metropolitan Plan see Esteban (2012), Acierno and Mazza (2011) and Nel·lo (2011c).

metropolitan area (i.e. for an area similar to the 164 municipalities in the Barcelona Metropolitan Territorial Plan) are not likely to produce results in the short term.

Summing Up

We have seen how in the last half century urban transformation in Metropolitan Barcelona has been one of the driving forces of change in Catalonia and Spain, in social, economic and environmental terms. In order to take the opportunities and face the challenges arising from this process, new forms of social and administrative organization were required. When democracy was reinstated in Spain, in the second half of the 1970s, an important number of initiatives were undertaken in this field, so much so that Barcelona became internationally known as an example of successful urban policies. However, after the 1992 Olympic Games the limitations of these policies started to evidenciate. In part these were the result of the metropolitanization process: the city had become a large metropolitan region whose problems could not be tackled efficiently by the single efforts of local administrations. New tools, provisions and resources were required in order to operate at the metropolitan scale. As shown, in the last decade some of these policies were put in place: the Neighbourhoods Act (2004), the Landscape Act (2005), the new provisions for Social Housing (2004 and 2007), the Barcelona Metropolitan Plan (2010), the new Metropolitan Government (2010), among others. However, the new situation created by the economic crisis and the policies that came with it make uncertain the future of these provisions.

References

Acierno, A. and Mazza, A (2011). *Governare la metropoli. Il Piano Territoriale Metropolitano di Barcellona*. Napoli: Edizione Scientifiche Italiane, Collana Quaderni di Tria, 3.

Borja, J. (2009). *Luces y sombras del urbanismo en Barcelona*. Barcelona: Universitat Oberta de Cataluña.

Burns, M. (2008). *The (re)positioning of the Spanish metropolitan system within the European urban system (1986-2006)*. Barcelona: Universitat Politècnica de Catalunya.

Cabré, A. (1999). *El sistema català de reproducció*. Barcelona: Proa.

Camagni, R., Gibelli, M. And Rigamonti, P. (2002). *I costi collettivi della città dispersa*. Florence: Alinea.

Capel, H. (2005). *El modelo Barcelona: un análisis crítico*, Barcelona, Ediciones del Serbal.

Colegio de Registradores de España (2013). [Online]. Available at http://www.registradores.org/colegio_registradores.jsp [accessed: 2013].

Donat, C. (2010). L'habitatge a la regió metropolitana de Barcelona, 1995-2006. *Papers. Regió Metropolitana de Barcelona*, 51, 44-60.

Esteban, J. (2012). El Pla Territorial Metropolità de Barcelona en el planejament territorial de Cataluna. *Papers. Regió Metropolitana de Barcelona*, 55, 14-18.

Ferrer, A. (2005). El urbanismo municipal en España. *Papers. Regió metropolitana de Barcelona*, 43.

Ferrer, A. and Sabaté. J. (1999). L'urbanisme municipal a Catalunya. *Papers. Regió metropolitana de Barcelona*, 32.

Font, A. (2007). Región urbana de Barcelona. De la ciudad compacta a los territorios metropolitanos. In F. Indovina (Ed), *La ciudad de baja densidad. Lógicas, gestión y contención*. Barcelona: Diputación de Barcelona.

Font, A. and Carreras, J. (2005). *Transformacions urbanitzadores. Àrea metropolitana i regió urbana de Barcelona*. Barcelona: Àrea Metropolitana de Barcelona.

Garcia Espuche, A (1998). *Un siglo decisivo. Barcelona y Cataluña 1550-1640*. Madrid: Alianza Editorial.

IDESCAT – National Statistics Institute of Catalonia (2011). *National and Municipal Censuses*. [Online]. Available at: http://www.idescat.cat/en/ [accessed: 2012].

Indovina, F. (1999). *Barcellona. Un nuovo ordine territoriale*. Milano: Franco Angeli.

Indovina, F. (2009). *Dalla città diffusa all'arcipelago metropolitano*. Milano: Franco Angeli.

López, J. (2003). La mobilitat de les persones a la regió metropolitana de Barcelona. *Papers. Regió Metropolitana de Barcelona*, 38, 11-27.

Marshall, T. (2004). *Transforming Barcelona*. London-New York: Routledge.

Muñiz, I., Calatayud, D. and Garcia. M.A. (2007). *Sprawl*. Causas y consecuencias de la dispersión urbana. In F. Indovina (Ed.), *La ciudad de baja densidad. Lógicas, gestión y contención*. Barcelona: Diputación de Barcelona.

Muñoz, F. (2007). La producción residencial de baja densidad en la provincia de Barcelona. In F. Indovina (Ed.), *La ciudad de baja densidad. Lógicas, gestión y contención*. Barcelona: Diputación de Barcelona.

Muñoz, F. (2011). De la urbanització dispersa a la ciutat de baixa densitat: un repte ignorat. In F. Muñoz (Ed.), *Estratègies vers la ciutat de baixa densitat: de la contenció a la gestió*. Barcelona: Diputació de Barcelona.

Nel·lo, O, López, J. and Piqué J.M. (2002). Las redes emergentes de articulación del territorio en la región metropolitana de Barcelona. In J. Subirats (Ed.), *Redes, territorios y gobierno*. Barcelona: Diputació de Barcelona.

Nel·lo, O. (1999). *Vint anys d'ajuntaments democràtics (1979-1999). Elements per a un balanç i per un debat de futur*. Barcelona: Federació de Municipis de Catalunya.

Nel·lo, O. (2001). *Ciutat de ciutats. Reflexions sobre el procés d'urbanització a Catalunya*. Barcelona: Empuries.

Nel·lo, O. (2002). Las áreas metropolitanas. In J. Gómez Mendoza and A.G. Olcina, *Geografía de España*. Barcelona: Ariel.

Nel·lo, O. (2004). ¿Cambio de siglo, cambio de ciclo? Las grandes ciudades españolas en el umbral del siglo XXI. *Ciudad y territorio. Estudios territoriales*, XXXVI (141-142), 523-542.

Nel·lo, O. (2005). La Nuova Politica Territoriale della Catalogna. *Archivio di Studi Urbani e Regionali*, 83, 39-70.

Nel·lo, O. (2007a). La nueva política territorial de Cataluña (2003-2006). In J. Romero and J. Farinós (Eds), *Territorialidad y buen gobierno para el desarrollo sostenible. Nuevos principios y nuevas políticas en el espacio europeo*. Valencia: Universitat de València.

Nel·lo, O. (2007b). La tercera fase de metropolitanización en España. In O. Rullán (Ed.), *Los procesos urbanos postfordistas*. Mallorca: Asociación de Geógrafos Españoles.

Nel·lo, O. (2010). Les dinàmiques territorials a la regió metropolitana de Barcelona (1986-2006): Hipòtesis interpretatives. *Papers. Regió Metropolitana de Barcelona*, 52, 16-27.

Nel·lo, O. (2011a). La ordenación de las dinámicas metropolitanas. El Plan Territorial Metropolitano de Barcelona. *Scripta Nova. Revista electrónica de Geografía y Ciencias Sociales*, XV(362).

Nel·lo, O. (2011b). The Five Challenges of Urban Rehabilitation. The Catalan Experience. *Urban Research and Practice*, 4(3), 308-325.

Nel·lo, O. (2012a). *Ordenar el territorio. La experiencia de Barcelona y Cataluña*. Valencia: Tirant lo Blanch.

Nel·lo, O. (2012b). La política territorial a Catalunya. Reptes, principis i instruments. In M. Castaner (Ed), *El planejament territorial a Catalunya a inicis del segle XXI*. Barcelona: Societat Catalana d'Ordenació del Territori.

Oliver-Frauca, L. (2010). La mobilitat i el transport. *Papers. Regió Metropolitana de Barcelona*, 51, 62-84.

Prieto, F., Campillo M. and Díaz, J.M. (2011). Tendencias recientes de evolución del territorio en España (1987-2005). *Ciudad y Territorio. Estudios territoriales*, XLIII(168), 261-278.

Rueda, S. (2002). Els costos ambientals dels models urbans dispersos. *Papers. Regió Metropolitana de Barcelona*, 36, 73-104.

Sarasa, S. (2013). L'impacte social de la crisi a l'Àrea Metropolitana de Barcelona i a Catalunya. *Papers. Regió Metropolitana de Barcelona*, 56, 10-87.

Serra, J. (2002). "Grandes aglomeraciones metropolitanas europeas", en *Papers. Regió Metropolitana de Barcelona*, 37, 7-16.

Smith, L. (2010). *The New North. The World in 2050*. London: Profile Books.

Trilla, C. (2002). *Preu de l'habitatge i segregació social de l'espai a l'àmbit metropolità de Barcelona*. Barcelona: Ajuntament de Barcelona.

Trullen, J. (2011). La metròpoli de Barcelona: economia. *Papers. Regió Metropolitana de Barcelona*, 54, 38-51.

Van den Berg, L. (1987). *Urban Systems in a Dynamic Society*. Gower: Aldershot.

Vila, P. (1937). *La fesomia geogràfica de Catalunya*. Barcelona: Generalitat de Catalunya.

Vilar, P. (1964). *Catalunya dins l'Espanya moderna. Recerques sobre els fonaments econòmics de les estructures nacionals*. Barcelona: Edicions 62.

Chapter 5
Budapest

Barbara Kovacs

City Profile

Budapest, as the capital of Hungary, is the administrative, political, economic, scientific and cultural centre of the country. Budapest is the largest city in Hungary, and the eighth largest city of the European Union, with 1.7 million inhabitants (17 per cent of the country's population). It occupies 525 km². The City and its urban region extend to 2,538 km², including the capital and 81 other settlements with 2.4 million inhabitants (24 per cent of the country's population). The Central Hungary Region is one of the seven Hungarian regions, containing Budapest and Pest County; with an area of 6,919 km². Central Hungary is home to 2.9 million people (29 per cent of the country's population). The major highways, motorways, main transport and train lines enmesh the country originating in Budapest. The city lies at the intersection of three Pan-European transport corridors. Eight lines of the national railway lines are part of the Trans-European Rail Network, and the 30 TEN-T Priority Axes and Projects contains three projects which affect Hungary. Budapest straddles the banks of the River Danube, a main waterway of Europe (Pan European Corridor VII). Budapest's Liszt Ferenc International Airport is the 48th largest airport in Europe with three terminals having served 8.2 million passengers in 2010.

Demographic and Social Features

Despite the Central Hungarian Region being the most populated area of the country, it has limited competences, the CHR is still just a statistic region. The population of the region is slowly increasing mostly as a consequence of internal migration. The fall in population during the 1980s was due to natural attrition outnumbering migration gains. Between the 1990s and the early 2000s, the suburbanization process shifted 15 per cent of the city's population to the agglomeration area. According to this tendency, experienced from the beginning of the decade, the decline of the population had slowed down, then after three decades – from 2007 – the population of Budapest it slowly increased. It is caused on one hand by the natural reduction running better, on the other hand, by the balance of the migration turning into positive, then into increasing level. In early 2011, the population of the Capital city was 323,000 people, or by nearly 16 per cent less than in 1980.

In the 1990s, the balance of migration was negative. In migration from Budapest to the outskirts of the city, Pest County, was the most affected; in 2009 more than 22,000 permanent citizens chose to move to the suburbs around Budapest. The population balance ensued from the international migration compensated, and from 2005 exceeded, the inland migration losses of Budapest – mainly against its agglomeration. For the first time since the 1990s the balance of the national migration was also positive in 2007, 2008 and in 2009.

Employment and the Structure of Labour

Between 1990-1996, the number of economically active members of the population in the capital dropped. A part of this decrease is to be derived from the decrease in the number of the total population. On the other hand, some of the economically active inhabitants became unemployed, or left their jobs, increasing the number of dependants as passive unemployed. By the beginning of 1998, this trend had modified to some extent. In parallel with the stabilization of the economy, the number and ratio of active earners increased somewhat within the population of the Capital, while the number and ratio of dependants and inactive earners decreased. The number of employees increased for the first time in 1998 during the 1990s, then, showing a slight fluctuation, it remained steady. Between the periods of 1998-2010 the number of white collar workers was increasing all the time, so in those years when the number of the employed in overall decreased, it occurred because of the decrease in manual workers. Employment figures showed the sharpest decline in construction and in industry.

As for the employment structure, six sectors increased their share: trade, financial intermediation; real estate market-economic services, education, health care as well as other communal, personal services. The most substantial decrease in the relative weight of individual sectors took place in industry and in the construction industry. The number of employees has decreased or remained the same in most sectors in the city. Between the periods of 1993-2002 the number of registered unemployed decreased, then as opposed to previous trend, it started to increase in 2003. The increase temporarily stopped in 2005, but at the end of year 2008 it started again. The economic crisis in 2009 had also an impact on the labour market of the city, but it was not as deep as the decrease in other segments of the national economy. The employment rate is still significantly higher and the unemployment rate is lower than the national figure (49.2 per cent and 11.2 per cent respectively).

Economic Structure and City Management

In addition to being an administrative centre, Budapest is traditionally the economic and intellectual centre of Hungary. More than one-third of the country's GDP is generated in Budapest (37.7 per cent). This figure significantly exceeds that of County Pest (10.4 per cent), the next in weight and that of the third, County Győr-Moson-Sopron (5.0 per cent). The City excels in terms of the value of per capita GDP (HUF 5,910,000 in 2008), which exceeds the national average by about 122 per cent, and the EU-27 average by 36.4 per cent on purchasing power parity. Out of the top 20 companies considering net sales, 12 have their headquarters in Budapest with total sales of HUF 10,220,760 million that is 68.8 per cent of the net sales of the top twenty. Its economy focuses on services: 81.5 per cent of the gross value added generated in the territory of the capital comes from services (commerce, catering, transport, telecommunications, financial and business services, etc.).

The Municipality Structure

Based on the current regulations in effect, the organization of the local governmental functioning of the city of Budapest is based on a non-hierarchical, dual system which consists of the central Municipality of Budapest and the municipalities of the 23 districts. The tasks of the Municipality can be divided into two large groups: On the one hand it fulfils the tasks which involve the entire capital as a whole or exceed the limitations of the districts, on the other hand it fulfils special tasks related to the role which the city plays on a national level. Budapest is responsible for the determination of tasks related to urban development and urban management and urban rehabilitation as well as for the harmonization of the implementation of tasks related to the management of dwellings in the ownership of the Municipality.

The obligations fulfilled by Budapest related to the special role it plays on a national level include the maintenance of public transportation and the technology of traffic management, the determination of its touristic concept as well as providing for the protection of local built values declared to be of national heritage. The obligations of Budapest include the undertaking of such public utilities and services which it only provides should one district refrain to do so (such as providing secondary schooling, vocational training or student boarding).

The General Assembly of the Municipality of the City of Budapest is authorized to constitute decrees in terms of the tasks affecting the city. The decree of the General Assembly constituted within the framework of its tasks may authorize the districts to create decrees as well. The "dual level" of the constitution of decrees results in the obligation of the districts to correspond their constitution of decrees to the regulations of the Capital and not exceed its framework of jurisdiction meaning that the decree of the districts may not contradict that of Budapest. The interests of the Capital – as a single settlement is represented by the General Assembly of the Municipality of Budapest. However the representative bodies of the local districts must be involved in issues effecting structure of the districts. The General Assembly as the decision making body must be informed about the position of the districts.

The basic concept of the allocation of functions/task within the individual dual system of the Capital is that the Municipality of Budapest is responsible for tasks and competencies necessary for the operation of the city as a single unit while districts provide for the basic services required by the inhabitants. This results in the fact that the number of inhabitants in the majority of the districts coincides with that of the larger cities. At the same time some districts do not maintain institutions providing for secondary level educational services. Due to the specific features of the Capital the flow of tasks is not streamed in a one way direction and is not absolutely unconditional.

The agglomeration of the Capital has a specific significance which includes the settlements surrounding the Capital. Depending on the area which the services of public utilities affect (for instance transportation, waste management, environmental tasks) the number of settlements pertaining to the agglomeration may vary. Unfortunately the agglomeration of Budapest has no institutional form, meaning that it functions based on partnership rather than on decision making authoritative jurisdiction.

The local governments/Municipalities of the districts are obliged to provide for the operation of kindergartens, elementary schools and institutions in charge of basic social and healthcare services. The districts also fulfil tasks that are divided between the dual system of local governments, for instance they maintain public roads in their ownership within the framework of their functions. The local governments of the districts along with the Municipality of the city of Budapest assists national and ethnical minorities in exercising/vindicating their rights and provide for the conditions necessary for the operation of minority local governments. Legislative proposals and proposals aiming modifications or the execution of regulations are mostly submitted to the Parliament by the Government even in cases where local governments are affected.

The Government as indicated in the Constitution is obliged to control the legitimacy of jurisdiction of the operation of local governments. The government carries out this duty through its territorial administrative bodies. The territorial administrative bodies fulfilling controlling tasks are not superior to the local governments and are not empowered to limit the practice of jurisdiction of the local governments or to alter or override their decisions. What may only be inspected by the above bodies is whether the operation, the system of organisation and the process of decision making (decrees and resolutions) are lawful from part of the local governments.

Developments and Policy Changes since Early 1990s

Political changes at the end of the previous century have had a major impact on the country and the social, economic life of Budapest as well. Hungary has switched to market economy. Meanwhile, some changes have taken place there in the process of urbanization, which called for redefinition of city markets. Changing structure of space and higher level individual services were the key features that have gained strength. At the same time urban society had gone through some changes as well, it has become more individual-oriented and internationally open. New features and values of city life have appeared, for example, quality of life, liveability, competitiveness, sustainability. It has had to face a new type of competition appearing on the internal market as well as the international market which urges a repositioning of Budapest.

At the end of the 20th century and at the beginning of the 21st century deindustrialization, the appearance of new transportation methods, new technical achievements, the evolution of the information society and the emergence of the IT sector had taken place and economic and social changes had created different demands. The city became the centre of leisure activity, recreation, culture, innovation, research-development and education as well. Because of the diversity of users and functions, the city has to comply with different market demands and therefore develop different attributes. Such market segments are: tourism, the innovation/research and development/education trio, housing, development of human and material infrastructure. This adaptation to new urban land use and new circumstances is still in process.

Changes in Economic Structure and Growth

The economic recession that has started in 2008 has had a serious effect on the capital within Hungary. The overall economic performance of Budapest in 2009 declined in most sectors, but to a lesser extent than at the national level. The economic performance of Budapest in 2010 was effected by opposite trends: the output of the industrial organizations increased less than the national level, the output of the construction industry and the number of homes built decreased even more than the national level.

Business Dynamism   In the years following changes in the political system (in 1989), the expansion in service capacities in the capital could partially offset some of the consequences of the economic recession, primarily the major decline in industrial output. The proliferation of enterprises, which took off at the end of the 1980s and accelerated during the 1990s, was most intense in Budapest. At the end of 2010 the number of registered companies in the capital was the 23 per cent of all enterprises in the country. Among the limited companies which represent the biggest share within enterprises, 41 per cent are registered in Budapest, among individual enterprises this figure is 13.9 per cent. Budapest plays an outstanding role as nearly 61 per cent of all businesses with foreign capital in the country and 51.9 per cent of equity capital is anchored within Budapest.

Investment Activities   In 1998, at its highest peak, the volume of investments in the capital was almost 50 per cent higher than in 1991. Up to the end of the 1990s such volume was largely in line with the nationwide trend. Since 1999 the investment volume of Budapest had greatly fluctuated, taking a different path from the national investment trends. While until 2006 the national data on a comparable base had shown an increase every year; in 1999, 2001 and in 2003 the volume of investments in Budapest had decreased, it has increased by more than the national figure in 2000, and less than that in 2002, 2004 and 2005. In 2010 according to preliminary data, the Budapest-based companies have spent 12 per cent less in current prices than in the previous year. Investments in Budapest made up nearly 41 per cent of the total investment expenditures of the country. In the capital the investment was HUF 723,000 per capita which is 2.4 times more than the national level.

Industry   The capital had formerly been the industrial centre of the country, but in the 1990s, production dropped by a higher rate than the national average. The direct cause of this was the great number of industrial units with excessive capacities in Budapest, mainly in machinery and light industry, developed primarily to satisfy the demands of COMECON markets. Following the collapse of these markets, the above industries went bankrupt and many companies were liquidated. In the second half of the 1990s, the relative buoyancy of industry in the capital can be attributed to the dynamic growth of production in three industrial sectors: machinery, the food industry and electricity generation. After the recession of 2008-2009, the output of the industries operating in Budapest rose in parallel with the national growth.

After a sharp decline in 1995-1997, production by construction companies with their headquarters in the capital rose during 1998. The new trend of expansion was due to the increase of investment projects – new constructions, expansions and renovations. In 2001, the volume of production in the construction industry continued to grow, but at a faster rate than a year before. Overall, in 2002-2003 and 2005-2006, there was a slight expansion in the volume of construction-installation works; but caused by the crisis, in 2009-2010 there was an unfavourable tendency that the total value of contracts of the companies was lower at the end of 2010 than in the previous year.

Tourism   Budapest is one of the most attractive destinations in Hungary for tourists; more than 29.9 per cent of all overnight stays and 52 per cent of all overnight stays by tourists are spent here. 31 per cent of the total hotel accommodation of the country is provided in Budapest. The number of guests and also the number of guest nights was higher in 2010 compared to the previous year. The increase in the number of foreign visitors was significantly higher than the increase in the number of domestic guests.

Commerce   The relative density of the network of retail outlets is linked partly to the role of the capital in tourism. In 2009, 19.9 per cent of all retail outlets and 16.7 per cent of catering establishments within Hungary operated within the administrative city boundaries of Budapest. This network, comprising of approximately 41,000 outlets provides services to the population as well as foreign and Hungarian tourists and partly meets the demand created by neighbouring settlements.

Banking Bank consolidation, which began in the first half of the 1990s is now complete and financial sector activities generate average profits. As a result of privatization, fresh capital, international experience and a new mentality have been introduced to the banking system. Financial institutions began to compete with one another, active market approaches have become characteristic and the modernisation of banking operations has also been achieved. All financial institutions in the country, except for savings co-operatives, some insurance companies and other minor institutions, have their seats in the capital. According to the 2008 figures, 254 foreign companies were performing financial services in Budapest, representing 81 per cent of the total such companies in Hungary. Regarding ownership structures, among companies providing financial services in Budapest, 66 per cent were solely in foreign hands, 23 per cent is in foreign majority and 11 per cent was majority owned by locals (data from 2007).

Urban and Regional Vision, Strategy Development and Implementation

In the past few decades Budapest has shown spectacular growth in certain sectoral areas such as Educational-Research and Development and Information Technologies. However in terms of the city as a whole or its everyday operation Budapest failed to develop as much as it could have been expected based on the facilities and the opportunities given. Only very little of the comprehensive objectives defined in the documentations of urban development had been realized. The reason for the this partial failure is that urban development had been inferior to economic development, which forced the objectives of urban development in a minor, secondary position where the framework of the strategy set urban development objectives behind economic progress. This did not make long term planning possible. A further reason for the lack of progress in terms of urban development is that the leadership of the Municipality must primarily concentrate to Urban Management instead of development and handle the anomalies of the inefficient practices of management which had been conducted in the past decades. In addition to the above, due to the strategy of placing urban development into a secondary position, such changes have occurred that altered the use and the structure of the city. Budapest did not realize the effect of these changes in time and failed to react appropriately to the different ongoing processes such as the phenomenon of suburbanization.

Reason 1: Upside down connection between urban and economical development As mentioned above, in the past few decades urban and economic development had been decoupled and the emphasis had been placed on the sectorial approach despite the comprehensive objectives defined in the approved documentations of urban development issued in the year 2002 and 2008. The economist politicians granted tax exemptions and territories to the sectors driving the economy as to encourage economic development. The politicians forming the leadership of the Municipality had been seeking for methods to increase the financial sources provided by the state strained by debt and deficit as well as from the European Union raising special conditions. The leadership also tried to find the way to attract large companies regardless of their profile into the city to generate local business tax, jobs and incremental investments. Based on this concept economic development is considered to be an investment which offers increasing income, economic growth and jobs while urban development is considered to be an expense which "doesn't yield" but yet requires financial investment. Up until now urban development consisted of two elements: projects of necessity and projects of spectacle. According to the above concept urban development is interpreted as the background sector of economic development therefore it has been forced to fulfil a secondary role inferior to economic development. The political sector draws up schemes thinking in 4-year term cycles and the current local economy has a very narrow set of assets therefore it is difficult to make long term coherent plans.

Reason 2: Re-action policy instead of pro-action The city expected the solution of the problem deriving from the lack of financial resources from external sources – mainly the European Union and state provided subventions. The planning of urban development was not intended to supply investors with investment opportunities and the economic model for the implementation of the developments had not been at its disposal. Economic planning which would have determined the conditions for development was also lacking. This had only allowed for a less coherent and wasted development of the city, where progress may only be visualized on the level of a few projects in comparison to the comprehensive objectives included in urban development documentations (see: Metro Number 4, The Heart of Budapest, City quarter of the Millenar, the Central Sewage Cleaning system of Csepel, Bridge reconstructions, etc.).

Reason 3: City management instead of development – current problems The tasks related to urban management may be divided into two main areas: to the area of public utilities and non-transportation related public services and to the area of individual and public transportation services. The management of corporations providing public utilities within the ownership of the Municipality had been conducted without drawing up a comprehensive, strategy based conscious scheme in terms of the proprietary and contractor role for Budapest in the past 20 years. Therefore the operation and the financing of urban management and public utility services had not been transparent and appropriately harmonized. Therefore the Municipality established the Transportation Centre Corporation of Budapest (BKK) for the management of tasks related to individual and public transportation as well as the Centre of Urban Management for Budapest (BVK) for carrying out tasks related to other non-transportation public utility and other non-public services in the autumn of 2010.

Reason 4: City management and development strategies are not resilient enough for change The delayed realization of the changes which occurred in terms of territorial use and the urban structure and the reactions following the above phenomenon required extra financial resources. Such phenomenon is the abandonment of the city and the outflow to suburban areas, the deterioration of dwelling areas in downtown Budapest and increasing segregation. The flow of the wealthier population to suburbia and to the agglomeration had changed the composition of urban and other living estates. In the case of some of the districts – the process of segregation dramatically increased at the beginning of the 1990s. At the same time, the inhabitants of the suburban areas still continue to commute to work in the city. They generally settle around the outskirts of the city near large shopping centres which influence the surrounding conjunction conditions and the circumstances of individual transportation.

Implemented Projects

The extension of Metro Number 3 at the beginning of the 1990s (an extension turned out to be shorter than originally intended) increased the value of the areas along Váci Street and so the city began to expand along the main road towards the North. This resulted in the relocation of commercial and service providing businesses and banks to the above area which had originally been considered to be suburban, turning it into a business boulevard. At this time new commercial complexities and shopping centres emerged such as the Duna Plaza along Váci Street which was the first one in line. In the past 15 years, 28 large (between 30-100,000 square metres) shopping centres have been built in Budapest. The West End City Centre Commercial and Business node established at the Western Railway Station consists of the Shopping Centre and surrounding transportation junction point which includes buses, trains and metro services. This is the first model of intermodal urban centres. The fever of plaza construction began to halt at the beginning of the 2000s however, its negative effect on small retail commerce had already become apparent – the turnover of downtown businesses dramatically decreased forcing numerous units to close.

The profile of the businesses along the ring roads has narrowed and many shopping units are vacant. One of the most significant objectives in terms of the renewal of public premises is to provide favourable conditions for the revival of small retail commerce: this is supported by the extension of the construction of the promenade networks, the Heart of Budapest programme currently implemented as well as the surface road-works and area management connected to the construction of Metro 4. The Municipality has created a separate subvention system for the reconstruction of valuable dwellings, meaning that more and more dwellings in private ownership, or which once had been in the ownership of the Municipality, are being renovated from year to year. As industrial production had been withdrawn from Budapest in the 1990s, it left behind tremendous areas of brownfield sites raising increasing demand for their development by the beginning of the 2000s. The two radically differing solutions for utilizing central brownfield areas were introduced by the MOM Park in 2001 and the Millenar Park in 2002.

The MOM Park which had been constructed on the site of the Hungarian Optical Works had primarily been established on a business basis. The Park includes living estates, and office construction and a shopping centre to satisfy local demand. The Millenar Park located in the centre of Buda focuses on the satisfaction of community demand and on the preservation of industrial values. A cultural and entertainment centre, a modern square for exhibitions and a park of high quality had been built by the re-utilization of the buildings once belonging to the Ganz Electronic Works.

The revitalization of the Gas Factory of Old Buda has emerged from external brownfield sites where the largest information technology centre in the country has been established within the past 10 years. This is where the dynamically developing Hungarian and Foreign Companies had located their headquarters, which are in close cooperation with a private university (Aquincum Technological Institute, ATI). At the turn of the millennium, a similar science park was formed at Lágymányos which consisted of a technology and informatics campus as well as one of the natural sciences: University Eötvös Loránd and the Technological University of Budapest. The huge Info Park which hosts the centre of large communication companies had been built in the neighbourhood and this is where the European Institution of Innovation and Technologies has been operating since 2008.

The Urban Centre of the Millennium had also been constructed on the site of the railway station of Ferencváros within the past 10 years where in addition to the offices and housing estates the greatest cultural centre of the country had been constructed. These are the National Theatre and the Palace of Arts. Another important task, which had emerged in the second half of the 20th century, in addition to the development of function-changing areas, is the rehabilitation of deteriorating historical urban sites. A determining factor throughout the above process apart from the aspect of urban management and finance is to fulfil social expectations. The density and poverty of the Roma population is greater within the external Southern ring of the city centre and therefore the rate of crime is also higher here.

The rehabilitation of the internal parts of District IX beginning from the middle of the 1990s had been very successful however this process halted by the middle of the 2000s. Great changes have been taking place in District VIII through the demolition of old buildings and the construction of new subdivided housing estates and educational institutions. In addition to the renovation of historical sites, the renovation of housing estates of panel buildings reaching the end of their useful life had also become absolutely necessary. The renewal of these estates is being achieved using significant amounts of EU and state funds along with resources provided by local governments within the framework of a national program. The most important task of urban management is to continue the programmes of the past 20 years and to make them more effective which serves the purpose of relieving strain on the historical city centre whilte creating true urban sub-centres in the temporary zones and establishing intermodal centres in the external zones.

Part of the development schemes concentrate on areas around railway stations. The area of the railway station of Kelenföld serves as the western gate of the city and will become the largest intermodal node of the nation by the year 2014 with the construction of Metro line Number 4. This will generate significant estate investment in the area. The Western Railway station wedged into the city centre separates the two historical districts of the city, District VI and XIII. The demolition of the railways and plants no longer in use will clear tremendous areas and will make the integral connection of the two areas possible, in harmony with the planned urban rehabilitation of District VI.

The largest railway station within external Ferencváros along with the surrounding industrial sites together with Western Csepel form the greatest potential area of development for Budapest. The value of the area is increased by the fact that the southern gate or exit of the city has good connections with the international airport of Liszt Ferenc and to the logistical centres being formed there. An alternative breakout point besides brownfield investment are the territories along the bank of the Danube River. New, first class category dwelling areas (housing parks) are being constructed (Marina Park) in the neighbourhood of the Office Building Quarter of Váci Street along the Danube Bank at Újpest. Several investors such as (Duna Passage – Foster and Partners, Duna City – Erick von Egeraat) are planning the establishment of housing quarters and business commercial centres in the coming 5-15 years in the South at the bay connecting to the campus of Lágymányos and along the Danube branch of Soroksár as an extension of the Millennium City Centre. Northern Csepel may become the major intermodal node of the city and the Danube. This is where the international port (harbour) can be found: which is the centre of the Danube passenger and cargo transportation still to be developed; this is where the most extensive public park of Budapest will be built, and may become the central zone of the Olympic Games to be organized in Budapest at a possible future date.

The objective regarding the middle downtown section is the improvement of the connection between the city and the Danube and the relieving of the docks. Since the transition of 1989, two new bridges have been constructed (Bridge Rákóczi located between the Millennium City Centre and the University Quarter in the South and Bridge Megyeri in the North as part of M0 Highway). At the same time two bridges have been reconstructed (Bridge Margaret and Bridge Liberty) while Street Andrássy (the boulevard of Pest) and the great Ring Road have been renewed and the Hungária Ring Road has been completed.

The beltway M0 bypassing the city has also been constructed, however the motorway sections and roads leading into the city (especially the motorway coming from the Airport into the city) and their urban surroundings are still unarranged. Metro Number 4, the project consuming nearly all the financial resources of Budapest allocated for development and enjoying state aid as well is still in process, but it is obvious that this investment affects the further development of the urban sub-centres along the line. Of the infrastructural developments, the improvements in the sewage system and the opening of the waste disposal site at Pusztazámor are especially significant.

State of the City

The Role of Budapest in European and National Context

The conventional north-south, east-west division of Europe is changing. The Eastern European, Balkan and White Russian markets are open to the West. The role of Hungary has changed within the Union by responding to the needs of Adria, Balkan, and the territories of the Black Sea, and with transferring the needs of the western parts of Europe to the east.

To increase the market, the main task is to develop sub-centres of the city and to make Budapest a distribution and transfer centre with interrelationships based on human resources, transnational networks, and coordination between institutions. This transfer role of Budapest means managing information flow between cities, sharing knowledge, cultural relations and education-innovation developments.

Main Question of Urban Development – Funds and Proactive Policy

We need to reverse the relation between urban development and economy development; we have to deal with urban development as an investment for future yields, not simply as an unwelcome expense. The task of urban development is to extend economic and social values with the integration of housing, commercial, recreational developments and services. The objective is to make the culture of a sustainable local economy, creating an income that improves the quality of life and healthy competition. The local taxation and local asset should have a prominent role so that the shortcut of market effects could give new impetus from the bottom up in the metropolitan area and nationwide.

A short-term view dominated the current system, the aim was to spend all the resources, rather than raising the economic (investment) inspiration. The core of an integrated, value-based economic and urban development plan is to generate new value, based on local skills, through investment-oriented developments, with the expansion of local resources. The self-expansion of the urban economy is based on self-financing systems for municipal projects, which are also resources. An internal resource connected to external financing gives a follow-up character for the city development. Projects with the contribution of financial and investment institutions should be set up to improve public property so that the public should not be at the mercy of any development of the private equity investment. It is also necessary to organize resident and business local communities in order to improve living and working conditions and the quality of life. A long-term sustainable urban development could be achieved only in close collaboration with the district and the main economic and municipal actors. It is important that in this system the participating partners are equal partners, to ensure the division of labour, in addition to initiating a capital partner. The capital primarily has to create a development framework by using the activities of other actors to reach the desired development.

Budapest and Region – Joint Spatial Development for
Increasing Competitiveness

Effective strategic planning and the practice of regional cooperation between Budapest and its agglomeration, the immediate and wider area covering the city, is still not established. There is a lack of effective regional cooperation which has become a hindrance to coordinated development and improvement. There are inter-municipal and regional relationships, but these are often informal and for most parties the benefits are sporadic. A "functional (large) urban areas," or large city region as a "metropolitan area" definition and delimitation is missing from Hungarian territorial planning acquis, despite a necessary major regional strategic development plan would be for creating opportunities in collaboration because of Budapest's particular situation due to the suburbanization.

The most important feature of a metropolitan area is a high quality network connection system of settlements. The traditionally established transport "availability" is no longer the sole consideration for the cooperation. The cooperation is about the flow of information, the common interests and common strategic decisions, and the creation of value, work, tertiary production, education, research and development, industry triangle. Each settlement has its own character, so the city regional cooperation system should be designed to specific functions, and unique abilities. In order to strengthen the position of Budapest in the European city network and to halt the process that was previously spontaneous and ill-planned, a controlled complex spatial plan and the impoundment of functional metropolitan area is required. The integrated development and regulatory planning of the metropolitan area (and/or traditional agglomeration) and the central core (the city) is the most important task.

Changes in Urban Structure due to Changes of Economic and
Social Circumstances

The composition of the residents of Budapest differs in many aspects from the residents in other parts of the country. On the one hand, as the capital city, it is one of the most significant points of international relations within the country, where national decision-making and management functions are concentrated. In this connection its relations and the proportion of market and financial services are developed, it provides a stable, determining role in research and development and educational activities. In Budapest the level of employment is higher, the unemployment rate is lower, the qualification of the employees is also higher compared to other territories of the country, and thanks to the international migration the population of the city is decreasing less even less than the population of the country.

For Budapest the outbreak opportunity lies in the development of the education-research-development triangle, in receiving foreign students and researchers, in establishing "hot houses" (innopolis centrals of the city districts), in the latter employment of the students. Sixty-three per cent of Hungary's researchers work in the capital city, out of 1,200 national researcher and developer positions, 550 are situated in Budapest and its close area. Out of the registered enterprises employing more than 250 people, every 6th-7th person, and out of the medium enterprises every 24th person, conducts research and development activity. The number of foreign researchers and representatives of business life living in Budapest and its close area increases by 10 per cent a year. The concentration of educational activity is high in this area. The university campus of southern Buda has improved exactly in such a "knowledge triangle"-based cooperation, where in 2008 the European Institute of Innovation and Technology (EIT) was established. This is the first institution of the EU that has its seat in Hungary.

The revitalization of the Óbuda Gas Factory along the Danube on the northern side of Buda, and the already operating Graphisoft park are aiming at a similar profile, which is supported by the private university in the park (called Aquincum Technological Institute, ATI). As part of the so-called Corvin-Szigony Project in Budapest District VIII, the Corvin Knowledge Park (combining medical, biotechnological, IT research activities), which is managed with the cooperation of the surrounding universities and research institutions, is the next element of future investment. However, compared with other parts of the country, the city is ageing more rapidly (as the population of the city grows significantly due to immigration and not because of reproduction), there are more pensioners, who are better educated, have higher living standards and consumption demands compared with the national average.

This new phase of ageing – outside of the social burden – leads to a new kind of demand, a new kind of economic and social strategy and requires new kinds of servicing functions. The so-called "Silver-Economy" has appeared, which might also raise the city's competitiveness, by providing services for a new kind of city utilization and by solving the complex transport-, infrastructure-, housing-related servicing issues. Economic and social changes have induced changes in the field of city utilization as well. Nowadays the city is not only a place for production, but a place for leisure and recreation as well, the annually organized international festivals, sport events (series of city running, the "National Gallop" – an event promoting equestrian sports, swimming and water polo championships, family sport days, Budapest Sziget Festival and other international music festivals, Wine and Pálinka Festivities, thematic city days, etc.) have become more significant, and their wide range strengthens the city's competitiveness.

Compact City with Subcentres

Budapest is a city with a traditional and extensive ring-road structure. The circular connections are determined by the country's settlement network, however the ring-road structures have been generated by city expansion in response to the growing population of the city. This characteristic structure, which includes the city's historical core, will remain protected, and therefore relieved from disproportionately heavy demands, caused by city expansion. In the course of the development of Budapest during the last 50 years, the city has lagged behind the creation of the necessary ring-type elements. The existing network of roads will be updated with its missing elements, and new structures must also be established. The principle is to develop a system based on density and the city's structure of polarities. On the territory of Budapest some pole areas could be created, by marking densely built in areas, where the concentration is higher, but the high-level of city supply is secured. These poles might provide complex services, new job opportunities, they could connect the settlements of suburb areas with the city centre as well.

As in every large city, in Budapest there can also be found city centres, which have developed from the centres of former separate settlements and which now play a strategic role in the city's operation and the utilization of its territories. These are the centres of those pole areas to be developed. The distances between the poles will be short, thus not only the car traffic will possibly decrease, but new transport means, such as electric vehicles and bicycles may also become possible. For travelling between the outskirts situated diagonally, far from each other, the radial-type network of metro lines, interlocking beneath the downtown will be absolutely necessary. For those who want to accomplish these travels by car, the boulevards, which does not cross the inner city parts, like Hungária boulevard and the M0 Ring Road will be available. However the quality and functional composition of subcentres is currently not viable. By increasing the density of Budapest, not only pole areas need to be established, but also the subcentres must be developed, in some places new, functional and multi-faceted subcentres (like in Albertfalva, northern Csepel, Pasarét, etc.).

Accessibility – Mobility

As a consequence of economic development, the transportation of commodities has transformed and the demand for it has increased significantly over the past few decades. Since Hungary has also become a member of the European Union, our country has vigorously joined the east-west and partly the north-south network of the transportation of commodities. As a result of its transport geographical situation and its size, the City of Budapest has to deal with a particularly huge burden, affected by freight transport. Western-Europe makes strong efforts to change the structure of the transportation of commodities, preferring favouring water and rail transport. Nowadays in Eastern- and Central-Europe as well, road transport is more dominant, but the disadvantages of this mode of transport are well-known.

Our opportunities for rail and inland waterway transport remain underdeveloped, so the aim is to transform the mode of freight transport which is so significantly related to our country. To this end, we have the opportunity provided by the European Danube Region Strategy coordinated by the European Commission, which has appointed our country, to be in charge of the development of shipping. The other opportunity for Hungary is the transport policy favouring more intense utilization of the railway network. There must be special areas of logistics set and established within the country, in order to provide an opportunity for a modern, comfortable and environment-friendly freight transport. Budapest has to play quite a significant role in this, as in the city or around it, beyond the converging railways and highways, the Danube itself is also a very useful transport corridor. The Capital City and its surroundings are therefore eligible to offer space for logistics locations of international importance as well. However, one the most important conditions is that the intermodality between the infrastructure of certain modes of transport – road, railway, water and air – should be secured.

For Budapest logistics provide a significant opportunity for development and innovation. Exploiting the opportunities provided by the north-south and east-west international transport corridors connecting and passing the European metropolises, it is necessary to "stop" the commodities crossing the region, to manage their logistics, to generate added value on the spot (trade, agency, bank, advertisement, printing, movie, fashion, packing, etc.), to improve employment and to support intended financial investment. The Budapest Mutlimodal Logistics centre represents conscious development of logistics, as it may be the biggest facility serving road and rail transport in the country. In addition, regarding the supply of the Capital City and its suburb area, the Csepel port could gain a more significant role, as a hub of the water, rail and road transport. The urban boom, which started in the middle of the 20th century, is followed by a phenomenon that we notice as the rapid development of motorization.

The outcome – a city, which is more liveable than today – can only be achieved by a joint, but diverse development of transport. We need to make public transport (metro, bus, tram, trolley, shipping) more comfortable, modern and cheaper, we need to prioritize bicycle and pedestrian transport modes (providing cycle routes, establishing bicycle rentals and extending pedestrian zones). By securing development opportunities of differentiated intensity, in accordance with the capacities of settlement structures, we need to improve the pole areas and decrease the distance between workplaces and residential areas. We need to develop the intermodal junctions of public transport into an important element of the city's structure. It is necessary to stop the car traffic coming from the suburb area to the Capital City, at the origin of settlement if possible, but at least at the outer zones of the Capital City, by establishing an improved network of P+R parking lots, and we need to create the opportunity for rail transport within the city, not just by improving the suburban railway. The most important objective of transport and city development is to relieve the city centre and to strengthen the relations with the suburb areas. To achieve it – in line with European directives – the development of the rail transport has priority. In Budapest there is no intermodality between the metro line and the railway, and therefore development of the network of metro lines, the enlargement and the integration of the suburban railway lines is crucial. Creating the connection between the International Airport and the city centre, by a rapid transit railway

(FEREX), is also an important development plan. The metro line 5 will be Budapest's first, RER-type rapid transit railway system, which will connect the whole metropolitan region, from north to south.

Effects and Influence of National and EU Policies

Hungary's Access Treaty was signed on 16 April 2003, and from 1 May 2004 Hungary became a full member of the European Union. To comply with the Community law, the EU does not make a difference between certain fields of law, however the preparations for integration – also by the EU – have contained specific fields, as environment protection, the single market, the four freedoms in the EU (the free movement of goods, services, capital and people). Therefore the regulations of local governments – in the field of environment protection (drinking water, wastewater treatment, local programmes of environmental protection, local noise and vibration protection, implementation of waste management-related local duties); in the field of industrial and commerce sector (the operation of fairs and markets, public procurement) and in the field of public services, secured by municipalities – have been specially recognized.

Budapest can manage EU funded developments through the National Development Agency (NDA). The NDA is an institute of national government, established in order to undertake long- and mid-term development and planning related tasks and operational programmes required for using financial assistance granted by the European Union and set up the institutional system required for the use of these. The institution is responsible inter alia for the following: co-ordination of the operational programmes: planning; monitoring of their implementation; finalisation of the calls for applications; selection of the developments, investments to be awarded support; operation of the related system of institutions; administration of the necessary EU consultations and preparation of the prescribed documents. Furthermore, NDA takes an active part in planning the budget for the 2014-2020 development cycle, in the establishment of what are the most favourable support and related resources for Hungary's particular requirements.

As a result, the development strategies (like the New Urban Development Programme of Budapest and the EU 2020 Strategy of Budapest), action areas and projects of the city have to fit to the priority areas of the New Széchenyi Programme which runs under control of the NDA. The main objectives of the New Széchenyi Programme are improving competition and creating one million new jobs within ten years along seven emerging areas: the health industry; green economy; housing; enterprise development; science-innovation; employment and transport development).

Chapter 6
Dortmund

Harriet Ellwein and Hildegard Mai

City Profile

Dortmund is a city in Germany, located in the federal state of North-Rhine Westphalia. Its population is about 580,000 making it the 7th largest city in Germany and the 34th largest in Europe. Dortmund was mentioned in official documents for the first time in the 9th century and became important as a "Freie Reichsstadt" (Free Imperial City) and "Hansestadt" (Hanseatic City) in the medieval period. During the Second World War, the city was largely destroyed and later reconstructed including a completely new city centre with modern infrastructure and some ancient, entirely renovated buildings such as the church "Reinoldikirche", one of the symbols of the city. Over the last decade, Dortmund has become one of the most dynamic cities in the new German economy and a rapidly growing location for new technologies. This is evident from the city's high position in a comparative ranking of German cities dealing with global market and sector foresights of a number of key sectors. Dortmund ranks 23th out of the 413 regions analysed and is the first in the Ruhr area.[1]

Located in the East of the polycentric industrial Ruhr area (also referred to as *Metropole Ruhr*), Dortmund is part of one of Europe's biggest urban agglomerations, with around 520,000 inhabitants. At the same time, Dortmund belongs to the Rhine-Ruhr Region with a population of c.11,000,000 inhabitants, and almost 100,000 people are within a one hour car journey of Dortmund. Furthermore, geographically, Dortmund can be understood as an interface between the huge metropolitan Ruhr area, on the one hand, and the largely rural region of Sauerland and Münsterland, on the other hand. In terms of accessibility, Dortmund has Europe's biggest canal port, an airport and six interstate highways (*Autobahn*).

Economic Structure

Dortmund's economic structure is clearly characterized by small and medium enterprises. An important feature of this structure is the absence of large firms. The economic structure can be described as diverse, relying on such different sectors

---

1 The statistical data used throughout this report are obtained from the *Bundesamt fuer Statistik* (Federal Office of Statistics), the *Bundesagentur für Arbeit* (Federal Employment Agency) and the *Stadtamt für Statistik Dortmund* (City Bureau of Statistics of Dortmund).

as logistics (also e-logistics), information and communication technologies, the metal-electro sector, micro and nanotechnologies and biotechnologies, but also the health care sector and financial services, above all banks and insurance.

Currently, about 80 per cent of workers (employees subject to social insurance) are employed within the tertiary sector and about 20 per cent within the secondary sector. This is a dramatic change compared to the year 1980 when 51.4 per cent were employed in services and 48.2 per cent were working in the industrial production sector. Most workers are employed in the modern service industries, such as banking and insurance, real estate, leasing, services for business enterprises and public and private services. Within the Ruhr area, Dortmund is by far the most important location for the insurance industry; more than two thirds of all employees in this industry work in Dortmund. Other important employers are the metal-electro sector, logistics and information and communication technologies.

Despite a relatively low share of manufacturing in the economy of Dortmund and a clear shift towards modern service industries in recent decades, manufacturing still has an important role in Dortmund's economy. In fact many services in Dortmund are related to manufacturing. Furthermore, the services in Dortmund might serve the manufacturing industries in the surrounding areas of the city where the manufacturing sector still has a relatively high share in the economy. Also, to the East and South of Dortmund, outside the Ruhr area, there are areas with a large share of manufacturing. Altogether, within a diversified economic structure, manufacturing remains significant as it is probably a major source of innovation and doubtless a major contributor to exports. This is very important, for Dortmund's export rate has experienced a tremendous increase from 25.6 per cent in 1997 to its current rate of about 50 per cent.

The city's relative economic performance can be evaluated positively, especially compared to most other cities in the Ruhr area. Since the middle of the 1990s, GDP per capita has increased to €32,637 in 2008, which is above the German average (€30,392) and the other cities in the Ruhr area with exception of Essen (€38,429). Dortmund's economic structure was diversified, also due to many successful start-ups. The city's political leadership has been very clear in formulating its policies according to the financial limits it has to deal with. For that reason, public debt has been kept under control in Dortmund: a situation, which is not the case for many German cities. Especially in the Ruhr area, but also in other regions undergoing structural change, local budgets are completely overstretched.

Demography

With a population of at least 580,000 people, Dortmund is the largest city in the Ruhr area. Since the first half of the 1980s, Dortmund's population has hardly varied, apart from the beginning of the 1990s, when it slightly exceeded 600,000, it has been approximately 580,000-590,000 people.

Demographic change constitutes a serious problem for Germany as a whole. Although many European countries have to deal with that challenge, Germany's situation appears particularly alarming. Without any doubt, for Dortmund, it is (and will be during the next decades) also a relevant topic and the city is working on appropriate solutions. Especially, Dortmund's Economic Development Agency has an outstanding role in this process. At the same time, although stagnation rather than increase in population is expected, as some forecasts demonstrate, until 2030, Dortmund is supposed to perform better than any other city in the Ruhr area. At the same time, and despite considerable achievements in economic performance, the city's social structure is still affected by the decline of its main industries in recent decades, which used to be main employers for thousands of people. Unemployment could be reduced, but still remains relatively high with 37,144 jobless persons in the year 2010 (13.1 per cent of active population), 39.2 per cent of them being unemployed over two years (long-term unemployment). Nevertheless, long-term unemployment decreased 15.1 per cent since 2008 and youth unemployment was reduced by 8.9 per cent during the same period.

The share of immigrants is about 15 per cent of the city's population. Within the federal state of North-Rhine Westphalia, it means one of the highest values, but it corresponds approximately to the share of immigrants at national level. It cannot be stated, however, that Dortmund is facing a specific integration problem. As with any other city in Germany, it is pursuing the goal of increasing attainment for immigrants in terms of education and insurable employment. Still, a problem, which may not be overlooked, is that of deprived districts in the Northern part of the city. But this is not necessarily a particular issue of immigrants rather than of generally poorly educated, long-term unemployed inhabitants, often regardless their ethnical origins.

Education and Research

At the same time, Dortmund has been successful in developing its universities, offering multiple opportunities for higher education. Currently, there are c.33,300 students in Dortmund (with an increasing share of foreign students in the student population), studying at the TU Dortmund University and at the Dortmund University of Applied Sciences and Arts. Additionally, there are about 1,200 students at the private university called International School of Management. Despite its name (with "TU" being an acronym for "Technical University") and clear focusing on teaching and researching in technical and natural sciences, such as engineering, informatics or chemistry, the TU Dortmund University is also well-known for its long tradition in economic and social sciences as well as journalism. For its part, the University of Applied Sciences and Arts does not only offer numerous degree programmes in technical disciplines, but also has a renowned faculty of design. Thanks to a long tradition in applied research and many intensive co-operations between science and business, both universities have also had tremendous impact on the development of Dortmund's economy.

Furthermore, there are almost 50 research institutes in Dortmund, many of which are non-university institutions, such as Fraunhofer Institute for Material

Flows and Logistics (IML), Fraunhofer Institute for Software and System Technique (ISST) or Max Planck Institute for Molecular Physiology.

Governance

To better understand the city's economic policy, it is necessary to make a general outline of role of local communities within the federal system in Germany. According to the German constitution, different tasks are conceded to every level (national, federal state and local). Within this multilevel system, local communities have two tasks: local self-government and transferred activities. Local self-government means the right to regulate in its own responsibility all matters concerning local community within the legal frame. There are tasks on voluntary and compulsory basis. Transferred activities refer to implementing laws, dictated by the national state and the federal state level. Altogether, local communities, de jure, dispose of a considerable room for manoeuvre. Nevertheless, de facto, they often have to reduce spending in voluntary tasks due to extremely limited financial resources.

As far as Dortmund is concerned, it is noteworthy to mention, that – despite budget limitations – the city is investing in its economic development by maintaining a modern, service-oriented Economic Development Agency with a broad range of activities, such as cluster and network management, location marketing, start-up competitions, human resources development initiatives or development of commercial sites. The city is implementing all those tasks on a voluntary basis. Compared to many other German cities, where local economic development agencies are not (or at least not directly) part of local government, and especially regarding its considerable financial and stuff resources, Dortmund's Economic Development Agency can be described as a special one. Another interesting feature of local economic development is co-operation with the Ruhr area economic development agency (*Wirtschaftsförderung metropoleruhr*), for example, in location marketing.

Developments and Policy Changes since Early 1990s

Historical Background

From the end of the 19th century until the last decades of the 20th century, Dortmund used to be known as one of Germany's leading centres in the sectors of coal, steel and beer. Until the 1980s, these three sectors formed the key industries in the city in terms of employment and economic output. At the beginning of the 1950s, Dortmund had the largest steel output of Germany, and also one of the biggest outputs in coal. In the 1960s, Dortmund was home to eight breweries, which produced 10 per cent of the German beer consumption. Moreover, the city had worldwide the second largest beer output after Milwaukee. However, since the 1960s, the pillar industries began declining which resulted in the closure of the last mine in 1987 and the closure of the last blast furnace in 2001. Also, the last two independent breweries of the city were taken over by a big enterprise. The last steel plant (ThyssenKrupp's PHOENIX, formerly run by Hoesch) was dismantled in 2001 and then rebuilt in China as well as the world's most modern coking plant.

Hence, these three traditional industries – coal, steel and beer – have nearly disappeared, with a high unemployment rate as a consequence. Similar processes took place in other parts of the Ruhr area and, although, it is still one of the largest industrial areas of Europe, the role of the mining industry decreased dramatically. In Dortmund, the end of activities in the coal mining and steel sector was also accompanied by a heavy decline in manufacturing activities. However, the metal-electro sector is a manufacturing sector, which still plays a major role in the economy of the city and the Ruhr area. It counts for at least two thirds of employment in the manufacturing sector in Dortmund.

To better illustrate the meaning of the decline of the three key industries of coal, steel and beer for the city, one should take a look at the difference in employment in these sectors in the 1960s and at the end of the 20th century. Employment in coal mining fell from over 35,000 to zero. In the steel industry it dropped from 35,000 to approximately 4,000. And Dortmund's beer industry had about 1,000 workers in 1999 compared to almost 5,000 in the 1960s.

Consequences of deindustrialization were manifold for Dortmund. Above all, the economic and social structure of the city changed completely. Additionally, almost 150 years of mining and industrialization had a strong impact on the city in terms of environment, with many polluted brownfields in various parts of the city. In this sense, the city was not only affected in environmental aspects, but also in terms of the cityscape and the structure of the city.

To meet the challenge of deindustrialization and to make Dortmund a liveable location, local authorities had to react by introducing different measures in all areas of the city's development, especially in the economic structure, human resources development, accessibility, environment and other spheres of life quality and infrastructure, like leisure facilities.

Despite a difficult situation at that time regarding Dortmund's further development, it was very important that the city could count on several significant institutions, such as the Dortmund University (now TU Dortmund University, founded in 1968), the Technology Centre (*TechnologieZentrumDortmund*, founded in 1984) and the Technology Park (*Technologiepark Dortmund*, founded in 1988), with all three located in close proximity to each other, regarding the importance of spatial proximity for spin-offs in particular and innovation processes generally. The decision to found a university in a city dominated by a working-class population, at that time, turned out to be crucial for the city's further development. It was because of the university that Dortmund could successfully develop a technology centre and a technology park, enabling by these means the city's evolution into a modern high-tech location with growth clusters. Clearly, one of TU Dortmund University's most important features is its openness towards business enterprises, especially compared to many other German universities.

There has been a long tradition of consent-oriented economic and social policies in Dortmund and from the middle of the 1990s there has been an intensive discussion about a re-orientation in economic development. It was clear that the era of coal mining and steel industry was at an end and the only solution was concentrating on creating new structures to promote new, knowledge-based sectors. This re-orientation was pushed primarily by the city government. The general goal was a clearer focus of the Economic Development Agency's activities on the city's growth potential in different sectors and a better connection of growth-oriented policies with employment-oriented policies. In this regard, new measures were planned in developing locations and sites, in promoting technologies and product development and in qualifying human resources. Furthermore, Dortmund's image as a location was not very positive due to a long tradition of coal mining and the steel industry, often associated with pollution, low levels of education and generally low quality of life. For that reason, the city had a difficult task to communicate on the regional, national and international level that Dortmund was a modern research and development location characterized by small and medium enterprises and distributed over plenty of free commercial sites. Moreover, it was a matter of creating a new identity and image. It is important to emphasize that local authorities were willing to invest in the Economic Development Agency despite a difficult budget situation. This future-oriented decision was not only reflected in considerable resources in terms of personnel and financing, but also in the extraordinary variety of tasks. Of course, to meet structural change the city needed more resources which could be invested through different programmes coming from the federal state of North-Rhine Westphalia and from the European Union (Dortmund as an Objective 2 region).

At first concrete policy reactions focused on promoting start-up companies and fighting unemployment through diverse measures. Since the middle of the 1990s, one of core areas was implementing cluster-oriented policies and creating new structures on the basis of the possibilities which existed at that time. For example, Dortmund's University already had one of Germany's leading faculties in informatics. In connection with steel production and supported by the technology centre and the technology park, numerous ICT companies had emerged since the 1980s and there were some notable achievements in creating new capacities in research and development (also in some other sectors). But if those companies had represented a kind of small sector within the steel cluster, after steel production had been closed in Dortmund, according to local authorities, the ICT sector was supposed to become one of the new leading sectors in Dortmund's economic structure.

The Dortmund-Project: A Comprehensive Strategy

The most important measure to implement all these cluster-oriented policies and, at the same time, the biggest milestone in Dortmund's structural change in the last two decades was the foundation of the "dortmund-project" in 1999. The story of the "dortmund-project" is a special one. It has its origins in the closure of ThyssenKrupp's plant PHOENIX, planned at the end of the 1990s and finally implemented in 2001. In return and thanks to great efforts of the mayor of the city, ThyssenKrupp agreed on investing in a public-private partnership (finally staying for three years), which was also joined by the city of Dortmund and the consultancy firm McKinsey. This public-private partnership was called "dortmund-project" and despite its name it evolved into much more than a mere project, becoming one of the symbols of the so-called "new Dortmund". But first, it was an intensive nine-month co-operation between the Economic Development Agency, ThyssenKrupp and McKinsey, accompanied by a working group with representatives from the Chamber of Industry and Commerce, the Chamber of Crafts, trade unions and further actors relevant in employment issues. This co-operation resulted in a concept, named "Fortifying Dortmund's economic performance through targeted development of growth clusters".

The main features of this concept were focussing on the three leading, knowledge-based sectors of ICT, microsystem technologies and logistics (especially by promoting start-ups and company growth), preparing available sites for these sectors with their special infrastructural requirements, development of qualification and research infrastructure and job placement for the new leading sectors. The "dortmund-project" fell directly under the city of Dortmund's mayor's office and, at the beginning, the city council decided to finance it for a decade. At that time, the main goal of the project was to generate 70,000 new jobs between 2000 and 2010. This number was not coincidental, but was chosen according to the loss of 70,000 jobs in the former three leading industries of coal, steel and beer since the 1960s.

The "dortmund-project" was established as a comprehensive project with three main pillars: targeted promotion of leading sectors (cluster and sector development, start-up competitions), human resources and capacity development according to requirements of the leading sectors and development of commercial sites (with the highlight of restructuring the huge former industrial PHOENIX area at the South of the city into a technology park and a lake with leisure facilities and housing). To support these three pillars, two further areas of the "dortmund-project" were introduced: location marketing within the region and on a national and international level, improving data availability and introducing effective control of all project activities. In this sense, as a comprehensive project, the "dortmund-project" clearly has transcended the boarders of traditional local economic development.

Regarding sectoral and cluster development, one should definitely mention Dortmund's new competence centres (being part of TechnologieZentrumDortmund) as absolute milestones within the process of the city's transition towards a modern research, development and high-tech location. Among others, the following competence centres are home to high-tech start-up companies: MST. factory Dortmund (micro and nanotechnologies), e-port-dortmund (e-logistics), BioMedizinZentrumDortmund (biotechnology), B1st-Software-Factory (ICT),

Zentrum für Produktionstechnologie (production technologies), KITZ.do (technology centre for children and adolescents). Dortmund's competence centres represent an attractive opportunity for high-tech start-ups and, therefore, are fully utilized. For example, several foreign start-up companies moved to MST. factory Dortmund, as they found unique conditions for research and product development. It was also thanks to MST.factory, that Dortmund was distinguished by EUROCITIES as Europe's most innovative city in 2006. Certainly, MST. factory has helped Dortmund evolve into Europe's second biggest cluster for microsystem technologies.

In 2008, the majority of the city council voted for the continuation of the "dortmund-project" beyond 2010. The main difference compared to the beginning of the project is its integration in the Economic Development Agency in the year 2005. Although, the objective of generating 70,000 new jobs could not be achieved (approximately half that number were created), there is general consent that the work of the "dortmund-project" can be evaluated positively.

When talking about the main achievements of the "dortmund-project", it is important to mention that some of them can be measured and expressed in numbers while others are more subjective, but still may not be neglected. On the one hand, many start-up companies were founded and thousands of new jobs were created, especially within the leading sectors ICT, microsystem technologies and logistics. Numerous commercial sites were renovated and prepared for further use by high-tech companies (being already partially the case). On the other hand, manifold measures were implemented to improve the city's basis in human resources. Some of them can already be denominated as successful. For example, the IT Center Dortmund, established in 2000, offers Germany's fastest degree programme in informatics. In contrast, other measures are long-term oriented and cannot be evaluated yet. Furthermore, location marketing has been one of central features of the "dortmund-project". Different examples indicate that the perception of Dortmund has changed positively within the region, but also in other regions. This can be observed in reporting on Dortmund by media on a national level. Also, commercial fair newspapers (e.g. at the Hannover Fair) often refer to companies from Dortmund. Moreover, in terms of local economic development in Germany, the "dortmund-project" is often referred to as a best-practice-case.

Last but not least, when referring to the main achievements of the "dortmund-project", which cannot be measured, it is necessary to point out that the "organizing capacity" of the city has improved, particularly in terms of dealing with structural change and fortifying a modern location profile. The city has definitely evolved as a learning organization.

Besides the "dortmund-project", various achievements should be mentioned when referring to the city's development since the mid-1980s. First, an extensive renewal of the city centre was implemented with such highlights, as the new City Hall, the new Concert Hall (*Konzerthaus*) and, above all, renewal of the U-Tower (*Dortmunder U*), a former brewery, which was converted into a centre of arts and different leisure activities. Also, an expansion of the airport and canal port took place. Regarding environmental development, an important measure with lasting impact has been the renaturation of the Emscher River (which used to be a sewer). It started originally within the ten-year programme (1989-1999) International Building Exhibition Emscher Park (*Internationale Bauausstellung Emscher Park*) by the federal state of North-Rhine Westphalia. This regional project to encourage structural change in the Ruhr area helped improve Dortmund's situation in terms of urban planning and in social, cultural and environmental aspects. Furthermore, Dortmund was a venue for various football matches during the World Cup (2006) and part of the cultural capital of Europe (Ruhr 2010) for the whole year of 2010.

Finally, concerning financial room for manoeuvre to master the challenge of structural change, sourcing from the European Structural Funds, the European Regional Development Fund (ERDF) and the European Social Fund (ESF), has been indispensable for the city and will be also very important in the future.

State of the City

Facing New Challenges

Doubtlessly, Dortmund's economic and social structure has changed dramatically during the structural change and, in sum, the city has been successful in meeting this enormous challenge. Dortmund is the most dynamic city in the Ruhr area in terms of population and number of start-up companies. GDP has increased and reduction of unemployment is not only reflected in more jobs, but rather in better jobs, many of them being part of new knowledge-based sectors. Dortmund has become a city of technology and *Technologiepark Dortmund* belongs to the best technology parks in Europe. Altogether, more than 280 companies and over 8,500 people are currently working in the technology centre and in the technology park (firms can relocate from the former to the latter after a successful start-up). In addition, 16,000 jobs are indirectly related to the park and the fiscal benefits, in terms of business taxes generated, are €438m. Overall every single Euro of public money invested in the technology centre (TZDO) and park (TNPD) has attracted seven Euros of private investments, making the TZDO and the TNPD among the best performers in Germany and Europe. Of course, working conditions are also much better than in former leading industries of coal, steel and beer. Furthermore, the city's infrastructure has been improved fundamentally and Dortmund's accessibility is even better than before. Finally, high organizing capacity between public and private partners and civil society can be observed in Dortmund.

Nevertheless, first, managing structural change is a dynamic process where new issues arise continually (including external matters like financial international crisis or global warming), and, second, despite largely successful policies targeting all aspects of the city's development, some important challenges still remain.

First of all, the fight against unemployment is not over. On the contrary, although unemployment has been reduced, it is still considerably above the national level.

Reducing the unemployment rate to less than 10 per cent until the year 2015 is one of the main new projects (if not the main project) of the city's government. A major problem with the labour market is a qualitative mismatch: there is an over-supply of low or unskilled people, on the one hand, and a shortage of highly skilled knowledge workers within the new growing sectors, on the other hand.

Also, there is socio-economic polarization and serious problems within deprived areas. Plenty of projects have been implemented to meet these problems, but it should be understood as a long-term, continuous process. Although there have already been many initiatives, local authorities are currently putting even more emphasis on overcoming social and economic disparities. Moreover, Dortmund's new mayor has made fighting right-wing extremism one of his priorities.

At the same time, serious budget restraints clearly reduce local government's room for manoeuvre. As shown above, Dortmund's political leadership has been very responsible in balancing running up debts, on the one hand, and investing in the city's development, on the other hand. To keep on investing in a responsible way and addressing all relevant issues concerning economic and social development, it will be important to attract more private capital and to link public initiatives to voluntary activities (with Dortmund having a solid civil society) in even a stronger manner than up to now.

As mentioned above, Dortmund's economic structure is characterized by small and medium enterprises. Actually, there are no headquarters of DAX-listed enterprises. This is particularly noteworthy considering the fact that 9 out of 30 DAX-listed enterprises have their headquarters in the federal state of North-Rhine Westphalia. However, absence of big companies with thousands of employees can also be considered an advantage for Dortmund in certain ways. Shocks like closure of a huge steel plant in 2001 are not possible anymore. Examples from the neighbour city of Bochum, where Nokia closed its plant some years ago and the future of Opel's plant is anything but certain, also demonstrate the dilemma of dependency on big enterprises.

Moreover, Dortmund was less affected by the financial and economic crisis in 2008/2009 than many other German cities because of its diversified economic structure. Additionally, Germany performed better than most countries worldwide, especially due to so-called *Kurzarbeit* ("short work"). This measure helped avoiding lay-offs by reducing working hours instead, with the government making up some of the employees' lost income. Generally, the city's budget experienced serious financial cuts, but Dortmund's economy performed comparatively well during the crisis. According to a company survey recently published by Dortmund's Chamber of Industry and Commerce, 92 per cent of companies consider their situation to be satisfactory to good.

Probably, one of the biggest challenges for Dortmund has to do with human resources development. Especially, such matters as brain-drain and demographic change take central stage concerning the city's further development. For that reason, it is indispensable to improve educational infrastructure generally and the intellectual climate in particular. The city is rather successful in keeping its graduates, but should advance in attracting skilled workers from other parts of Germany and from abroad. In this sense, at least at first sight, absence of big enterprises seems to be a disadvantage.

Managing Structural Change

Since the early 1990s, the city has worked a lot on improving its human resources development, realising e.g. such projects as LernDo!, a best practice model which develops and implements practical realization of lifelong learning. Currently, based on the idea of investing in people and education instead of heavy infrastructure, there are manifold initiatives targeting human resources development at different levels. The main idea of those initiatives is sustainable improvement in the supply of skilled workers coming from the local (and regional) level. To meet this goal, the city of Dortmund has developed an integrated approach, which includes the whole education chain of a person. For example, a technology centre for children and adolescents, named KITZ.do, was opened in order to develop interest in technical and natural sciences at an early stage and in a different way than within traditional school education. In 2010, over 5,000 primary and secondary school students took part in manifold activities at KITZ.do. The core idea is to inspire children and adolescents to study technical and natural sciences considering decreasing interest in such disciplines not only in Dortmund, but virtually in all parts of Germany.

At the same time, the city would not benefit just by achieving more interest in studying technical and natural sciences. It is important that young people study in Dortmund and also stay there after graduating. For that reason, the city's Economic Development Agency is implementing various projects to make students and graduates stay in Dortmund. For example, there are different activities to bring students together with local companies, which could become attractive as employers in the future.

Another important field of human resources development refers to improving supply and demand in trainee jobs. Here, the city is tackling the problem of mismatch by acquainting high school students with different professions and companies. In this sense, the most important measure is the *jobtec* project, which includes a fair where high school students can get in contact with companies that offer training. Different measures target human resources development in specific sectors with particular importance for Dortmund's economic structure, such as ICT and logistics. Computer science classes have been intensified at high schools and there is also a contest for ICT trainees called JOY.

To improve data availability regarding demand for skilled workers in Dortmund's leading sectors, an annual company survey called "Skilled Worker Monitoring" was introduced in 2008, allowing for a realistic view on skilled worker shortage in the city. Thanks to this dialogue between the city's Economic Development Agency and companies from Dortmund's high-tech sectors, tools to deal with the skilled worker shortage have been readjusted, also regarding vocational education and training.

Further initiatives are about promoting female employment and increasing employment opportunities for people in socially deprived districts in the Northern part of the city. By these measures, the percentage of (skilled) workers is supposed to increase.

Transforming the former industrial PHOENIX site into an attractive multifunctional location is a good example of how Dortmund has managed to improve its image by establishing itself as a modern city with an active marketing strategy. It is also thanks to this project that Dortmund is no longer perceived as a city of industrial decline and severe pollution problem, but as a modern location with innovative, knowledge-based companies, new leisure opportunities and good living conditions. PHOENIX is the central site development project within the "dortmund-project" and, at the same time, Dortmund's biggest urban planning project. The main goals are profiling it as an integrated project in terms of urban planning, characterized by high quality in working, living, leisure and environment and supraregional marketing as a location with important quality features for technological development, on the one hand, and quality of life, on the other hand. Thanks to intensive renovating and restructuring of the former industrial area, both parts – PHOENIX Lake and PHOENIX West – are already used as a technology park. Although there is still a lot of work to be done (completing buildings and the landscaping of the site to attract further high-tech companies to the technology park), PHOENIX Lake is already a new attraction and popular destination for many inhabitants. Also, many apartments have already been sold, while PHOENIX West is home to two competence centres: MST.factory (micro and nanotechnologies) and the Centre for Production Technologies. Because of fast growth and significant expansion, some companies have already left the MST. factory to build their own buildings in close proximity to competence centre at the PHOENIX West site. This is precisely what local authorities were striving for when designing this project. To promote PHOENIX, Dortmund's Economic Development Agency uses such renowned property fairs as MIPIM fair in Cannes and EXPO REAL in Munich.

Altogether, the meaning of the PHOENIX project is manifold. First, it is about further development of Dortmund as a city with growth clusters in knowledge-based sectors. Second, it means completely new living and leisure opportunities for the city's residents. Third, a profound renovating and restructuring of the PHOENIX site led to a significant improvement in terms of environment (restoring of environmental damage caused by the steel industry, development of new green areas). Fourth, and this is extremely important for the city's image in terms of external perception as well as of its self-image as former industrial site, PHOENIX is a symbol of a fundamental transformation of a location, characterized by traditional heavy industries and pollution into a modern city with future-oriented sectors and a high quality of life. This successful development of PHOENIX has also disproved external estimation of this project, originally considering it a bad investment.

The PHOENIX project is also a good example for what is currently the main issue regarding further cluster and sectoral development in Dortmund: cross-clustering. When developing the former blast-furnace-site of PHOENIX West into a technology park with expertise in micro and nanotechnologies, it soon became obvious that, in the long term, the strategy of focussing on a single technological corridor would not be sufficient to develop a vivid and fast growing competence area. At the same time, there has also been demand for entrepreneurial support in the field of production technologies. Therefore, two different incubators – one for micro and nanotechnologies and one for production technologies – were founded at PHOENIX West. Both incubators were developing very well. Until now, cross-clustering activities at that site have not been fundamental yet. However they are supposed to increase due to high-tech companies' continuous interest in this new technology park and good collaboration opportunities with Dortmund's universities. In this sense, a challenge for the city is also attracting international companies.

Cross-clustering at PHOENIX West may not be comprehended as a single activity in this respect, but rather as a part of a new strategy for Dortmund, developed in 2008. The same year, this strategy to compete for global markets, in regard of economic globalization and demographic change, was approved by the city council to be implemented until 2018. There are four strategic goals within this strategy: interlinking technologies and sectors, supporting companies, interlinking knowledge and advancing on developing quality of work and life in the city.

Interlinking technologies and sectors is considered an essential task also in view of the increasing importance of efficiency technologies. This market's central feature is connecting different technologies such as micro technologies, on the one hand, and production technologies, on the other hand, with the former being enabling technologies for the latter. For that reason, Dortmund's task is to establish links between its different clusters – the so-called cross-clustering.

The initiative "Efficiency", established in 2010 and aiming at bringing together representatives from different clusters to create new projects and products and to enter new markets, is the city's main project for cross-clustering. At the same time, it is also Dortmund's major initiative in terms of promoting the change towards a Green City with sustainable and efficient technologies and buildings.

The first step was identifying Dortmund's main efficiency markets for local enterprises. Such markets are characterized by a critical mass of enterprises and R&D, potential for co-operation between old and new technologies and future potential for economic growth. Currently, four markets fulfil these criteria: simulation (e.g. simulation of production processes), mobility (e.g. development of new light materials for e-mobiles), energy (e.g. energy reduction in intelligent buildings) and resources (e.g. sensor technology to save resources like materials).

Dortmund's Economic Development Agency is responsible for the implementation of the initiative "Efficiency", working on bringing people and enterprises together by offering events for exchange, creating networks, initiating projects and doing location marketing. The following activities have already started for the four efficiency markets described above. In "simulation", the network KOSIM has been founded. In "mobility", there are projects for electro mobility infrastructure like a test centre and mobile solutions. In "energy", the focus is on information about the energy efficiency of buildings. Some information events are in progress as a first step towards an energy efficient building network (Green Building Initiative). The "resources" market is focused on green microsystem technologies and materials.

The example of the network KOSIM gives a better understanding of what those projects are about. Here, the question is how firms can avoid losing the competitive advantage of "innovation" through cost-intensive testing and sample production. In this regard, simulation has a key role to play. It enables companies to reduce development costs significantly and, therefore, to compete globally. Many companies already use the potential of the "Competence Network Simulation Dortmund" as a reliable partner. By these means, local and regional scientific and technical competences in the field of simulation are being pooled and demand-oriented for enterprises. One clear advantage of this network is that companies involved can better coordinate their offers and, consequently, they could win a large order for a simulation system of the Lufthansa airline.

Another example for cross-clustering is DORTMUND.KREATIV, an initiative for creative industries, an important and vivid economic sector in Dortmund. In 2007, the Economic Development Agency decided to target this sector and developed a strategy to build networks for creative and technology enterprises (e.g. through events and meetings) and to bring them in touch with potential customers. In this context, the idea of the format "DORTMUND. KREATIV.marktplatz" was born. It is about companies from the sector of creative services (e.g. communication design, photography, website design and event management), presenting themselves to other sectors, such as logistics, micro and nanotechnologies, biotechnology, trade or production technologies.

Last but not least, one of the most important current examples for cross-clustering and for further development of Dortmund as a modern city with growing knowledge based sectors, is the initiative called "Der Innovationsstandort e.V." ("The Location of Innovation"), founded in 2008. It is a network of organizations from the world of business and the world of academia which can be described as is its particular strength. After only three years, "The Location of Innovation" ("Der Innovationsstandort") can be already considered as an example of a successful innovation network. Within the network there are five working groups developing five key topics and, by doing so, targeting the most important challenges in terms of innovation co-operation: communication between science and business, network marketing, transfer of human resources, funding projects and advances in education.

Cooperation with other Policy Levels

Co-operation with other policy levels is very important for Dortmund. Together with the government of the federal state of North-Rhine Westphalia, the city is working intensively on cluster development, among other issues. Co-operation is also crucial in terms of funding: North-Rhine Westphalia is receiving c.€1.3 billion from the European Regional Fund (ERDF) from 2007 until 2013. Together with further funding from the federal state government and private sources, about €2.5 billion is available during this period. Within the federal state of North-Rhine Westphalia, Dortmund is the most successful city besides Aachen in winning grants from the so-called Objective 2 programme. Until the end of 2010, 39 cluster projects from Dortmund have been chosen in competitions, receiving more than €40 million (project costs about €70 million) with grants varying from €9,000 to €2,7 million. One of the main reasons for this success is strong co-operation between business and universities and the latter's orientation towards applied research. Also, active research co-operation with such renowned institutes as Fraunhofer has been important for winning grants as well as capable networks, a good information base and expertise in applying for funding.

During the last decade, Dortmund's reputation has improved on a national and international level. The latter has been possible thanks to events, such as World Cup in Football (2006) and the cultural capital of Europe (Ruhr2010), but also because of continuous and intensive commitment to such important European networks and institutions like EUROCITIES and Euricur.

Chapter 7
Dublin
Jamie Cudden

City Profile

The Dublin region is situated to the east of Ireland and occupies an area of 92,200 hectares. The region is located on the coast bordered by low mountain ranges to the south and farmland to the west and north. The city is famous for its music and pubs and is home to the Guinness brewery. Dublin's strong literary heritage is very much alive in the present day and the city was named a UNESCO City of Literature in 2010. Dublin is the administrative and political capital of Ireland, housing the national government and president of the state. It is the most populous city in the state and national economic driver of Ireland accounting for 38 per cent of the national economy. It also acts as a European and international gateway for the many multinational firms that have established their headquarters in the city.

The Dublin Region comprises the administrative areas of Dublin City, South-Dublin County, Dun Laoghaire-Rathdown County and Fingal County. The region is home to 1.27m people accounting for almost 28 per cent of the national population and accounts for 37 per cent of jobs nationally. The Great Dublin Area, which includes the surrounding counties of Meath, Wicklow and Kildare, is home to 45 per cent of all jobs in the State.

The population of Dublin and the State grew at record levels from the 1990s, driven by high levels of natural increase and a sustained period of immigration from the mid-1990s to the present. Ireland is one of a small group of countries in the EU where the population is young and is forecast to grow strongly (+46 per cent by 2060). It has the one of the lowest old age dependency ratios (16.8 per cent in 2010) and one of the highest fertility rates (2.1 in 2010) in the EU and is not typical of average European demographic trends (EUROSTAT, 2011).

In the last number of years Dublin has proved an attractive destination for inward migration from other EU states. While the free movement of labour within the EU and Ireland's facilitative policy after EU enlargement resulted in large inflows of economic migrants from Eastern Europe, there were also significant inflows from Asia, Latin America and Africa during the Celtic Tiger period, 1990-2007. The region experienced an increase of over 367 per cent of non-Irish Born residents over a 20 year period up to 2006. Non-Irish born residents accounted for 17 per cent of the total population in 2006 up from 5.5 per cent in 1986.

The current economic downturn and decline in employment prospects has resulted in higher levels of emigration in recent times. This is especially true for those who lost their jobs in the construction sectors and lower skilled services sectors. Between 2007 and 2010 the numbers of immigrants arriving in Ireland dropped by over 70 per cent while emigration flows increased by 80 per cent between 2006 and 2010 (CSO, 2011). Despite a slowdown in the level of immigration in recent years, modern Dublin has retained a significantly more diverse population than at any other time in the city's history.

The Celtic Tiger

Beginning in the early 1990s, unprecedented economic growth saw the level of Irish real GDP double in size over the course of a little more than a decade. This period of growth was coined the "Celtic Tiger" with average GDP growth rates of about 6-8 per cent per annum (see CSO, 2011). The Irish economy evolved from being one of the poorest countries in the EU to being one of the richest during this period (Ireland's GDP per capita for 2010 is now 125 per cent of the EU-27 average having peaked at 146 per cent in 2006).[1]

There were a number of key reasons for Ireland's economic growth over this period, including:

* Membership of the EU and access to the Single Market.
* Success in attracting foreign direct investment and major multinationals.
* A young, educated population of working age.
* Increased participation in the labour force, especially by females.
* Co-ordinated social partnership agreements.
* Public Finance stability.
* Reversal of trend of emigration to one of immigration.

Dublin's and indeed Ireland's economic growth from the 1990s up to 2007 had strong positive implications for employment growth. In Dublin the numbers in employment increased from 340,00 to 616,000 while employment in the state grew from 1.16 to 2.1 million in employment. The unemployment rate dropped from about 14-16 per cent in the 1990s to historically low levels, averaging 4.5 per cent in 2007.

The End of the Celtic Tiger, 2008 – Present

The Irish economy faces serious challenges which have been complicated by major banking and fiscal crises. The scale of this challenge is unprecedented, and has few international parallels. The Irish economy contracted for the third consecutive year in 2010, leaving real GDP and GNP around 12 per cent and 13

---

1   GDP is artificially inflated in the Irish context due to the large presence of multinationals that repatriate their profits abroad. GNP is a more accurate measure of Irish economic performance however international comparisons predominantly use GDP.

per cent respectively below 2007 levels. This compares to economic growth of between 6 and 8 per cent per annum between 1990 and 2006. Recent economic figures for 2011 show the national economy returning to growth, GNP grew 1.1 per cent during Q2, 2011 while GDP increased by 1.6 per cent during the same period.

Since 2007 Ireland has witnessed a major decline in its economic performance and a resulting contraction in the numbers in employment. This was largely linked to a collapse in the housing market and the construction sector. In 2008 output fell for the first time since 1983. House prices increased by over 400 per cent in the late 1990s up to 2007 and investment in housing as a percentage of GNP rose from around 6 per cent in 1996 to almost 15 per cent in 2006. The construction industry in Ireland, at its peak in 2006, represented 24 per cent of national GDP employing one in seven people. This compares to just 4.9 per cent of GDP in the US for the same year and less than 1 in 17 people in employment (SLMRU, 2011). A number of indicators relating to property and construction have displayed falls of over 90 per cent in activity since 2007 (including building commencements, planning permissions, housing completions). The construction boom resulted in an oversupply of residential units across the country.

Unemployment levels, the number on the live register and redundancies have hit record highs although the pace of decline in key unemployment indices has begun to moderate somewhat over the past year. Despite this, there is no doubt as to the continued scale of the problems in the labour market in Dublin. The city faces enormous challenges in relation to the record numbers of people who are now unemployed, underemployed or in precarious work situations. The risks and consequences of a sustained high rate of long term unemployment and forced emigration remain very real and urgent.

The numbers in employment in the Dublin Region have declined from about 620,000 to 525,000 in just 3 years (CSO, 2011). The national unemployment rate has tripled to 14 per cent from 4 per cent in 2007, with almost half of those unemployed for over a year. Unemployment in Dublin is currently 12.7 per cent (2011) and is back to levels not seen since the 1980s. A collapse in house prices by over 50 per cent from their peak in 2007 (CSO, 2011) has placed many households in negative equity. Over 7 per cent of all residential mortgages are currently in arrears of over 90 days.

The national government has established an agency called The National Asset Management Agency (NAMA) in response to the Irish financial crisis and the deflation of the Irish property bubble. NAMA's function is to acquire property development loans from Irish banks in return for Government bonds with the view to improving the availability of credit in the Irish economy. The original book value of these loans nationally is €77 billion. NAMA will be offering many of these properties/developments for auction in due course which will include hotels, development sites, offices, retail and residential housing units across the city. The economic difficulties caused by a collapse in the domestic economy and a banking system crisis coupled with the global downturn and credit crunch meant that Ireland was no longer able to finance its borrowing from the global markets.

This resulted in Ireland entering into an €85 billion joint EU/IMF financial support package in 2010.

Exports are expected to continue to drive economic activity over the medium-term although this will be very much dependent on international economic conditions. Ireland is now the second most globalized country in the world and is on course to being the most globalized country by 2012 (Ernst and Young, 2011). In 2008 Ireland accounted for just under 3 per cent of total global service exports and about 1 per cent of total global merchandise exports in 2008. This compares to a population which accounts for just 0.07 per cent of the global total. During 2010 exports reached the highest level ever with €161 billion of exports an increase of almost 7 per cent over 2009.

Regaining Competitiveness

Towards the end of the economic growth cycle (2000 onwards) Ireland and Dublin recorded a significant loss of international competitiveness. High levels of wage and price inflation combined resulted in a dramatic increase in the cost of living.

Ireland's economy has begun to regain competitiveness over the past two years, as wages have adjusted and costs have fallen. The latest competitiveness indicators for Ireland show a marked improvement in cost competitiveness over the past year. In particular, there has been a sustained depreciation in the real effective exchange rate helped by a weaker euro exchange rate and more importantly by weaker inflation in Ireland relative to our main trading partners.

The Irish economy continues to retain many underlying strengths, including a skilled labour force with one of the highest levels of formal education in the OECD, much improved physical infrastructure, a good regulatory environment for enterprises and an excellent reputation for ease of doing business.

In addition, certain aspects of the cost of living have decreased in recent years and months. In Dublin, house prices have dropped by over 40 per cent since their peak in 2006 (CSO, 2011). Residential rental prices have fallen by 20 per cent while office and retail rents have seen a decrease of over 50 per cent over the same period.

Employment Profile

The city has high levels of employment in knowledge intensive industries particularly in software, IT, financial and business services. It has an internationally recognized financial services centre (IFSC) directly employing over 32,700 people. The Dublin region dominates in the national context in the sectors of Financial, Insurance and Real Estate Activities, Information and Communication. Services (market and non market) dominate employment in the Dublin City Region, accounting for 86 per cent or over 4 in 5 persons employed.

The top three employment sectors in Dublin in 2010 were in Wholesale and Retail trade (15 per cent), Human Health and Social Work Activities (13 per cent) and Financial Services and Real Estate (10 per cent).

Research and Knowledge

Dublin is a city with a strong reputation for education and its University and Research Institutes have excellent reputations internationally. It is the knowledge hub of the state and an important location for international students attracting almost 60 per cent of the national total (14,361 of which 10,300 are full time). The tuition fees generated by these students were €146.5 million while the living costs add another €170 million per year. Dublin City Council is collaborating on strategies with Dublin's universities to grow the international education sector.

Dublin continues to perform strongly in knowledge intensive sectors and will continue to demand specialist skills. There currently exist skills shortages in a number of sectors. Occupations difficult to source include scientists, engineers in design, production, quality control and validation, water and waste treatment and energy; senior software engineers and developers; IT professionals with business acumen; industry specific sales and IT development in areas such as biopharma; healthcare professionals and sales; and financial professionals. Vacancies in these areas often arise in narrow specialist areas (National Skills Bulletin, 2011).

Nonetheless, there is broad recognition reflected in national and sub-national policy that Ireland, led by Dublin, is continuing to evolve toward a knowledge intensive economy.

Foreign Direct Investment

Foreign Direct Investment (FDI) supported by the state Industrial Development Authority (IDA) accounts for 140,000 jobs directly created by foreign companies operating in Ireland with an additional 100,000 jobs supporting these firms (IDA, 2010). Over half of FDI investment is centred on the Dublin Region. IDA-supported multinational companies make up:

- Thirty per cent of Gross Value Added in the Irish economy accounting for more than two-thirds of all exports, at €110 billion annually;
- Contribute nearly half of all corporate tax revenues; spend €7bn on payroll; and account for €19 billion in total spend in the Irish economy.
- IDA client companies spend nearly €1.2bn per annum on R,D&I, accounting for nearly three-quarters of all R,D&I spend in the country by business.

Ireland's low corporate tax rate (12.5 per cent) combined with an excellent reputation for its education system and wide skills base especially in high value manufacturing, global business services and R&D has ensured long term success in attracting and retaining Foreign Direct Investment.

Ireland has the youngest workforce in Europe, with 36 per cent of the population under 25 years of age (IDA, 2010). Investment in education and training from the 1970s onwards, the establishment of the IFSC and low corporation tax regime in the 1980s followed by a continued investment in research and development in particular in the areas of science and technology have contributed to Dublin's success in attracting FDI. There are real opportunities for Dublin to position itself as an early adopter of new technological trends such as cloud computing. The cloud computing industry has the capacity to create 8,600 jobs by 2014 and to generate €9.5 billion in Irish sales annually (Ireland's Competitiveness and Job Opportunity: Cloud computing Goodbody on behalf of Microsoft, 2011).

Dublin city is emerging as a major destination for internet businesses. The city has attracted the International and European headquarters of firms such as Google (with over 3,000 employees in Dublin), Zynga, Facebook, Microsoft, IBM, Amazon, LinkedIn, Big Fish Games, eBay, Gala Networks and PayPal, earning it the title as the up and coming 'Internet and Social Networking Capital of Europe'. Despite the economic downturn, Dublin continues to attract new project announcements and expansions. In 2010 these included companies such as AXA, Zurich, IBM, LinkedIn, SAP, WebRoot and Riot games. In September 2011, Twitter announced their intention to establish international headquarters in Dublin.

The draw of Dublin as an attractive destination for FDI investment in Ireland is clear. The 2007-2010 figures show that over 50 per cent of total national FDI investment is locating in the Dublin City Region (FT, FDI benchmark). In the national perspective the Dublin City Region accounts for 67 per cent of all software and IT projects and approximately 60 per cent of all financial and business services announcements.

Dublin's Performance in International Metrics

Dublin continues to be recognized as one of the most liveable cities in the world. In the Mercer 2010 ranking, Dublin was ranked in joint 26th position. Dublin's economy was ranked 91st in the world in terms of size of GDP by PwC in 2008 with a total GDP of about €61 billion (PricewaterhouseCoopers, 2009). Cambridge Econometrics ranked Dublin as the 6th highest GDP per capita among 67 European cities. In 2009, Dublin's GDP per capita dropped to eleventh highest among the same group of cities and remained high at €44,240.

Research published by Peter Taylor and the Globalization and World City Networks (GaWC) demonstrates Dublin's strong performance as a truly global city (alpha minus city classification) that is extremely connected in the global economy (in relation to advanced producer services). Dublin was ranked 4th in an international survey looking at the capacity of cities around the world to attract and benefit from international populations (BAK – Basel Economics, 2011). The British Council's OPENCities project compares 26 cities worldwide, looking at factors including diversity policies, quality of life and education.

During the period 1993-2007 a ranking of the top 150 global metros ranked Dublin's economic performance 6th. However the severity of the economic downturn in Ireland has seen Dublin drop to 144th position for the period 2007-2009. The city is currently placed 150th for 2010 (Global Metro Monitor and LSE Cities, 2010). A 2009 Eurobarometer perception survey on quality of life in over 70 European cities demonstrates the startling change in the employment situation in Dublin in the last number of years. In the 2006 survey Dublin was ranked the top city in the EU for '*ease of finding a job*'. In the most recent survey in 2009 Dublin was placed in the bottom tier of cities on the same indicator. Furthermore, during the last quarter of 2009, some 61 per cent of people in Ireland surveyed cited 'Unemployment' as the most important issue facing the country.

Tourism

From the late 1990s to 2008 Dublin saw a surge in growth in tourism numbers, in particular for those visiting for a short stay city break. However 2009 and 2010 have seen a major decline in the numbers (down over 12 per cent) reflecting the impact of the global recession.

There were almost 3.9 million international visitors to Dublin in 2009 and according to Euromonitor International's Top City Destination it was the 19th most popular international city destination in 2008. The European Cities Marketing Benchmarking Report placed Dublin the 9th most popular city in Europe in terms of bed nights in 2007. Dublin was not placed in the top 15 cities in 2010.

International Connectivity

Dublin was ranked the 16th most connected city in Europe by York Aviation in 2009. In 2010, Dublin airport served 177 routes with 63 airlines and handled over 18.4 million passengers, which was a 10 per cent decrease in passengers on the previous year. The airport is ranked 10th busiest in Europe and 17th in the world. A new €600 million terminal at Dublin airport opened in 2010 capable of handling 15 million passengers.

Developments and Policy Changes since Early 1990s

Background to Dublin from the 1990s

Ireland and Dublin experienced difficult economic times in the 1980s when unemployment in Ireland stood at 17 per cent in 1986 while emigration peaked in 1989 (e.g. Redmond et al., 2007). The inner city was in decline, suffering from high levels of unemployment, and widespread drug problems. The reorientation of the national economy towards knowledge (in particular information technology, biotechnology and financial services) in the 1990s proved successful in lowering unemployment rates, increasing economic growth levels by an average of 8 per cent per year between 1995 and 2002. Investment in education and the creation of an attractive financial environment sowed the seeds for this success. The publication of the 'Technology Foresight Ireland' document in 1999 identified knowledge as a key driver of growth (ICSTI Ireland, 1999). This report helped shape subsequent National Development Plans (2000-2006 and 2007-2013) which invested heavily in research and technology. The Technology Foresight document facilitated the development of specific clusters, which would be based on the development of strong links between the third level colleges and industry, agriculture and the financial services sectors.

Ireland's R&D expenditure trebled in the decade to 2008 to €2.6bn and approximately 1.66 per cent of GNP; Business Expenditure on Research and Development (BERD) doubled to an estimated €1.68bn; Higher Education Research and Development (HERD) spending quadrupled and was reflected in the numbers of research articles produced (Department of the Taoiseach, 2010).

In 1987 against a backdrop of spiralling unemployment, mass emigration and large national debt a tripartite agreement between the social partners – Government, trade unions and employers – was reached. The *Programme for National Recovery 1987-1990* was the first social partnership agreement and focused on wage moderation in exchange for lower levels of income tax and policies to stimulate employment. Since then there have been seven further agreements and negotiations on wider matters of social policy have involved further representative groups including farmers, environmental organizations and the community and voluntary sector. Although a matter for debate, social partnership has been widely credited with contributing to Ireland's economic growth during the Celtic Tiger period.

Urban Regeneration Programmes in the City

Regeneration of the city core was a key policy initiative of the 1990s. Dublin's inner city experienced a sustained period of decay during the 1970s and 1980s with a major outflow of population and a suburbanization of the wider region. The late 1980s and 1990s saw a sustained effort to regenerate the city centre and improve the economic vitality of the city centre. The national government introduced many incentives to encourage market led development in inner city Dublin through rate rebates, capital allowances and income tax relief. There were a number of areas designated as urban renewal areas in Dublin. This increase reflects the high level of apartment building in the inner city from the late 1980s onwards, due in large part to tax and other fiscal incentives. Between 1991 and 2011 the population of the inner city increased by over 62 per cent.

Although the city has experienced unprecedented levels of economic growth, problems of social inequality and exclusion still prevail. The city is characterized by pockets of social housing which remain poorly integrated and which experience high levels of deprivation. Since the early 1990s, Dublin's inner city has changed from being an area of widespread poverty to one of a close-knit patchwork of considerable affluence and disadvantage at the micro level. One of the lasting legacies of the Celtic Tiger period is an urban sprawl that extends out beyond the traditional city boundaries.

Docklands and the IFSC

The Custom House Docks with the International Financial Services Centre (IFSC) was the major flagship scheme of urban renewal in Dublin in the 1980s. This previously derelict docklands site was the object of a major integrated development comprising business, residential and recreational functions. The creation of a new IFSC was added to this objective and a single purpose development agency established, with effective planning functions for the area under its administration.

Ireland's International Financial Services Centre was established in 1987 with the creation of the IFSC tax incentive zone. Companies locating in this zone benefited from a 10 per cent corporation tax regime which continued up until the end of 2005. From 2006 all companies operating in the international financial services sector pay corporation tax at the prevailing rate of 12.5 per cent. Ireland's tax regime has played a key role in the continuing success of the IFSC. The IFSC located in the centre of the city incorporates office accommodation, educational institutions, executive housing, restaurants and shopping facilities.

The Dublin Docklands Authority led the regeneration and development of the area. The area has also benefited from a light rail LUAS extension, the Samuel Beckett Bridge, a National Convention Centre, the Grand Canal Theatre and the O² (Dublin's largest live music venue).

An Economic Success Story: The IFSC

The International Financial Services Centre (IFSC) is one of the major economic success stories of Dublin and Ireland. It is located in the docklands area of Dublin and contributed 7.4 per cent to the Irish GDP in 2009. There were over 32,700 employed by over 500 companies with two thirds or 22,000 of these jobs located in Dublin (Accenture, 2010). The IFSC was ranked the 13th leading Financial Centre in the world in The Banker magazine 'International Financial Centre's Rankings' in 2009. Despite the economic downturn and problems in the domestic financial sectors, employment in the IFSC has remained steady over the past three years. The main activities of the IFSC include asset financing, banking, captive insurance and reinsurance, corporate treasury, fund administration and management, life insurance and securities trading.

Temple Bar, Cultural Quarter

The 1990s witnessed the renewal of Temple Bar as a newly rejuvenated cultural, artistic and entertainment quarter. Enhanced financial incentives existed in this area for refurbishment and considerable amounts of public finances were committed to developments under the programmes. This area also possessed a single purpose development agency, Temple Bar Renewal Ltd that controlled spending of public funds and had the responsibility of maintaining a functional mix and promotion of desired activities in accordance with the prepared plan for the area. For the general designated areas the local planning authority retained planning control over all renewal schemes and often provided land for development purposes. In these areas, development by normally private interests was required to comply with controls as established in the existing development plan. The early success of urban regeneration initiatives encouraged their duplication and prolongation and played a role in the overstimulation of the real estate market resulting in oversupply and property market collapse.

The Digital Hub, Knowledge Quarter

The Digital Hub involved the development of a 'knowledge location' close to the centre of the city with the aim of developing it as a world class cluster of digital media companies. It is located in an area of the city which was in need of economic and social regeneration. The hub offers incubation space for start ups in digital media and serves as a flagship for the entire digital media industry in Ireland. Around 1,000 people are currently employed in the Hub with 84 companies and 79 per cent SME composition. One of the catalysts for the development of the digital hub was the establishment of MIT's media lab Europe. A separate state body called the Digital Hub Development Agency (DHDA) was established to deliver the Digital Hub concept in 2000.

This project has had its difficulties from its establishment in 2000 with the dot com bust and in 2005 the closure of the Media Lab Europe. A major redevelopment phase of the Digital Hub was initiated from 2005 with the establishment of a public private partnership to develop the lands owned by the DHDA. This proposal of a high rise mixed use development of over 1 million square feet incorporating enterprise, retail, residential, community and learning space fell through due to the recent collapse in the property sector.

Nevertheless the digital hub while not achieving its full ambition has come a long way since its inception. It was a particularly challenging ambition to mix the redevelopment and regeneration ambition with its core function to grow and develop the digital media sector in Dublin and Ireland. Despite its criticisms it has grown into a dynamic enterprise zone. However in order to reach its full potential the main stakeholders are currently rethinking its future direction.

Ballymun Regeneration

Ballymun was a response in the 1960s/1970s to the Dublin housing problem. The development consisted of 2,814 flats in seven 15-storey tower blocks, nineteen 8-storey spine blocks, and ten 4-storey walk-up blocks as well as 1,987 standard housing units. The area has since been characterized by low levels of social infrastructure and economic activity. One of the largest regeneration projects in the city, Ballymun Regeneration, was set up in 1997 to plan and implement a regeneration programme to develop a new town and facilities for the 30,000 people who will live there. Ballymun Regeneration Limited is responsible for developing and implementing the Masterplan for the physical, economic and social regeneration of Ballymun. There are two clear phases of development – 347 units prior across 7 hectares to 2014 and 2613 units to be accommodated across 23 hectares at a future date.

Grangegorman

Another major development in Grangegorman has the potential to transform the north inner city. This comprises over 30 hectares of land just over 1 km from the city centre. This development will place innovation at the heart of the city-region with the development of a vibrant city quarter and urban campus with education, accessibility, diversity and community services at its core. This centralized campus will bring the faculties of Dublin Institute of Technology into one location (20,000 students are currently located at 39 sites across the city). The Grangegorman planning scheme was approved by the City Council in July 2011, while the Masterplan project has won the Chicago Athenaeum 2010 American Architecture Award.

State of the City

Spatial and Planning Policy

One of the consequences of the rapid economic boom and speed of population growth was a proliferation of unplanned development of housing, offices and industrial space across the greater Dublin region. The lack of co-ordinated planning has resulted in many new communities having limited access to adequate social infrastructure. Increasing commuting times and congestion were serious problems towards the end of the Celtic Tiger period. The national government introduced the National Spatial Strategy (NSS) 2002-2020 to address the dominance of development in the Dublin urban region. The NSS has been the subject of much controversy with some arguing that it damages the international competitiveness of the Dublin City Region. The NSS identified eight gateways and nine medium sized hubs spread across the country. Despite the ambition of the National Spatial Strategy, Dublin has continued to grow and dominate in the national context.

Planning in Ireland is carried out using a tiered system as described from National Spatial Strategy to Local Area Plan. Nonetheless, a State centric approach to economic development has largely underpinned development frameworks. The National Spatial Strategy (NSS) is the current national planning framework. The NSS is linked to the investment priorities of the National Development Plan.

The lifetime of the current NSS extends to 2020. The next tier of planning is the Regional Planning Guidelines. The RPGs inform and direct City and County Development Plans. The RPGs which impact on the Dublin city region cover a wider area known as the Greater Dublin Area (GDA). The GDA is comprised of the two NUTS III Regions of Dublin and the Mid-East.

The metropolitan area represents a largely continuous urban fabric in terms of built up land extending from the core Dublin city centre area outwards. The NSS defines the metropolitan area as the physical area of Dublin city and suburbs and directs policy towards consolidation of this area. While the Regional Planning Guidelines have been in place since 2004, in 2010, to ensure that city and county development plans are consistent with the policies and recommendations of the RPGs for the GDA, local authorities must prepare evidenced based "Core Strategies." These core strategies are designed to consider all parts of planning and economic development including the quantum, distribution and phasing of proposed development.

Reform of Planning and Development

Past planning and development practice were a contributory factor in the unsustainable development market which subsequently collapsed. High levels of speculative activities, often linked to questionable zoning and planning decisions, contributed to a property market collapse necessitating a subsequent rescue of the Irish owned and managed banking sector and property market at a major cost to the Irish taxpayer which threatens the financial future of the state. Discussion on the rescue plan has forced policymakers to reconsider the planning and development system which played a major part in current market failures. Reform of the planning and development system has commenced with proposals developed in the Planning and Development legislation of 2010 – including core strategies to ensure compliance with strategic level policy direction.

Progress in Infrastructure

Dublin and Ireland have benefited from significant investment in infrastructure during the sustained period of economic growth. The National Development Plan formed the blueprint for infrastructure and national development over 5 year periods. The national road infrastructure saw the most significant investment over the period.

While major progress was made during the economic boom years (catching up from an extremely low base) there will be a continuing challenge to maintain investment in critical infrastructure in the city. For example, in Dublin City Council there has been a 50 per cent cut in its capital budget for 2011-2104 from 2 to just over €1 billion. The National Development Plan (2007-13), now discontinued, will have missed many of its ambitious targets for infrastructure investment over the period. One of the most ambitious transport infrastructure programmes in the history of the state, Transport 21 has effectively been discontinued with only a small selection of projects proceeding. Dublin was to receive €14 billion under this plan. The critical areas that require infrastructure investment include: Public Transport, Communications infrastructure (broadband), Energy, Waste and Water.

Impact of EU Policies and Funding

Since joining the EU in 1973, Ireland received approximately €17bn in EU Structural and Cohesion Funds (to the end of 2003 when Ireland no longer qualified for Cohesion Funding due to improved economic circumstances). During the period 1993 to 2003, the Cohesion Fund invested some €2bn in more than 120 infrastructure projects in Ireland.

Many significant projects in Dublin were supported by the Cohesion Fund up to 2003: 12 water supply projects were supported and 31 waste water treatment projects carried out nationally. In Dublin this included the Dublin Bay Project (Ringsend Wastewater Treatment Works); Roll On/Roll Off Berths at Dublin Port; the M50 (Dublin Ring Road), M1 (Dublin-Belfast) and improvements on the N4 (Dublin-Sligo), N7 (Dublin-Limerick) and N11 (Dublin-Rosslare).

The Dublin Region and Ireland have been very active in accessing European funding – ERDF and ESF. The Dublin Region (part of the South and Eastern Region) has moved from a convergence to competitiveness region. The Europe 2020 agenda priorities are very much aligned with the national and regional policies in Ireland in the areas of research and development, innovation and sustainability. For example, while with regard to the FP7 mechanism, among the EU-27, Ireland ranks 8th in terms of applicant success rate and 10th in terms of EC financial contribution (European Union, 2011).

Governance and Role of the City in Economic Development

Despite Dublin's dominance in terms of its economy and population it is a city largely governed by national rather than local/regional stakeholders. The Irish state is highly centralized with national agencies being responsible for key areas of service delivery. Many of these national agencies will retain more than a passing interest in the affairs of the city and its governance as Dublin is the seat of national government. National stakeholders will be involved in the governance of the city region in a way that will not happen in other cities.

Dublin does not have a directly elected mayor and locally elected public representatives in Ireland play a much less significant role in the policy formulation and decision-making processes than their European or American counterparts. The ability of citizens to influence both the policy formulation and decision-making processes beyond casting their ballot is very narrow. The majority of decisions made by the local government tend to lie in the domain of the manager of the local authority (in the case of Dublin city this is the Dublin City Manager, John Tierney).

Local government in Ireland is not involved, to any significant degree, in the delivery of services such as Policing, Health, Education, Public Transport or Social Welfare. The main areas of responsibility for local government are Housing and building, Road Transportation and Safety, Water Supply and Wastewater Treatment, Planning and Development, Environmental Protection, Recreation and Amenity. This lack of local level autonomy and established weak horizontal and vertical linkages between the multitude of existing local and regional boards and agencies (health, education, transport, planning, policing, enterprise, local authorities) will continue to undermine the effectiveness of the delivery of services in a streamlined and cost-effective manner.

The City supports national economic development policies through its planning and development remit and its management of key infrastructure areas such as water, waste, roads and traffic and major urban regeneration projects. The lead agencies in economic delivery in Ireland are the IDA (Industrial Development Agency), Enterprise Ireland (focusing on export led enterprise and high growth potential), the City and County Enterprise Boards (small scale enterprise, entrepreneurs), FÁS (training and skills) and Forfás (policy advisory board for enterprise and science).

The economic downturn has resulted in a radical rethink of the medium/long term priorities of Ireland and Dublin. Since the downturn there has been a number of national policy documents focusing on the smart economy, innovation and Irelands international linkages/relationships. There is an increasing emphasis on developing Ireland's export potential now that the domestic economy is flat.

The middle and long term priorities for the city have certainly shifted to increased collaboration and a greater economic development role for local government. There has been an increased recognition of the need for Dublin to develop stronger leadership and coordination in the absence of a directly elected mayor and strong regional governance structures. There is a move towards maximizing existing assets in the city and increasing collaboration with the extensive FDI clusters (leader firms) in the city region.

Policymakers have recognized the opportunities and potential of sustainability as a key driver of economic growth, in particular identifying the economic opportunities of sustainability. For example, projects such as the 'The Green Way' are being developed as a collaborative venture involving industry, academic institutions and public/semi-state players in the North Dublin region.

Creative Dublin Alliance

The overarching framework for enhanced regional collaboration falls under the remit of the Creative Dublin Alliance established in 2007. The Creative Dublin Alliance aims to build a network of diverse urban leaders that gather to identify, discuss and distribute solutions in response to the challenges that Dublin faces. The City Council has the responsibility for the management and objectives while members are responsible for collaborating, bringing their expertise to projects and distributing the projects across the alliance. The alliance was developed in the absence of formal governance structures in the city region. This triple helix alliance is a clear demonstration of the willingness of local government to engage with both academia and industry in the pursuit of common policy objectives and stronger lobbying for the Dublin region. A number of strategic projects have been identified by the Creative Dublin Alliance and are currently being delivered. These include:

Innovation Dublin Festival   The city is increasingly recognizing the importance of supporting, nurturing and showcasing innovation and talent in the city. A major annual festival brings together the public, private, academic and not for profit sectors to exhibit innovative projects and solutions that are being developed in Dublin. The first Innovation Dublin was held over seven days in October 2009, and 12 days in November 2010. Innovation Dublin 2010 had an international focus with IBM global final of SmartCamp and the Globe Forum international conference on innovation and sustainable development both hosted in the Dublin Convention Centre. In 2011, Innovation Dublin will move into its third year. The initiative has become a platform for seminars, workshops, discussions, exhibitions, performances, showcases and competitions related to innovation and creativity. The overriding aim of the festival is to provide Dubliners – entrepreneurs, students, researchers, artists and small and large corporations – with an opportunity to discuss, promote and celebrate innovation in the city.

City Identity Project   To create an identity for Dublin that is defined by an authentic, relevant and distinctive vision for the city and that is supported, reinforced and enriched by all communication between Dublin's stakeholders locally, nationally and globally.

Economic Action Plan   The Economic Action Plan sets out the key priorities for the development of Dublin as an internationally competitive city region. Its aim is to: 'position the Dublin City Region, the engine of Ireland's economy, as a significant hub in the European knowledge economy through a network of thriving sectoral and spatial clusters providing a magnet for creative talent and investment'. This was the first attempt to bring together the myriad of organizations that operate across the Dublin region to focus their attention on a co-ordinated economic action plan for the Dublin Region.

The Dublin City Indicators Project   The Dublin City Indicators project is a key benchmarking exercise that enhances the evidence base of city performance. It allows for the continued monitoring of Dublin's performance in the national and international context. The project provides for peer learning and collaboration and will allow the city authorities to gauge the position and progress of Dublin in terms of its innovation, liveability and attractiveness as an investment location.

Dublinked   is a Dublin Regional initiative to develop a networked community of researchers and innovators across the corporate, academic and public sectors, created by Dublin City Council and the National University of Ireland, Maynooth. IBM is a key participant in Data Dublin. It aims to establish an open data portal creating an innovation framework to support smart city research and develop solutions to the city's challenges. The main areas of focus are currently in public lighting, digital money, water, energy and transport.

The TCD/UCD Innovation Alliance   This is a primary example of cooperation across the city region's universities and academic institutions. The Innovation Alliance is a Trinity College and University College Dublin partnership working with the education sector, the State and its agencies alongside the business and venture capital communities to develop a world-class ecosystem for innovation that will drive enterprise development in Ireland.

The Green Way   is being developed as a collaborative venture involving industry, academic institutions and public/semi-state players in the North Dublin region. The vision of the Green Way is to create jobs and trade opportunities by activating and developing an internationally recognized Cleantech cluster which will support existing green economy companies in the region, foster and accelerate green economy start-ups and facilitate multinational corporations capable of bringing green economy jobs and investment to the region. The founding partners of the Green Way include Dublin Airport Authority, Fingal County Council, Dublin City Council, Ballymun Regeneration Ltd, Dublin City University, Dublin Institute of Technology and North Dublin Chamber of Commerce. The cleantech cluster is already home to many large cleantech/ICT companies such as IBM who have developed their first European "Smarter Cities Technology Centre" in North Dublin. Other MNCs with significant cleantech divisions within the cluster area include Wyeth, Siemens, Intel and Hewlett Packard. Some of the key domestic companies include NTR, Glen Dimplex, OpenHydro, Solarprint and Ecocem.

The Green Way is focussed on leveraging the existing ICT base of major companies and R&D centres in the region to develop the cluster as a centre of excellence for green data centres, cloud computing capabilities, sensor and monitoring technologies and smart grid applications. The cluster is also focussed on leveraging the involvement of Ireland's two largest local authorities (Dublin City and Fingal County), the Dublin Institute of Technology and Dublin City University and a major International Airport campus (Dublin Airport Authority) to develop the region as an attractive 'deployment platform' for Smart City and cleantech applications in relation to the management of waste, water, transport, energy and data assets.

Already there are many pilot projects under development such as Dublin City University Cleantech Innovation campus and the DIT Dublin Energy Lab. The Dublin Airport Authority (DAA) are regenerating the airport zone as a hub for Cleantech Foreign Direct Investment and have also launched Dublin Terminal 2 which will assist in connecting to emerging Cleantech centres in Europe, China, India and the US.

The Global Green Interchange project (GGI) is a two year project to coordinate, facilitate and accelerate the positioning of Dublin as a world-class centre for green finance and enterprise and will act as a catalyst for sustainable innovation alongside the Green Way.

Establishment of a Research Observatory   Under the direction of the Creative Dublin Alliance (see above) The Office of International Relations and Research at Dublin City Council has established a 'Research Observatory' which brings together the main researchers from within the major multinational enterprises, local government and academic institutions for the purposes of driving a research agenda across the city region.

Positioning Dublin as an Open City – Pursuing an Internationalization Agenda

The city has recognized the importance of internationalization to the national and regional economy and established an Office of International Relations and Research. This unit is central in positioning Dublin as an Open City and is engaging with all stakeholders in the development of a framework to agree a set of actions that will enhance Dublin's position as an open and internationalized city. The agenda is based on the three pillars of internationalization – innovation, inclusion and integration which are in turn underpinned by strong regional leadership and governance.

Some examples of actions under the openness agenda include Dublin's participation in international networks, city twinning agreements (Beijing, San Jose), international festivals (Chinese New Year, Russian Festival), city accreditations (UNESCO City of Literature, Design Capital (Pivot Dublin), Citizen Engagement initiatives such as Your Dublin Your Voice, City of a thousand Welcomes, One People One Voice.

References

BAK Basel Economics (2011), Open Cities monitor. [Online]. Available at http://opencities.britishcouncil.org/web/index.php?monitor_en. [accessed: 2011].

CSO (2011) [Online]. Available at http://www.cso.ie/en/. [accessed: 2011].

Department of the Taoiseach (2010). *The Report of the Taskforce on Innovation*, March 2010. [Online]. Available at http://www.forfas.ie/media/Report_of_the_Innovation_Taskforce_Summary.pdf [accessed: 2012].

Ernst and Young (2011). *Globalization Survey 2011*. [Online]. Available at http://www.ey.com/Publication/vwLUAssets/The_world_is_bumpy/$FILE/ Growing_Beyond-The_world_is_bumpy-new_strategies_for_growth.pdf [accessed: 2012].

European Union (2011). *Innovation Competitiveness Union Report*. [Online]. Available at http://ec.europa.eu/research/innovation-union/pdf/ competitiveness report/2011/executive_summary.pdf [accessed: 2012].

EUROSTAT (2011), *Population Projections 2010-2060*. [Online]. Available at http://europa.eu/rapid/press-release_STAT-11-80_en.htm [accessed: 2011].

ICSTI Ireland – Irish Council for Science, Technology and Innovation (1999). *Technology Foresight Ireland – An ICSTI Overview*. [Online]. Available at http://www.forfas.ie/publication/search.jsp?ft=/publications/1999/ [accessed: 2012].

IDA – Investment Agency Ireland (2010). *IDA horizon 2020 strategy*. [Online]. Available at http://www.idaireland.com/news-media/publications/library-publications/ida-ireland-publications/IDA-Ireland-Strategy-2020.pdf [accessed: 2012].

Global Metro Monitor and LSE Cities (2010). *Global Metro Monitor: the path to economic recovery*. Metropolitan Policy Programme, London: The Brookings Institution.

PricewaterhouseCoopers (2009). *Global City GDP Rankings (2008 – 2025)*. [Online]. Available at http://www.ukmediacentre.pwc.com/Media-Library/ Global-city-GDP-rankings-2008-2025-61a.aspx [accessed: 2011].

Redmond, D., Crossa, V., Moore, N. and Williams, B. (2007). *Dublin as Emergent Global Gateway: Pathways to creative and knowledge-based regions*. Amsterdam: Amsterdam institute for Metropolitan and International Development Studies.

SLMRU – Skills and Labour Market Research Unit (2010), *National Skills Bulletin, July 2010*. [Online]. Available at http://www.fas.ie/NR/rdonlyres/9ABC5EE1-CF20-4AA5-ACA4-C5B81DD9FE5E/1087/EGFSNnational_skills_ bulletin_2016.pdf. [accessed: 2012].

Chapter 8

Helsinki

Eero Holstila, Anja Vallittu, Sanna Ranto, Tanja Lahti
and Asta Manninen[1]

City Profile

Helsinki was founded in 1550 and has been the capital of Finland since 1812. The city has about 0.6 million inhabitants and is the centre of economic and cultural life and administration in the country. The dynamics of the city is based on a growing population, a high standard of living and welfare services, functional urban infrastructure and innovative industries. The City of Helsinki is also the centre of knowledge and research in Finland. The proportion of inhabitants with tertiary education is one of the highest in European cities and even globally. The City of Helsinki is also a science and student city with several universities and applied science institutions. Helsinki was appointed the World Design Capital for 2012.

The Helsinki Metropolitan Area is composed of four municipalities: Helsinki, Espoo, Vantaa and Kauniainen. This area is the core of a larger functional urban region: the Helsinki Region which is composed of 14 municipalities and has 1.3 million inhabitants altogether. The development of the Helsinki Region is stimulated by its close connections to other metropolises. Geographically, the nearest of these are St Petersburg in the east, Tallinn in the south and Stockholm in the west. The Baltic Sea also connects the Helsinki Region to many other Northern European metropolitan regions. The Helsinki Region is an international traffic junction and a gateway to culture and tourism in other parts of Finland.

Demography

The population of Helsinki is 588,549 (1 January 2011) and it is the most populous municipality in Finland. The population has been growing and during recent years the growth has clearly been based on migrants from abroad (Urban Facts, 2011).

In the history of the City of Helsinki, 1990 was the first year during the Finnish independence that the number of people immigrating to Helsinki exceeded the number of people moving abroad. Foreign population has increased rapidly in Helsinki in the 2000s. Nowadays one in ten people in Helsinki are

1 The authors thank Marko Karvinen and Sini Askelo for their contributions to this chapter.

non official language speaker, born abroad or hold a foreign citizenship. There are citizens of approximately 165 countries and native speakers of 150 different languages among Helsinki's immigrant population (City of Helsinki, 2009). The population of the Helsinki region is also growing: in the 2000s, the rate has been around one per cent annually. Nativity is 1.8 times as high as mortality in the Helsinki Region. The annual birth rate is 12 per 1000 inhabitants. Net migration is positive for the Helsinki Region, and it accounts for half of the region's population growth. By 2030, the population of the Helsinki Region is forecasted to grow by 18 per cent. The fact that large age groups are reaching the age of retirement is going to almost double the number of 65 year olds or older in the next 20 years. On the other hand, the number of children is expected to grow, too: below 15 year olds by 17 per cent by 2030, and those of working age are expected to increase as well. In 2011, the demographic dependency ratio was 0.40. The demographic dependency ratio is expected to reach 0.54 by 2030 primarily owing to the growing number of old age people (Urban Facts, 2011).

The Helsinki Region is characterised by its highly educated population, high standard of living, diverse services and highly specialised economy. As high a proportion as 44 per cent of Helsinki Region population aged 25-64 has completed a degree at tertiary level. The population of the Helsinki Region has a higher percentage of children and youth as well as working age population compared to the rest of Finland. Consequently, the Helsinki Region has a lower percentage of pensioners than has the rest of Finland.

The population of the region is growing: in the 2000s, the rate has been around one per cent annually. Nativity is 1.8 times as high as mortality in the Helsinki Region. The annual birth rate is 12 per 1000 inhabitants. Net migration is positive for the Helsinki Region, and it accounts for half of the region's population growth. By 2030, the population of the Helsinki Region is forecasted to grow by 18 per cent. The fact that large age groups are reaching the age of retirement is going to almost double the number of 65 year olds or older in the next 20 years. On the other hand, the number of children is expected to grow, too: below 15 year olds by 17 per cent by 2030, and those of working age are expected to increase as well. In 2011, the demographic dependency ratio was 0.40. The demographic dependency ratio is expected to reach 0.54 by 2030 primarily owing to the growing number of old age people (Urban Facts, 2011).

Socio-spatial differences have stayed relatively small in the Helsinki Region. The main factor behind this development is housing production, which has applied the policy and guidelines of building both owner-occupied and social rented housing in the same neighbourhoods. The so-called positive discrimination is another tool used in Helsinki to curb socio-spatial differentiation: neighbourhoods that score low in social ratings are granted more money for day care centres and schools and for the support of social well-being. Such areas are mainly located in eastern Helsinki.

Economy

One-quarter of Finland's population live in the Helsinki Region, while more than one-third of the total output is generated in the region. Gross domestic product (GDP) per capita was €48,675 in Helsinki region in 2008, which was 1.6 times the average of the EU27. Gross value added (GVA) per capita was €42 950 in 2008. Of 15-64 year olds in the Helsinki Region, 78 per cent belonged to the labour force in 2010. The rate of employment was 73 per cent and the rate of unemployment was 6.3 per cent (Urban Facts, 2011).

The service sector employs 81 per cent of Helsinki's workforce. There are 738,000 jobs in the Helsinki Region. The largest industry in terms of jobs is wholesale and retail trade. Knowledge-intensive services are typical of Helsinki where one inhabitant in ten works in the field of professional, scientific or technical activities. Almost half of all Finnish workers in this sector live in the Helsinki Region. From a nationwide perspective, Helsinki specialises particularly in the production and distribution of knowledge, arts and culture, in finance, scientific research, wholesale trade and air transport (Urban Facts, 2011).

The Helsinki Region accounts for more than 40 per cent of the investments in research and development done in Finland. The level of investments in research and development is quite high in Helsinki – 4.5 per cent of the gross domestic product (2009). The corresponding figure in Finland is 3.7 per cent (Urban Facts, 2011).

Helsinki is one of the cities which have grown noticeably faster than the average of western metropolises. Employment increased by 37 per cent (1.1 per cent per annum) and output by 189 per cent (3.7 per cent per annum) from 1980 to 2009. The annual growth rate of employment was 0.5 per cent points and of output 1.7 per cent points higher in Helsinki than in the western European countries (Laakso and Kostiainen, 2011).

The trend of employment has been significantly more varying in Helsinki than the average trend in the western European countries and metropolises. Helsinki was severely affected by the economic crisis of the first half of the 1990s. In addition, both the trough of the ICT sector in 2002-2003 and the latest recession, in 2009, hit Helsinki harder than they did the western European countries as a whole. By the same token, however, growth during the 1980s and after the crisis of 1990s was very rapid.

Finnish exports fell dramatically in 2009 and this affected Helsinki, too. However, Helsinki specialises, to a large extent, in services for business and households, both of which were affected less than manufacturing and construction. Consequently, the effects of the recession on employment were not as dramatic as they were on output: employment declined less than 2 per cent, while the corresponding drop in output was 8 per cent, in 2009. Production stopped declining in the Helsinki Region in autumn 2009, but economy picked up slowly. Despite a recent recession, production was 6 per cent higher in 2009 than it had been in 2005 in the Helsinki Region and 3 per cent higher in Finland as a whole. Since early 2010, the volume of production in the Helsinki Region has been growing (Urban Facts, 2011).

Accessibility

The accessibility of Helsinki has been considerably improved thanks to good flight connections to Asia. Good flight connections to Asia also established good flight connections within Europe. The Helsinki-Vantaa Airport has also undergone considerable renewal work and got increased capacity. Drawing on these improved assets, the City of Vantaa has developed their concept of Aviapolis, which has brought new jobs in the area.

Also the train connections are excellent from Helsinki to all major towns in Finland and to St Petersburg and Moscow, too. By Allegro train it takes only 3.5 hours from Helsinki to St Petersburg. In addition Helsinki and Tallinn are researching possibilities to create a permanent rail connection from Helsinki to Tallinn and to the rest of continental Europe by Rail Baltica in the future. Helsinki has also good shipping connections to the other Baltic Sea cities.

Public Administration

Finland has a political system with local governments and the state as the two governmental layers with elected representatives. Municipalities operate with a high degree of autonomy; local self-government is anchored in the society. Municipalities have the right to levy various taxes (and have the power to set the rates), including tax on income and corporate tax. They also have planning autonomy, implying a high degree of freedom in decisions concerning the locations of housing and business. Municipalities can perform the functions laid down for them by law either alone or in cooperation with other local authorities. They may also utilize other service providers.

In return, municipalities are responsible for the deliverance of many community services, like education, health care, social welfare, culture, environmental and technical infrastructure, and water supply. However, highway maintenance, legislation and police forces fall under the responsibility of the central government. Municipalities are governed by elected councils that answer to the voters only. Total expenditures of local governments mount up to 30 per cent of all public spending in Finland.

Developments and Policy Changes since Early 1990s

Focus on Internationalization

In the early 1990s, Finland went through a very deep economic recession that caused a rapid rise in unemployment in Helsinki. Finland was just joining the European Union, and yet the future looked very uncertain. The Helsinki City Council was aware major changes had to be made. It was acknowledged that Helsinki's position as a capital was not enough: Helsinki must be able to create an international profile and become the motor of the Finnish economy. In 1994 the City Council approved an internationalization strategy, which implied a turning point in the city's development policy. A crucial priority of the programme was to consolidate Helsinki's position as a hub of knowledge, science and innovation. The city started intensifying its cooperation with the local universities, above all the University of Helsinki. A common development company for the region, Culminatum Ltd, was established to promote the science-into-business philosophy. The shareholders of the company were from the very beginning the City of Helsinki and its neighbouring municipalities, the Uusimaa Regional Council, the Chamber of Commerce, the local science parks and all the universities and polytechnics of the region.

Since its foundation in 1995, Culminatum Ltd (today Culminatum Innovation) has been doing preparatory work for development projects that involve key actors in the Helsinki Region, and worked on bringing resources together. Two important functions of Culminatum Innovations Ltd are to develop knowledge-intensive corporate clusters in the framework of national programmes for centres of expertise and to develop Helsinki's metropolitan region as a world-class innovation ecosystem.

The 1994 strategy defined arts and culture as the driving force of the city. During the great recession, cultural expenditure was usually trimmed, but Helsinki decided to invest in culture instead and opt for the status of European Cultural Capital in 2000. A process that inspired large social circles began, and culminated in the 2000 Cultural Capital Year. The year left an awareness of the power of arts and culture also as a motor for innovation and economic development. At the same time, expertise in arts and culture management accumulated in the city, a fact which is shown by, for example, Helsinki's position as the World Design Capital in 2012.

The strategy programme also emphasised various measures designed to make Helsinki more international. The city administration ran a massive programme of international affairs education among the leadership of offices and departments. Helsinki joined the EUROCITIES organization in 1995 and was an active member of it onwards. The goal was to be given presidency in the organization, and this was achieved in 2000 when Mayor Eva-Riitta Siitonen began her two-year period as the president of the EUROCITIES organization.

Helsinki city has also the International Relations division, which co-ordinates the City's international affairs, supervises international city policies, and organizes hospitality. In addition to the staff in Helsinki, the International Relations division includes the Helsinki EU Office in Brussels, and the division directs the Helsinki Centre in St Petersburg.

Arts and Culture from the Early 1990s until Today

Helsinki is home to national shrines in arts and culture, including the national art and historical museums, theatre and opera stages and orchestras. In addition, the City of Helsinki has similar institutions of its own – except for an opera. These institutions have large audiences and usually received state grants – and often economic support from the city, too. The City of Helsinki has eight cultural centres scattered over the town. These centres have a wide array of functions, and part of them are specialised in fields such as children's culture or internationalism. The clients of the cultural amenities in Helsinki come from Helsinki Region and the rest of Finland – and even abroad.

The cultural sector in Helsinki is large, varied, dynamic and adaptive. It is well described by the following examples: annually, 55 festivals in various fields are held in Helsinki, where there are 30 professional theatre groups, 4 circus groups, around 90 art galleries hosting almost 1,500 exhibitions a year, and over 100 live music events in an average weekend. In recent years, various spontaneous non-institutional arts and residents events at grass root level have emerged on the cultural stage in Helsinki, such as various street events and pop-up restaurants.

In the field of arts and culture education, the newly established Aalto University brought together the local universities for economics, technology and design with a view to generate innovations and business and increase the competitiveness of the metropolitan region. A projected new arts university is expected to produce similar advantages from cooperation between various fields of art.

In 2007, the number of people working in public and private cultural services (Nace 2008) in Helsinki amounted to 56,000. This was 14.5 per cent of all jobs in Helsinki. Private businesses accounted for about half of these jobs.

With 39 per cent of national corporate turnover in the field of arts and culture, Helsinki strongly dominates this field in Finland. According to statistics of 2009 the turnover of such companies in Helsinki was €5.3 billion, which was 9 per cent of the total turnover of companies in Helsinki. The 2009 economic recession impacted less on companies in Helsinki than in the rest of Finland, and the arts and culture business suffered less than others.

Arts and culture businesses are often small companies with less than five employees. In terms of staff and turnover, the largest fields are printed media, advertisement and radio and television. The most successful fields, i.e. those with the strongest growth in staff and turnover between 2007 and 2009 were performing arts (concerts, theatre and opera), entertainment agencies and manager services, as well as graphic design.

The principles included in the Cultural Strategy for the City of Helsinki 2010-2017 regard arts and culture as a part of basic public services, the civic society and sustainable development, and as a promoter of community spirit and health. Arts and culture is felt to generate economic growth and have a distinctive economic impact. The city carries significant responsibility for the funding of arts and culture, but additional forms of funding can be found, too.

The arts and culture sector is a strong actor in Helsinki. The authorities seek various ways – educational, local and functional – to consolidate the resources of arts and culture and back up new innovation. Since the 1990s, there has been strong progress in the internationalization of arts and culture, in cultural exports and in local activities. This is partly a result of people's own activities, partly of work done by Musex, Frame and other organizations for the promotion of cultural exports. In 2011, the biggest international successes have been scored in the export of digital games. The global success of one company has encouraged other developers in the games business. Foreseeable trends in future include corporate clustering and an increase in the cultural experience business, in the degree of entertainment, and in the need for manager services and other services supporting the production of cultural content.

Knowledge City, Student City

In 1994 the City of Helsinki adopted an overall strategy to develop the city as a Knowledge City. In parallel, and at the same time, the City adopted a new internationalization strategy. By 2000, a strong growth in enterprises and jobs in the information sector and also in clusters of culture industries was observed. Its role as one of the European Cultural Capital Cities in 2000 also gave an extra boost to growth and dynamics in Helsinki. Significant investments in education and R&D were made.

An innovative example on "science in society", on improving the impact of scientific research and getting research outcomes turned into practice, is about cooperation in urban research bringing together universities, universities of applied sciences (polytechnics) and the major cities in the metropolitan region as well as the ministries. This began in 1998, when the City of Helsinki, the Ministry of Education and the University of Helsinki agreed to intensify their co-operation in the field of urban research. The first agreement generated six new professorships at the University of Helsinki for a term of five years. In 2003, this model was further extended. A new agreement was reached between the Cities of Helsinki, Espoo, Vantaa and Lahti, the University of Helsinki, the Helsinki Technical University and the Ministry of Education. According to the new agreement, nine professorships in urban research were achieved, seven professors accommodated at the University of Helsinki and two at the Helsinki Technical University (now Aalto University). The research fields were: European metropolitan planning, urban history, social policy, urban sociology, urban economics, urban ecology, urban ecosystems, urban technological systems, and urban geography.

The urban professorship model has been further developed and enlarged. By 2010 the professorships in urban research were made permanent and maintained by the University of Helsinki and the University of Aalto – Aalto University being created in 2010 from the merger of three Finnish universities: The Helsinki School of Economics, Helsinki University of Technology and The University of Art and Design Helsinki.

The present and enlarged structure of cooperation in the field of urban research is developed in the frame of the national metropolitan policy. On the agenda are key questions related to the request of improving the impact of urban research. These are: How does supply and demand meet? How to make them meet better?

How to improve the communication of research findings and how to turn scientific knowledge into practice?

At present, an agreement has been achieved between a large number of key stakeholders – the cities, universities and universities of applied sciences in the region and four ministries – with the aim to strengthen urban research and to advance the use of urban research findings and scientific knowledge.

Regional Cooperation

In the 1970s, the four cities of the Helsinki metropolitan Area decided to establish a joint body: the Helsinki Metropolitan Council (abbreviated as YTV in Finnish). The council was an example of statutory co-operation. This body was redesigned in 2010 resulting in two new authorities. Helsinki Regional Transport Authority (HSL) began operating on 1 January 2010 and is responsible for the planning and organization of public transport services in its member municipalities, as well as for the preparation of the Helsinki Region Transport System Plan. In the start-up stage, the member municipalities of the joint local authority are Helsinki, Espoo, Vantaa, Kauniainen, Kerava and Kirkkonummi. Later on, the rest of the municipalities in the Helsinki region may join in. These municipalities include Järvenpää, Nurmijärvi, Tuusula, Mäntsälä, Pornainen, Hyvinkää, Vihti and Sipoo.

Helsinki Region Environmental Services Authority (HSY) is a regional authority providing environmental services for residents and companies in the Helsinki area. The principal duties comprise water and waste management as well as providing some regional information services. HSY began its operations on 1 January 2010 and it brings together the waterworks of Espoo, Helsinki, Kauniainen and Vantaa as well as the waste management services and the information services provided earlier by the Helsinki Metropolitan Area Council (YTV).

There are three bodies for cooperation in the Helsinki Region. These are the Helsinki Metropolitan Area Advisory Board, the Helsinki Metropolitan Area Cooperation Assembly and the Helsinki Region Cooperation Assembly. Regional cooperation aims to secure the Helsinki region's international competitiveness. It is based on a shared view of the region's municipalities on the challenges of the area and a shared goal to promote the area's development. Regional cooperation focuses particularly on land use, housing and transport issues as well as regional services.

The Helsinki Metropolitan Area Advisory Board is a cooperation body of leading elected politicians of the four cities (Helsinki, Espoo, Vantaa and Kauniainen) in the Capital Region of Finland. Items on the agenda are prepared at the mayors' meetings. The Advisory Board has meetings monthly. The activities of this Board are based on a cooperation agreement, a common vision and a joint strategy. The Advisory Board deals with issues concerning strategic cooperation and steering of the most important joint municipal organizations. The main pillars of the strategy are common welfare services, international competitiveness, land use, housing and transport. The activities of the Advisory Board are based on decisions made by the City Councils of the cities involved.

The Helsinki Metropolitan Area Cooperation Assembly is another cooperation body of leading elected politicians of the four core cities in the Capital Region of Finland. The Cooperation Assembly has approved a Common Vision and Strategy for the Helsinki Metropolitan Area. The vision is implemented through the launch of cooperation projects. The strategy is incorporated into each city's operating and financial plan and helps to steer the cities' strategic planning in the coming years. Items on the agenda are prepared at the mayors' meetings.

The Helsinki Region Cooperation Assembly is the cooperation body of the leading elected officials of fourteen municipalities in the Helsinki Region. Participating are the cities of the Helsinki Metropolitan Area (Helsinki, Espoo, Vantaa and Kauniainen) and ten adjacent municipalities called KUUMA municipalities (Järvenpää, Nurmijärvi, Tuusula, Kerava, Mäntsälä, Pornainen, Hyvinkää, Kirkkonummi, Vihti and Sipoo). Regional cooperation focuses particularly on land use, housing and transport issues as well as regional services.

The cities of the Helsinki Metropolitan Area have implemented their regional strategies in many ways. Good tools for implementation have been for example in 2002-2009 the Urban Programme for the Helsinki Metropolitan Area and in 2010-2012 Regional Cohesion and Competitiveness Programme for the Greater Helsinki Area. Although these regional development programmes have been quite small they have been nimble and enable to implement many concrete regional projects based on the joint strategy. The main aim of these programmes has been to improve the international competitiveness and cohesion of the Helsinki region. The basic funding of the programmes has been covered by the cities and the State. However this form of cooperation will end in 2012 mainly due to the State budget cuts.

State of the City

From Innovation Strategy to Prosperous Metropolis

In 2003, authorities in the Helsinki Region acknowledged that the region needed a common innovation strategy. The task of preparing the strategy was given to Culminatum Ltd, whose 30 owners are all key actors in the innovation environment. This work became an extensive learning process actively involving several hundred people representing the cities of the region, local universities and companies and some national organizations.

The 2005 innovation strategy paved the way for a university reform whose flagship, the Aalto University, opened in early 2010. To promote user-driven innovation the Forum Virium Helsinki was founded in 2006, a consortium involving a dozen large companies working on the development of digital service applications. The City of Helsinki supports this initiative and relies on it as a sparring partner in the renewal of the city's service processes. Subsequently, the cities of the Helsinki Metropolitan Area have specified their own roles by drawing up, within Culminatum's framework, the Menestyvä metropoli (Prosperous Metropolis) programme, which brings together the measures taken by the cities to consolidate the international competitiveness of the region. This programme also formed a model for the metropolis policy launched by the former Finnish National Government. The tool is a common statement of intent for competitiveness shared by the ministries and cities and containing around ten development targets or projects for the years 2010 and 2011. One example of shared projects in the statement of intent is the Helsinki World Design Capital 2012.

Metropolitan Policy

New Metropolitan Policy was launched in Finland in 2007 with the aim as follows: To address the special issues affecting the Greater Helsinki Area, a metropolitan policy was launched to identify solutions to the problems associated with land use, housing and traffic, promote business and internationalization and prevent social exclusion. Multiculturalism and bilingualism will be promoted. The letter-of-intent procedure between the central government and the Greater Helsinki Area and cooperation based on partnerships with the individual administrative sectors was reinforced and extended.

There were six letter-of-intent agreements between the Central Government and the municipalities in the Helsinki Region. The agreements dealt with land use, transport, housing, immigration and competitiveness issues. The letter-of-intent agreements were:

- Contract of Intent between the Municipalities of Helsinki Region and the State to Increase Housing and Plot Supply;
- Making the central land use solutions and transport investments of the municipalities of Helsinki Region more compatible;
- Preparation and implementation of the Metropolitan Area competitiveness strategy;
- Preparation and implementation of the programme entity on immigration policy;
- Programme to combat long-term homelessness as well as steps to strengthen social integrity included in the suburban development programme;
- Developing social and health care between the Municipalities in the Metropolitan Area (Helsinki, Espoo, Vantaa, Kauniainen, Kerava and Kirkkonummi) and the State.

In addition, Metropolitan Policy has included the Metropolitan Region Urban Research and Cooperation Program 2011-2014 which has focused on urban research concerning the specific needs of the metropolitan region.

Government Report to the Parliament on the Metropolitan Policy was finalised and approved by the Government in 5 November 2010. This kind of report to the Parliament on this particular subject was the first in its history. The present national government, established on 22 June 2011, will continue the implementation of the metropolitan policy and strengthening the metropolitan policy. Special attention is to be paid to land-use and housing, transport, and international competitiveness. Acting for social cohesion and in anticipation to prevent risk of segregation is one major focus area. Improving employment of immigrant population is also an important goal.

Helsinki World Design Capital 2012

The World Design Capital (WDC) designation is a biennial city promotion project that celebrates a city having used design as a tool to reinvent itself and to improve social, cultural and economic life. Late 2009 Helsinki was nominated as WDC 2012 among more than 40 bidding cities. The bidding process for the WDC year 2012 was a boost to strengthen the organizing capacity of the Helsinki metropolitan region. The theme of World Design Capital 2012 is "Open Helsinki" creating open platforms that enable people to take part in designing a better, happier and increasingly liveable city.

WDC 2012 is a huge cooperation process between all the partners of the innovation ecosystem. It is a joint venture between cities of Helsinki, Espoo, Vantaa Kauniainen and Lahti. Aalto University and University of Helsinki play a crucial role as founding members of the International Design Foundation which the home of WDC Helsinki office. The support and funding from the National Government lay the solid ground for the process. Dozens on NGOs have joined the initiative. Most important is the strong interest from the business community. World design Capital Helsinki has about 20 corporate partners supporting the process by 6 million euro.

Finland is a country of strong design tradition. Design is simply a part of the way of Finnish life. The idea of WDC Helsinki 2012 "Embedded design in life" extends the concept of design from goods to services and systems. The program of the year 2012 consists of events and projects turn design into a tool for cultural, social and economic development. The goal is to strengthen the innovation capacity of the region by introducing user-driven perspective to the Finnish innovation model. From the perspective of urban policy WDC Helsinki 2012 is not only a year of attractive international and local events in the region. It is a big opportunity to start processes that can lead to long lasting positive effect on the economic, social and cultural development in Helsinki. The effects of World Design Capital Helsinki 2012 are expected to become remarkable in four directions:

- Improving the organizing capacity of the Helsinki region by offering a platform to all partners to join under a shared and challenging vision.
- Making Helsinki as a metropolitan city more attractive internationally by increasing global contacts and giving visibility to Finnish design and innovation abilities.

- Encouraging city departments to adopt design methods to make city smarter so that services and infrastructure will give every citizen opportunities for better everyday life.
- Improving the competitiveness of Helsinki based international and local companies by the means of partnership with WDC status.

Open Data, Open Access: Helsinki Region Infoshare

Helsinki Region Infoshare (HRI) – Open regional data (www.hri.fi) is an example of innovation in an open environment allowing for open and free access to public data to all, and also being an example of good cooperation in the region between municipalities and across sectors as well as with state government bodies.

Helsinki Region Infoshare aims at making information, especially various urban and regional statistics focused on the Helsinki Region, its municipalities and sub-districts freely available by offering easy access in a user-driven way. Actually, Helsinki Region Infoshare aims at a new, open model for sharing and re-using public data. The point of departure for this challenging project is at least three-fold. Firstly, the broad cooperation in the region requests for good information basis covering the whole region. Secondly, we believe that open data, openness and open cooperation is a competitive advantage stimulating new businesses, products and services and improving already existing ones. Thirdly, open access to statistical information and public data is essential to the society and to the public enabling participation, interactivity and commitment. In addition, open data and open access support harmonization of data and improve operation efficiencies on all levels. Open access to information can also lead to new services and businesses, and it may advance research and development. All in all, sharing public data between as many users as possible – and for free – will benefit society and public policy, citizens, service developers and businesses alike.

Helsinki Region Infoshare is a research and development project running from 2010 through 2012. The core municipalities Helsinki, Espoo, Vantaa and Kauniainen of the Helsinki Region, Forum Virium Helsinki and The Finnish Innovation Fund (Sitra) are participants in this project, which is coordinated by the City of Helsinki Urban Facts (www.hel.fi/tietokeskus). Forum Virium Helsinki (www.forumvirium.fi) is responsible for project planning, providing R&D-services and coordinating subprojects. The project is funded by the cities of Espoo, Helsinki, Vantaa and Kauniainen, as well as the Finnish Innovation Fund Sitra. In addition, the Finnish Ministry of Finance has given the project a municipality cooperation grant.

The open data are mainly statistical data, giving a comprehensive and diverse outlook on different urban phenomena, such as demography and living conditions, economics and wellbeing, employment and transport. A good proportion of the data offered is GIS based allowing for varied use and applications. After 2012 the target is that offering open data and open access will becomes part of the ordinary operations of the municipalities in the Helsinki Region. The service itself and the major part of the data will be made available also in English.

University Reform

Established in 2010, the Aalto University is a new university with centuries of experience. The Aalto University was created from the merger of three Finnish universities: The Helsinki School of Economics, Helsinki University of Technology and The University of Art and Design Helsinki. Aalto University School of Science and Technology has been divided into four new schools starting from 1 January 2011. The six schools of Aalto University are all leading and renowned institutions in their respective fields and in their own right.

The combination of six schools opens up new possibilities for strong multi-disciplinary education and research. The new university's ambitious goal is to be one of the leading institutions in the world in terms of research and education in its own specialized disciplines.

There is also under way the establishment of a new university for the arts. This new university will start from the beginning of 2013 and it will be created from the merger of three universities: Finnish Academy of Fine Arts, Sibelius Academy and Theatre Academy Helsinki. The new university will accommodate music, visual art, theatre and dance.

Municipal Reform

A process of local government restructuring is underway in Finland. Finland's generous suite of public programs and services are predominately delivered by local governments, i.e. municipalities. The restructuring underway aims to pass responsibilities horizontally from small municipalities to major municipalities as Finland works to reduce the number of local authorities in the country.

Citizen Participation

Helsinki City Board has established a Democracy Group to compile various democracy initiatives in the city, aiming to enhance opportunities for citizen participation. The group compiles numerous activities in the city administration that advance democracy into one consistent democracy project.

The Democracy Group's activities stem from the strategy programme 2009-2012 approved by Helsinki City Council, particularly from the programme's section Democracy and Participation. The group is a short-term body whose term extends from the beginning of April 2011 to year-end 2011. The tasks laid out in the strategy programme are:

- To create opportunities for direct democracy such as referendums;
- To improve the operational basis of citizen organizations and political parties;

- To seek to test good practices of participatory democracy during the current Council term;
- To build online services for electronic feedback and participation that allow citizens to become involved in the development of the city;
- To improve citizen's opportunities to review preparatory work and decision making;
- To advance and support young people's own, self-conceived projects;
- To organize regional service panels in various districts to gather resident feedback on core services.

New Residential Areas

Today, Helsinki is experiencing a phase of great opportunity. The new harbour in Vuosaari to the east of the city centre gave the city the opportunity to build a significant number of dwellings and premises on excellent spots close to the very heart of the city and the water front. The constructing will take place the next 20 years. Moreover, Helsinki has grown considerably in the East due to new land in Sipoo, where there will be totally new residential areas and a considerable number of new homes to Helsinki dwellers.

The new residential areas, e.g. Jätkäsaari and Kalasatama, combine proximity to the heart of the city with a thrilling environment. Thus these new waterfront districts are likely to become a real asset to Helsinki Kalasatama, already under construction, will accommodate 18,000 residents and 10,000 jobs. The Kalasatama metro station began its operations in January 2007. Jätkäsaari, only minutes away from the central Railway station, will host 20,000 residents and 7,000 jobs.

There will be more new residential areas, among others Keski-Pasila and Kruunuvuorenranta. Pasila will experience construction continuing until the 2040s, and by then it will have 12,000 new inhabitants and jobs for over 50,000 people. Kruunuvuorenranta will be built opposite the downtown area of Helsinki on a former oil terminal. Kruunuvuorenranta will be both a cosy residential area and an attractive recreational area for all Helsinki inhabitants. The area has six kilometres of shoreline and it offers its own cultural history in the form of estate parks and true natural wilderness. It is estimated that by 2025 Kruunuvuorenranta will host 10,000 residents and 1,000 jobs.

Sustainability and the Baltic Sea

Since the 1990s, the City of Helsinki has participated in international cooperation projects, which have improved wastewater treatment in the cities of Tallinn and St Petersburg. In 2007, Helsinki and the city of Turku launched a campaign called the Baltic Sea Challenge, which activates municipalities and other public sector actors, businesses, educational and research institutions, NGO's, civic organizations and citizens to draft action plans and implement specific projects and actions for the protection and rehabilitation of the Baltic Sea.

Helsinki will cooperate with the other metropolises in the Baltic Sea region to achieve the objectives in the joint Baltic Sea policy. The cornerstones of the EU Strategy for the Baltic Sea Region are to make this part of Europe more:

- Environmentally sustainable (e.g. reducing pollution in the sea);
- Prosperous (e.g. promoting innovation in small and medium enterprises);
- Accessible and attractive (e.g. better transport links);
- Safe and secure (e.g. improving accident response).

The Strategy aims at coordinating action by Member States, regions, the EU, pan-Baltic organizations, financing institutions and non-governmental bodies to promote a more balanced development of the Region.

References

City of Helsinki (2009), *Diversity and Innovation*. Human Resources Centre, Immigration Division. Helsinki.

Laakso, S. and Kostiainen, E. (2011*). European Metropolises. Recession and Recovery*. Urban Facts: City of Helsinki.

Urban Facts (2011). [Online]. Available at http://www.hel.fi/hki/tieke/en/etusivu [accessed: 2011]

Chapter 9
Manchester

Dave Carter

City Profile

Manchester is the largest city in the North West of England, seen as the 'original, modern' industrial city, the home of the industrial revolution and the economic powerhouse of the region, based on a number of key economic drivers, including world-class universities, knowledge-based sector growth (including creative/digital and medical/bio-tech), a vibrant city centre, skilled workforce and Manchester International Airport. Despite continuing challenges due to economic recession Manchester has experienced significant economic and population growth in the last few decades, growing from 423,000 people in 2001 to 498,800 in 2010, with a projection of it reaching 519,000 by 2015.

Manchester's transformation in the past two decades has been considerable, where, by working with both the private sector and government, Manchester has secured the assets and investment to move the city from post-industrial decline to the economic engine of the North of England. Over the two decades Manchester has:

- Developed the largest and busiest regional airport in the UK;
- Secured over £2bn of investment to rebuild Manchester city centre following the 1996 terrorist bombing of the city centre;
- Developed the Oxford Road Corridor area, where the University of Manchester is the home of more Nobel Laureates than any other university in the UK;
- Invested in creating Metrolink, the first of the UK's new generation of light rail transit systems;
- Secured the Bank of New York's significant investment in the city;
- Created the environment for the move of five BBC developments to MediaCity;
- Commissioned an extensive £1.35m independent review of its economy through the Manchester Independent Economic Review;
- Created a formal city region wide governance system through the Combined Authority;
- Transformed Manchester Science Park into the UK's fastest growing science park outside of the South East;
- Redeveloped Manchester Central into one of the largest conference venues in the UK.

Not many cities internationally – and certainly no city outside London in the UK – could lay claim to such achievements. However, the city now faces the deepest global recession since World War II following the 2007 financial crash and the resulting recession has left its marks on Manchester's economy that can only be healed by a sustained focus on economic growth.

Economic projections produced for Manchester suggest that, while economic output will bounce back relatively quickly (GVA will be back at the 2008 level by 2012), even with favourable economic conditions, without intervention, it will take until 2014 for the number of jobs to return to the pre-recession peak. At the same time it will be vital to raise the demand for higher level skills from employers so that they are better able to compete internationally.

The recent Manchester Independent Economic Review and the interventions agreed in the Greater Manchester Strategy have helped guide the development and implementation of innovation across GM, increase the rate of knowledge-based activity to drive Manchester forward as a global innovation hub. The establishment of a Manchester Innovation Fund that involved the National Endowment for Science, Technology and the Arts (NESTA) has supported innovative ways of working and developed projects have helped to develop high-tech innovations, open data infrastructure, and advanced and micro manufacturing. These projects have only begun to boost the number of high-worth, high-profile companies and individuals in the city and develop local networks to spread of innovation and knowledge spill-over and exchange. Our current priorities following on from this include the rapid roll out of the high-speed digital infrastructure needed by businesses to compete in the global market.

Economic activity generated in the Manchester area (which includes the other municipalities in the southern part of the Greater Manchester metro area) was worth some €40 Billion in 2008. Manchester has a diverse and growing employment base, with above-average rates of new business start-ups. In 2009 there were 304,800 people employed in the city and, while these numbers fell as the recession hit, the knowledge-based sectors have retained their position, accounting for some one-third of all jobs in the city, compared to a Core Cities (the eight largest cities in England excluding London) average of one-quarter. Manchester is also a major transport hub for road, rail and air, and has seen major investment in new public transport routes, including Metrolink (tram) and bus, such as the free city centre low-carbon 'Metroshuttle' bus routes. This has resulted in public transport increasing its share from some half of all journeys in 1997 to some two-thirds of all journeys in 2009.

The city covers an area of some 117 km^2 and has a population density which is over eight times the average for the north-west region. Its population growth, of about 2 per cent per year on average between 2001 and 2010, is more than three times the average rate of growth in England and Wales. The age profile of the city is also changing and over this period the proportions of the population aged 15 to 64 (close to working age), children aged under 4 and residents aged over 85 have all increased, while the proportion of children aged 5 to 14 and residents aged 65 to 84 have decreased. The largest increase is in the 20 to 29 age group, rising by some 61 per cent. Since 2001 inflows of internal migrants have been largest for the 15 to 24 age group, including students, peaking in 2003/4. Net inflows of international migrants (not age-specific) is most likely to account for the rest of the growth in young adults, and EU expansion in 2004 saw a large increase in the inflow of migrants from Eastern Europe.

Manchester continues to be a popular location for young adults and especially for students with more than 73,000 students attending higher education in the city in 2008/9, making up more than 14 per cent of the estimated mid-year population of the city in 2010. Manchester has a lower proportion of residents aged 65 and over, 10.1 per cent compared to 16.9 per cent in England and Wales, a proportion which is decreasing while the nationally this is increasing.

Manchester has been an ethnically diverse city for more than a century and many ethnic minority residents are the third or fourth generation to be born here. All broad ethnic groups grew in number between 2001 and 2010, growing overall from just under 20 per cent in 2001 to over 22 per cent in 2010. Increases were recorded (from the mid-2000s onwards) in the number of residents from the EU Accession States, Black African, Asian, Indian and Chinese groups, while decreases were recorded in White Irish, Black Caribbean, Mixed White and Black Caribbean and Mixed White and Black African groups.

Manchester suffers significant levels of deprivation. The UK Index of Multiple Deprivation (IMD) 2010 is based on seven domains of deprivation relating to income, employment, health and disability, education, skills and training, barriers to housing and services, crime and living environment. The IMD 2010 ranked Manchester as the fourth most deprived district (out of 326) in England overall, the second most deprived in terms of income and the third in employment deprivation. Deprivation is also spatially concentrated, with neighbourhoods in the north and east of the city (the traditional industrial areas) and the southernmost part of the city, Wythenshawe (the 1930s built public sector peripheral housing estate, at its time one of the biggest in Europe) representing the most deprived.

In terms of governance Manchester (and the other nine districts of the Greater Manchester metro area) are all single-tier authorities meaning that there is no formal metro area or regional government structure between Manchester and national government. In 2009, however, the Government announced that Greater Manchester would become a pilot 'City Region', with the potential to gain greater powers and responsibilities. This was supported by the ten districts and seen as a process which would help to create the conditions for recovery in the aftermath of the recession. In April 2011 the ten Greater Manchester authorities were the first in the country to develop a statutory Combined Authority to co-ordinate key economic development, regeneration and transport functions. Other related developments include the creation of a business-led 'Local Enterprise Partnership – LEP' which will coordinate economic development activities across the metro area and the creation of a new transport body – Transport for Greater Manchester (TfGM) – to deliver across the metro area. Each individual local authority will retain its single-tier status in terms of relative independence in delivering other services, such as education, social welfare, planning, housing strategy etc., but will liaise and coordinate more closely with the other districts through the Combined Authority

Developments and Policy Changes since Early 1990s[1]

In the mid-1980s Manchester City Council embarked on a radical new approach to regeneration. A new Economic Development Department was established and work was commissioned to bring together people with new and innovative ideas, from research bodies, business, trade unions, the voluntary sector and the wider community, to advise the City Council leadership on how to tackle economic restructuring and the consequent impacts which were resulting in massive levels of unemployment, poverty and alienation. Out of those discussions, which also included many 'heated debates' on priorities, a number of practical proposals emerged in the late 1980s (1987-89), including:

- There should be more of a focus on area and neighbourhood based working, devolving intervention to local areas and encouraging cross-sector working where the public sector would work on a more proactive basis with local communities, businesses and other public sector bodies, e.g. health;
- The idea of a 'creative city' emerged, demonstrating the economic importance of the 'arts and cultural industries', such as the idea that Manchester should look to cities such as Amsterdam and Barcelona as '24 Hour Cities' for inspiration and practical ideas for new initiatives;
- Innovation being identified as another key theme, acknowledging the lack of a coherent collaboration strategy with higher education in particular and the need to address this with some practical initiatives such as the development of Manchester Science Park (MSP) and the recognition that information and communications technologies (ICTs) could play a significant role in creating new infrastructures and services and, consequently, future economic growth.

These three themes were at the heart of the new Economic Development Strategy for the City and provided the foundation for the City Council's new 'Economic Initiatives Group (EIG)' focusing on local (neighbourhood focused) action, creative industries and technology and innovation. They are still at the core of Manchester's neighbourhood regeneration strategy 20 years later, underpinning the two core objectives of the City Council, namely generating sustainable economic growth and reducing dependency through tackling worklessness, inequalities and social exclusion.

---

1   This section is largely based on Carter (2013).

Greater Manchester is now moving into a new phase of its economic development, working closely with Government and with other 'core cities' in England it is developing a 'prospectus' of devolutionary initiatives that provides a new framework within which the 'smart city' agenda can thrive alongside cutting edge science and innovation as part of a new knowledge economy.

As the functional economic area outside London and the South East that has the most potential for growth, Manchester plays a key role in the economic performance of the North of England, and providing the national economy with a strong source of growth, diversity and resilience. In 2008 the city region generated over £44bn of GVA in 2010 representing 5 per cent of the national economy. Greater Manchester also generates 40 per cent of the North West's total GVA. Manchester is of national significance – and is a larger economic unit than Wales, Northern Ireland or the North East of England – meaning that it is central to the UK's efforts to rebalance from its current overreliance on financial services and London.

Manchester has a strong set of economic assets that currently drive our dynamic economy and that we will use as a platform for further growth. Greater Manchester has a high concentration of skilled, knowledge based jobs within a diversified, private sector economy. The city has particular strengths in advanced manufacturing, life sciences, creative and digital media and financial and business services. We have an exceptional higher education offer with the largest student population in Europe of over 100,000 students across five Universities and with the University of Manchester as one of the world's leading research institutions. Manchester is now developing an investment strategy which draws on a clear evidence base and set of strategic priorities to support economic growth and increase productivity. This reflects the changing financial climate, where the availability of both credit and grant funding is severely curtailed, but more importantly is the best way to ensure that we meet our full economic potential over the long term.

Manchester is creating a pipeline of projects that deliver against our priorities – covering physical development, business support, housing, transport and broadband – over the short, medium and long term. The projects meet traditional investment criteria and drive new jobs in Greater Manchester and increased GVA. In parallel we are drawing together funding streams – both public and private – to create an investment framework to use in the most efficient way to deliver our economic priorities.

In 2011 the launch of the EU's Digital Agenda for Europe (European Commission, 2011) provides a high level strategic framework for supporting the development of 'a flourishing digital economy by 2020' through 'policies and actions to maximise the benefit of the Digital Revolution for all'. As part of this local action is being encouraged so that cities and regions produce 'Local Digital Agendas' to set out their aspirations for change, while at the same time focusing on practical action and initiatives which will deliver that change supported by user driven open innovation through the use of digital technologies.

This comes at a time when Manchester is reviewing its own 'Digital Strategy', originally produced in 2008 focusing on three key priorities:

- Digital inclusion: continuing to tackle the 'digital divide' where, even when people generally have increasing access to the Internet and digital services, inequalities persist with large sections of excluded communities no longer having or using copper based landlines (over 50 per cent of households in some parts of Manchester) and, consequently, having limited or no access to the 'digital world' and where access to skills and jobs in the digital economy is still very limited;
- Digital industries: building on Manchester's strengths as the largest and most dynamic cluster of digital and creative businesses outside of London to support further sector based growth, through the independent Manchester Digital trade association (Manchester Digital, 2011) and other sector based initiatives, and to find ways to overcome barriers to growth, such as the lack of business finance to support new investment and start-ups and the need for better access to skills and pathways to employment in the sector;
- Digital innovation: generating investment for innovation and new infrastructures and working with the research community on Future Internet development to support Manchester as a 'Smart City' in areas such as smart energy, cloud computing and very high speed next generation access (NGA) digital infrastructures (fibre and wireless) and networks.

This review will take the form of a Green Paper: "Smart Cities: creating an inclusive and sustainable knowledge society: A Local Digital Agenda for Manchester" which is published in September 2011. This is the result of six months work in consulting with local stakeholders and partners, following a workshop organised by Manchester Knowledge Capital and the Manchester Digital Development Agency (MDDA) in March 2011, together with a range of discussion held with partners in the EUROCITIES Knowledge Society Forum (KSF), European Smart Cities projects and the European Network of Living Labs (Open Living Labs, 2011). Following that there will be further consultations with stakeholders and partners, local, nationally and internationally with the aim of publishing the Local Digital Agenda for Manchester early in 2012, outlining priorities and an action plan for realizing a digitally enabled and empowered Smart City, both in the short term and to 2020 and beyond.

In the late 1980s when the City's new Economic Development Department was formulating its priorities for action to drive economic change technology was largely seen as something that was neutral and passive, a product of economic change rather than a catalyst for that change. Information and communication technologies (ICTs), or telematics (the convergence of telephony and informatics), were not particularly seen as being central or even that important to economic growth. There were examples in other parts of Europe, however, as well as in North America, where the power of micro-computing was being linked together with the 'plain old telephone system' (POTS) to create the first open networks that were more widely available outside of universities, the wider research community and the military.

Manchester was particularly influenced by developments in Scandinavia and Germany, where 'X25' networks were providing the first open access email and conferencing systems, such as the 'GeoNet' system in Germany with its email, fax and telex gateway in the UK, and the Electronic Village Halls in Denmark and Sweden taking ICTs out to local communities to support rural development and with links to one specific community project in the UK, the Notting Hill Information Technology Education Centre (ITEC). Manchester commissioned research from the Centre for Employment Research (CER) at Manchester Polytechnic (now Manchester Met University – MMU) to review these developments and to make recommendations about how such developments could be used to support economic development and social inclusion in Manchester.

In spite of some advice CER received, such as that 'there would be no commercial access to the Internet for at least 10 years', this was in 1989, the report was very positive and Manchester embarked on a proactive strategy of encouraging some of the pioneers of this early use of 'telematics' to bring their skills and infrastructure to Manchester. This resulted in the move of Poptel (the UK's first worker cooperative Internet Service Provider), working in partnership with GeoNet, to Manchester with the 'Manchester Host' computer communications and information system. The Manchester Host was launched in 1991, the UK's first locally based, globally accessible public access system offering email, bulletin boards and on-line databases, focusing heavily on community based users and information providers, as well as working with business and the public sector.

A network of Electronic Village Halls (EVHs) was set up in local neighbourhoods in Manchester in 1992, providing access to ICTs and (pre Web) Internet services and Manchester City Council was one of the first UK local authorities to have a website in 1993. In 1994 a new community based organization was established, the Manchester Community Information Network (MCIN), to support capacity building work in local areas and with the voluntary and community sector (NGOs) generally, enabling them to produce electronic content and to make that accessible via the Web and associated on-line networks.

At the same time Manchester Science Park (MSP) became the home for the first 'Internet Exchange' outside of London, still the only facility of this scale and capacity outside of London, and this is a key asset in Manchester's continuing development as a digital city. As a recent report commissioned by the MDDA to review Manchester's 'Internet Hub' capacity said:

> That such an open infrastructure approach works for Manchester is evident in the history of the digital sector and the process that led to Manchester becoming the foremost Internet hub in the UK outside of London. Manchester attracted some of the earliest Internet service providers who saw potential in strong local market awareness – to some extent the result of public sector intervention. Those

ISPs created a market for Internet transit and hosting services that attracted investment by carriers and led to the creation of hosting businesses like Telecity, a hugely successful Manchester start-up. The same ISPs spawned a growing number of web design and software businesses that took advantage of the new market opportunities. Those in turn increased further the demand for hosting and transit capacity, and the city council joined others in promoting an initiative to establish MaNAP, the first significant Internet exchange outside London. The peering activity around MaNAP and the increasing number of carriers who chose facilities in the Science Park as their point of presence led to falling Internet transit costs. This increased the attractions of Manchester as a centre for digital businesses, increasing demand for hosting, and so on in a virtuous growth spiral.

Three factors were critical in bringing this about:

- The role played by SMEs as innovators and market creators, and their need for open infrastructure to support a competitive supply chain and offer opportunities to add value;
- The early emergence of the hosting facilities at the Science Park as a 'meet me' point for carriers to bring connectivity, overcoming the problem of 'where shall we meet?'.
- The leadership role played by the city council and the universities, in creating awareness through projects like the Manchester Host, in the creation of the first hosting facilities on the Science Park, and in the creation of MaNAP.

The work of the technology and information society team within the City's Economic Initiatives Group continued to focus on developing a balance between traditional 'high tech' (largely 'technology push') innovation and 'accessible tech' (largely 'demand stimulation') open innovation. In the latter case it was often the voluntary sector (NGOs) which was particularly innovative using digital technologies to develop networks of creatives, electronic arts initiatives and e-enabled community activities. The early digital business networks coalesced into the Manchester Digital trade association, launched in 2001, and largely survived the 'dot com' boom and bust, but there was a growing recognition by this time that accessibility to digital technologies had to be improved significantly if any competitive edge developed by the city was to be sustained. This meant not only improved networks and services for business but also for all local residents, especially those who, in spite of economic growth during the late 1990s, were still socially excluded, and for public sector services.

Continuing work that Manchester was doing with other European cities provided growing evidence of the need for more proactive approaches to investing in digital infrastructure and services. Firstly, through Telecities, of which it was a founder member and hosted the founding conference in 1993, and more widely through EUROCITIES where the late Councillor Brian Harrison, the first Chair of the City's Economic Development Committee in the 1980s, went on to be chair of the

EUROCITIES Economic Development Committee (1996-98). The development of community based digital networks and infrastructures in places such as Amsterdam (through its Digital City project 'Digitale Stad' in 1994 and the Waag Society MediaLab), Barcelona (with the Barcelona Community Network – BCN), Bologna (with its citizens community network) and Stockholm (with its municipal fibre company – Stokab) convinced senior decision makers in Manchester to take a much wider look at this agenda and how it could benefit Manchester, building on the second great digital revolution, the coming of broadband and the 'always on' availability of the Internet and Web services.

Current debates at the time (late 1990s) tended to focus on the more optimistic view that e-services will be able to empower citizens and provide for their full participation in an emerging 'digital democracy', while there was concern that continuing inequalities, especially at a spatial level, were ignoring the realities of power which could be seen to support, what was called at the time, 'an information aristocracy', with elite access, rather than an effective 'digital democracy'. It was felt then that if there is not full accessibility to the new digital infrastructures and services for all citizens then the outcome will simply reinforce existing patterns of inequalities with 'information haves' and 'have nots' in our communities. This is still seen as a real challenge to realising the idea of a 'Smart City' today.

State of the City[2]

*Urban Regeneration and Inclusion through Innovation: the Case of
East Manchester*

All of Manchester's work on managing the transition from a post-industrial city to a thriving knowledge economy is based on the premise that urban regeneration is an essential prerequisite for tackling social exclusion and economic restructuring. Cities across the world face similar challenges in terms of finding coherent and effective policies and strategies that will support and sustain economic growth and connect the opportunities created by economic growth with the needs of their citizens. The emergence of the information society has added new complexities to this process, on the one hand adding to the speed and scale of change while on the other hand providing new tools and processes which can help to mitigate the impact of that change.

Manchester has experienced new economic growth developing side by side with persistently high levels of unemployment, poverty and social exclusion. It has the fourth highest rate of multiple deprivations (apart from parts of Merseyside and London) and the highest rate of child poverty in the UK. This 'tale of two cities' syndrome (as it has been referred to) threatens to undermine the longer term sustainability of economic development and growth. It is in this context

---

2 This section is largely based on Carter (2013).

that Manchester's work on the information society and 'digital development' continued to be an important cross-cutting theme within its City-Region Economic Development Strategy and Action Plans. The central aim is that digital technologies should be used to increase citizens' access to skills, jobs and services and support greater participation in civic life, including in the regeneration process itself.

Manchester is the UK's second largest metropolitan area outside of London, with a population of over 2.6 million in the Greater Manchester city-region. At its core is the City of Manchester, the first industrial urban area in the world and the 'original, modern' city. Alongside the city's transformation from industrial to knowledge economy is the legacy of high levels of unemployment and poverty from the experience and impact of the economic restructuring of the 1970s and 1980s. Much of this legacy is concentrated in the traditional industrial manufacturing area of the city, in East Manchester, once home to more than 100,000 its population had declined significantly, to less than 30,000 people by 2000.

East Manchester was, and is, a regeneration challenge of regional and national significance. An area of 1,100 hectares situated immediately east of Manchester's City Centre, East Manchester presents an opportunity for regeneration on a scale and diversity almost unprecedented in an English city. There are unique opportunities for the renaissance of the area as a focus for the knowledge-driven economy of the twenty-first century. These opportunities have been generated by there being a range of regeneration initiatives focusing upon East Manchester to address many of the physical, economic and social problems in the area. These, in turn, build upon the stimulus provided by a buoyant economy within Manchester and the major investment attracted through the staging of the Commonwealth Games in 2002 and related legacy projects. The strong commitment by government to the success of cities and to tackling the most acute areas of deprivation is also a key factor driving this impetus, as is the partnership working between generated between the local community and local and national government.

A major influence on Manchester's approach to digital development and, most recently, work of the concept of the 'Smart City' is the experience gained in East Manchester where the City Council formed an Urban Regeneration Company (URC), New East Manchester (NEM) Ltd, a public-private-community partnership operating on a not-for-profit basis. An online community network, run in partnership with local citizens organizations and representatives, known as 'Eastserve' was established there in 2001. This was the location for the Commonwealth Games in 2002, which brought much needed investment and new facilities and resources in to the area, which had been the major industrial area of the city for more than 100 years until industrial restructuring brought factory closures, massive unemployment and environmental degradation over a 25 year period up to the late 1990s.

The 'Eastserve' initiative was one of a range of legacy projects, where the investment attracted by the Commonwealth Games, including the City of Manchester Stadium (subsequently the home of Manchester City Football Club –

MCFC), would continue to have positive impacts in supporting local residents to gain skills and access to employment, including through ICT projects. Even in 2001 many residents in the East Manchester area used cheap mobile phones rather than fixed telephone lines. The initial survey work undertaken by the area regeneration partnership (in 2001) revealed that more than 25 per cent of homes no longer used landlines. This led to changes to the initial aims and objectives of the project which had been to provide PCs to households with dial-up Internet access. This meant that a system of wireless broadband connectivity was required which then enabled households to access the Internet and on-line services.

More than 2,000 of the area's homes were Internet enabled through wireless broadband Internet connections, as well as 17 local schools, eight 'UKOnline' community access centres and 10 public access points in libraries and other centres. They all connected to a 100Mbps licensed wireless backbone linking four tower blocks around the East Manchester area from where bandwidth is distributed over a wireless network. Schools and public buildings receive an online community service, developed by Eastserve, and relay it to other residential locations. These locations are grouped in clusters and communicate with one another wirelessly via a radio dish antenna connected to a wireless bridge.

Underpinning this approach was the provision of micro-loans through the local Credit Union which enabled people to buy computer equipment which, because they were paying for it, increased the 'value' that they put on this and enhanced their sense of ownership over the process and its results. Many of the people involved had never saved before or, in some cases, did not have bank accounts, so the project also had a positive impact on the Credit Union, increasing membership from a few hundred to some 2,000 people.

At the time this was one of the largest community based all-wireless broadband networks in Europe and the largest community regeneration initiative using digital technologies in the UK. In spite of being one of the poorest areas in the city, the take-up of broadband the area is far higher than the city-wide rate and residents are using their new skills to improve their access to training and jobs. In one of several evaluation studies of the impact of the project it was shown that Eastserve users are:

- More aware of job opportunities,
- Want access to more training;
- More likely to seek work;
- More likely to take part in other educational opportunities;
- More likely to be looking for new challenges;
- More interested in running their own businesses.

Over 40 per cent of residents have now had basic ICT training because of EastServe, more than double the rate of most areas in the City, and 20 per cent of these were moving on to extended courses which provide opportunities for accreditation, again more than double rates for initiatives in other parts of the city.

Learning the lessons from the work in East Manchester influenced thinking about how to extend this and develop similar initiatives in other parts of the city and how to develop a city wide strategy for what was now termed 'digital development'.

Following a city wide review of services and structures following the Commonwealth Games the City Council decided to change the way it delivering its Economic Development Strategy, focusing future work in strategic initiatives in defined Area Regeneration Partnerships and in sector initiatives. This led to the Technology and Information Society Team in the Economic Initiatives Group becoming the core of the new Manchester Digital Development Agency (MDDA), set up as a city region wide initiative in 2003 with the mission:

> To make Manchester a leading world class digital city, having one of the most competitive broadband infrastructures in Europe, attracting and sustaining investment in ICT and e-commerce across all sectors of the economy, generating new businesses, developing new learning cultures, promoting social inclusion and providing all residents with the skills and aspirations to play a full role in the information society (Manchester Digital Development Agency, 2005).

In 2005 the Government published the UK Digital Strategy, which included proposals for a UK 'Digital Challenge' where local authority led partnerships would be invited to put in innovative proposals for accelerating digital development at a local level. The MDDA was responsible for coordinating a response to this, working in partnership with other public sector bodies, including the other municipalities in the city region, other public sector bodies, business and the voluntary and community sector. In January 2007 Manchester City Council submitted the ONE-Manchester Partnership Digital Challenge proposal to Government with plans for developing: 'universal, affordable next generation broadband access' which 'is essential to connect all residents and businesses of the Manchester City-region to the social, educational, informational and economic opportunities they deserve'. This established the foundation for the creation of a Manchester Digital Strategy with a vision of creating the city-region as 'the most advanced "next generation" connectivity in the UK, providing a sustainable base for high growth business, innovation, transformational public services and an inclusive knowledge society'.

The thinking at that time was that Manchester, as the 'original, modern' city, faces many challenges in sustaining its economic growth and in connecting the opportunities created by this growth with the needs of local residents, maximizing local benefit. Not least of these challenges is the way that ever accelerating developments of digital technologies are creating what has been referred to as a digital 'paradigm shift' in the global economy. Various terms are being used to describe this – the 'Web 2.0' world, 'wikinomics' and the new 'long tail' economic world where millions of micro-businesses and e-traders create as much economic wealth and opportunity as the traditional large corporate companies.

It was felt that, in many ways, Manchester should be well placed to be a prime mover in this world, celebrating the 60th anniversary of the invention of the world's first real computer, the 'Baby', on 21 June 2008, and being a real digital pioneer in the 1990s with the UK 'firsts' (as detailed previously) such as the Manchester Host (1991), the Electronic Village Halls (1992) and the Manchester Community Information Network (MCIN – 1994). The ONE-Manchester Digital Challenge proposals aimed to capitalise on this and to set out a 'route-map' for a third wave of development which would use the very latest digital technologies to support further economic growth, tackle the digital divide and create inclusive sustainability.

This in turn led to the development of Manchester first specific Digital Strategy, approved by the City Council in March 2008, with proposals for a 'Next Generation Digital City' aiming to make Manchester a world-class exemplar of how to lead this third wave around four main themes:

- Sustaining economic growth, especially through the digital/creative sector, new micro-businesses, digital social enterprises and creating e-traders;
- Promoting digital inclusion, ensuring that all residents can access the on-line services, technologies and applications that they need;
- Continuing to transform public services through innovative uses of digital technologies;
- Promoting inclusive sustainability where digital technologies are used more innovatively to support sustainable energy communities, intelligent buildings, teleworking, improved mobility, telecare and a greater quality of life generally.

Cooperation: From a Networked City to a Networking City

The newly produced Digital Strategy together with discussions on the lessons being learnt from the East Manchester work were both happening at the same time as Manchester's work within EUROCITIES had brought it into contact with the network in Helsinki which was working with the MIT Media Lab to develop the idea of Living Labs.[3] During the 1990s Manchester was successful in a number of EU funded projects, coordinated through Telecities and EUROCITIES, including:

---

3   Living Labs grew out of an initiative in 2000 by Nokia Research Labs, the VTT Finnish national research centre and Helsinki City Council to find new ways of trialling and testing ICT products and services through mass participation of users. The University of Salford had long been collaborative partners with VTT and invited Manchester City Council to join a new EU collaborative research project called 'Intelligent Cities' in 2001 which was subsequently funded by the EU's 6th Framework Programme (FP6). As a result of the project a European Network of Living Labs (ENoLL) was established in 2006 with the Manchester Living Lab as one of the first 20 members. There are now more than 200 Living Labs in the network.

- The European Digital Cities project (FP4);
- The INFOCITIES project (TEN-Telecom);
- The Intelligent Cities ('IntelCities') project (FP6).

One of the consistent partners in much of this work was the City of Helsinki, and their partners from Nokia and VTT, were also involved. Having seen and understood what they were doing with their Living Lab concept, i.e. getting research out of the research labs and into the hands of real people in local neighbourhoods, there were clearly a number of parallels with the work going on in East Manchester. As well as being a very good basis for knowledge exchange these collaborations also convinced the Helsinki network to talk to their European partners, including Manchester, about launching a European Network of Living Labs. Manchester joined in with this at the beginning in 2005 and then became a founder member of the network when it launched in 2006.

The Living Labs 'movement' is driven by the idea of user-driven open innovation, where users are involved at all stages of the innovation process, from design, implementation to application and service development. This brings some of the traditions and experiences of co-creation within software development, e.g. within the open source community, into the wider world of new product and service development and delivery. This is a welcome development as, despite some encouraging trends with public awareness and use of user generated content and social networking, the development of new services and applications remain dominated by the multinational corporate sector leading to a pattern of 'development from above'. If the new infrastructures and applications are to benefit a much wider spectrum of public involvement than is currently the case, there is a need for civic commitment and public support, including financial resources, at all levels to support 'development from below' in applications and services, especially if the full potential of the 'Web 2.0' paradigm is to be realised. There is, then, a distinct 'applications gap' at the level of local citizens, too many of whom still sit on the wrong side of the 'digital divide'. The most effective way of bridging this gap is by stimulating greater engagement and experimentation, empowering users to develop digital literacy and competences for themselves and to use these to create their own content and services.

The objective of such initiatives is to provide a wide range of insights which can be usefully drawn upon by others in developing alternative systems, geared to different local needs in different places. Local experimentation therefore becomes part of city-wide and region-wide 'learning networks' whereby the insight gained in one environment can be transferred with suitable adjustments to another. If these 'learning-networks' can then link up – nationally and internationally, then there is the basis for a potentially powerful counter-balance to vested interests, in terms of corporate and state interests, which can be much more proactive in taking an advocacy role in relation to consumer, citizen and wider democratic interests. Developments in advanced communications need to be accompanied by a strategy for development from below which seeks to realise the indigenous potential of cities and regions. Social innovation in the community – involving local government, schools and colleges, public libraries, the voluntary sector, consumer groups and trade unions is a necessary counterpart to organizational innovation led by industry, commerce and government.

Both the idea and the practice of Living Labs, especially in the Manchester context, is then a very significant one, providing a mutually beneficial way of organizing key parts of the innovation process and involving people locally, whether residents, students or businesses, in the co-creation and co-production of new applications and services.

This work became central to discussions within the Living Labs network about how to engage with new ideas and approaches, particularly those coming out of the EU's Future Internet Research and Experimentation (FIRE) community. There is a 'third wave' of Internet development underway, where the 'Internet of Things', i.e. networked objects, meets 'web-centric services', often referred to as the 'Internet of Services/Internet of People'. The challenge is how these developments can be translated into practical initiatives that meet the wider goals of the Living Labs movement, to co-create and co-produce new 'Future Internet' enabled services that deliver a more inclusive and sustainable knowledge society. At a local level the challenge is to harness these to deliver local benefit, promoting digital inclusion, helping the digital sector to grow and create skills and jobs that are accessible to local people and providing the required digital infrastructure to support innovation and future growth.

This is why the MDDA and its partners have been refining the vision originally outlined in the first Manchester Digital Strategy in 2008 to focus on the concept of 'Smart Citizens in Smart Cities', using digital technologies to promote community engagement, capacity building and social capital. To use the four level social capital model this includes:

- Firstly, creating a common vision and a sense of belonging for all communities through imaginative uses of digital technologies to help to transform lives;
- Secondly, ensuring that diversity is appreciated and positively rewarded through improved accessibility of digital technologies to support social networking;
- Thirdly, engaging people from different backgrounds through the use of digital technologies which enables them to have similar life chances;
- Fourthly, encouraging strong and positive relationships to be developed between people from different backgrounds in the workplace, in education and within neighbourhoods by using digital technologies to break down barriers and promote social cohesion.

The MDDA's projects continue to combine innovation through new initiatives, including the Manchester Living Lab, so that it can be the way by which people and businesses can easily connect and collaborate with MDDA projects and other initiatives, together with the further development of well established practice, especially in terms of digital inclusion, such as the 'Selling on the Web' courses.

The starting points for this are:

- **Access:** ensuring that all local residents, plus those who come to Manchester to work, study or visit, have the most accessible and affordable ways to use the Internet open to them, including through local access centres, next generation access (NGA) networks and wireless connectivity;
- **Business opportunities:** enabling existing digital businesses to safeguard existing jobs and create new ones, developing pathways into employment through training and skills programmes, including apprenticeships, and generating new business opportunities by supporting new start-ups and social enterprises and promoting new trading opportunities and promotional activities, including through the Manchester Digital trade association and the annual 'Big Chip' awards;
- **Capacity building:** using digital technologies to build social capital and to support community engagement so that there is real local benefit generated by innovation which, in turn, increases digital inclusion, provides access to skills and jobs and improves the quality of life, including through 'green digital' and open data initiatives, working in collaboration with local partners such as the Manchester Digital Lab (MadLab).

Examples of MDDA project development in these areas include:

- **'Fibre to the People'** – the Manchester Living Lab pilot project which is starting in the Corridor area (around Oxford Road, Ardwick and Hulme wards and Knott Mill) to roll out next generation access digital infrastructure using point to point, open access fibre networks and advanced wireless connectivity;
- **Manchester 'Internet Hub'** – ensuring that Manchester can develop its 'Internet Exchange' capacity to be a globally competitive 'Internet Hub' based on enhancing connectivity across the city, especially between Manchester Science Park, Sharp and Media City UK;
- **Low Carbon Open Data Network** – 'Lodanet': extending the wireless connectivity around the Corridor area to collect real-time environmental data using low-cost, low-power sensing equipment and providing open access to the data through a range of online services;
- **Smart Innovation and People** – 'SMARTiP – 'Smart Citizens in Smart Cities' – a European project connecting up digitally supported community engagement initiatives in Manchester and four other European cities working in partnership with Peoples Voice Media's 'community reporters' project and the University of Manchester;

- **Green Digital Charter** – a European wide initiative to reduce the environmental impact of digital technologies and to develop innovative 'smart energy' projects, such as Internet based interactive smart meters, that can improve energy efficiency and get people involved in new and imaginative ways of reducing their personal and collective carbon footprints;
- **Digital and Creative Skills** – bringing together businesses in the digital and creative sectors, including through Manchester Digital, education and training providers, community networks and other major employers to develop more innovatory ways for people to gain skills that can help them get access to jobs, set up their own businesses and get access to advanced learning opportunities through non-traditional routes, including apprenticeships.

Manchester's current digital projects aim to support the city region continuing to be the engine of regional growth. In order to remain competitive, however, Manchester believes it needs to remain ahead of the curve in terms of digital access, infrastructure and services. This requires a proactive approach at a number of different levels:

- Early, affordable access to 'the next generation' of open access fibre-based digital networks for business, public services and the wider community which are capable of delivering the support required for Future Internet enabled services to generate economic growth. Bandwidth demand is increasing exponentially which means that, given the lead times for infrastructure developments, cities need to be acting now;
- Increasing the capacity for innovation – especially as the digital and creative industries and the knowledge economy are so important to the UK economy. Cities are the places where these sectors cluster and in so doing, create new ideas for products and services and high-value employment opportunities. Easy access to Next Generation Digital Networks is a catalyst for cross-sector collaboration and experimentation. Our ambition is to turn Manchester into a Digital Test-Bed, an open innovation 'Living Lab' for Future Internet next generation services and applications, whether ultrafast broadband, smart energy, e-health or new virtualized capacities through 'cloud computing';
- Creating an enhanced ability to generate and share new ideas – NGA is not just about 'superfast' download speeds. In cities particularly, clusters of high tech digital companies are involved in creating and sharing digital media content and in developing and owning their own infrastructure so symmetric connectivity with fast upload speeds and open access networks are equally as important as faster download speeds;
- Making digital greener and more sustainable: NGA is equally about new green infrastructures, as cities are the primary producers of carbon emissions and, consequently, need to be using NGA to underpin the shift

to a low carbon economy by developing new and more sustainable ways in which people can work, study and live. Virtual business networks, for example, using applications such as 'telepresence' can deliver both carbon reductions and access to wider markets. Manchester's work on leading a European wide initiative in partnership with Eurocities (www. eurocities.eu) to develop this theme around the 'Green Digital Charter' is another example;

- Developing more efficient public services – NGA is key to enabling city service providers to maximise the ability for citizens to self-serve and to provide efficient access to expensive specialist resources, such as expert medical care, using innovative new services such as telemedicine. A further benefit to cities could be the sharing of expertise and collective response to the market in digital networks and specialist services, including shared infrastructure around data hosting, disaster recovery and virtualization, including cloud based applications and services;
- Exchanging knowledge and expertise – cities are ideally placed to mobilise and aggregate demand for NGA services for the Future Internet 'Smart City' and to provide the strong leadership required to make this happen. The 'Core Cities' network is currently working on an initiative to develop closer engagement between City Leaders, Government, Communications Service Providers and the Internet industry as a whole. In particular, Manchester is keen to continue to working with other cities to influence government policy to recognise the national importance of investment in urban infrastructure to complement the rural 'last third' agenda. Consequently we are establishing a forum within 'Core Cities' where this engagement can regularly take place and the emerging 'Smart Cities' agenda can be shaped through city leadership and regional networking.

A transformational digital infrastructure for the region will require three components:

- **Access networks:** serving businesses and citizens that will take us through the next 20 years and that will offer the maximum opportunity for local businesses to play a role in the supply chain. This effectively means 'fibre to the premises' (FTTP) networks supported by the latest wireless technologies. These fibre networks need to be fully open: shared by competing providers and not dominated by any one company or technology;
- **Digital hubs:** where these networks connect with each other and with the rest of the internet, where digital businesses can host the new applications and services on servers connected to these networks, and sometimes where the businesses themselves can locate. These hubs will play a similar role to Internet Exchanges (of which Manchester has the only significant one outside London in the UK), but more of them will be needed, closer to the end users;

- **Backbone networks:** connecting these hubs to each other and with the internet exchange in Manchester. These networks also need to be fully open, available to technology companies and service providers to adapt with different technologies and to compete with each other. This is the primary role of the proposed NGA deployment in the Manchester city region.

By bringing low cost, open access connectivity to several important regional centres, starting with the Manchester city region, such a network can effectively spread the benefit of the South Manchester Internet Exchange (currently clustered around Manchester Science Park) to other parts of the region. This would dramatically improve the business case for the development of hubs and access networks in these areas – initially creating a city-region-wide digital development zone in Manchester and then systematically extending this to other NGA projects across the region.

This underpins the work that MDDA is doing to develop the scale and scope of the Manchester Living Lab through projects which deliver local benefit around the core themes of its work programme. The new Manchester Green Paper (referred to previously, in section 2 above) aims to produce a 'Roadmap' for the Local Digital Agenda in Manchester, covering existing projects being undertaken by the MDDA and initiatives being developed in collaboration with local partners. The 'Roadmap' aims to map existing work going on in the city region, which is relevant to the 'Smart Cities' agenda, and to identify how this fits into the future vision, the challenges and gaps which exist and the future solutions and innovation needs in terms of realizing the targets and aspirations of the Manchester city region.

The 'Roadmap' is seen as a first stage in the process of developing the Local Digital Agenda for Manchester and the Green Paper is in place to stimulate discussion and consultations so that these responses can be used to validate proposals for future work and that this will be able to inform the production and implementation of the Local Digital Agenda for Manchester. This is, in turn, linked to innovative new approaches in other policy areas, particularly the City's new Environmental Strategy, where the local digital agenda can provide a strong cross-cutting theme for innovation through digital technologies.

Manchester's commitment, as exemplified in 'Manchester: A Certain Future', the city's Climate Change Action Plan for 2010-20, is to implement a detailed set of action to make Manchester a greener, cleaner, healthier, wealthier and greater city. The aim is to become a low-carbon city by 2020, reducing carbon emissions with 41 per cent less CO_2 than in 2005 and where 'low-carbon thinking' is embedded in all aspects of how people live and work in the city.

The Green Paper also sets out what are seen as the real challenges for realizing the 'Smart Cities' vision in Manchester, particularly in terms of creating: 'active citizen engagement in the planning, development and delivery of future internet-enabled services in ways which are accessible, empowering and sustainable'. There is certainly a much wider appreciation of why this is being suggested or, in some cases, demanded, but this has not yet been matched by action at any widespread or systematic level. This is why Manchester is committed to the three step approach outlined below:

Firstly, identifying and analysing good practice, e.g. 'OpenApps' development, 'Apps4' places,[4] which are felt to be relevant and (potentially) transferable to pilot projects being developed at a local level.

Secondly, acting as a catalyst to generate new pilot projects that build on existing good practice at a local level but which also embrace new developments from across Europe and globally which are identified through supporting networks, such as EUROCITIES and the European Network of Living Labs (ENoLL).

Thirdly, drawing out the lessons learned to identify how best to use and re-use the results from pilot projects, both in terms of enhancing the scope and scale at a local level, through extending their reach and developing new business models applicable locally, and in terms of wider replicability across Europe.

Making an Impact: European Policies and Funding for Manchester as a Future Internet enabled 'Smart City'

The experience gained through the delivery of projects supported through European networks and EU funding, as above, over the past five years has enabled Manchester to develop a new focus for its work around the idea that citizen engagement, 'smart citizens', needs to be at the centre of Manchester's proposed "Local Digital Agenda", creating a virtuous circle whereby:

- **Digital inclusion** generates skills and aspirations across all sections of society and re-engages people in all aspects of civic life, and;
- **Digital industries** generate new employment opportunities and pathways into these through skill development with local people and the institutions that support this, particularly schools and colleges, and;
- **Digital innovation** is the engine of this growth, with new next generation open access digital infrastructures and services, such as smart energy and smart health/wellbeing, underpinning this and enabling more sustainable growth while supporting greater community engagement which, in turn, supports digital inclusion, especially through Manchester Living Lab initiatives.

The key to realizing this, as a 'Smart City' strategy for the city region, is to sustain the momentum of work done to date through:

- **City leadership** (continuing support from the main decision makers at the highest level);

---

4   Examples include: http://www.verkkodemokratia.fi/apps4finland and http://www.gov20.de/apps-4-berlin/

- **Investment** in new digital infrastructures and services (even in spite of the economic crisis, where new and more innovative approaches and business models will be needed more than ever);
- **Exemplar projects** and activities which really stimulate interest and engagement (two examples in Manchester currently would be the Manchester Digital Lab, MadLab, and the Future Everything Festival).

The Future Internet enabled 'Smart City' is about the transformation of urban living through the imaginative use of digital technologies and ensuring that this can make a significant contribution to sustainable economic growth both immediately and in the longer term. At the same time these technologies also provide opportunities to transform the lives of local residents and the neighbourhoods where they live. This is why the focus on tackling the digital divide and promoting digital inclusion is continuing to be seen as a priority, highlighting the need to ensure that citizens have the capacity, skills and motivation to take advantage of these technologies and that there is a real commitment to focus not only on the transformation of public services in terms of 'business process' but also on co-production, the direct and active engagement of users in the design, delivery and, where needed, the ownership of services.

Some of the policies, as outlined above, are in place to facilitate and support the transformation process of Manchester into a 'Smart City', but there is still much to be done to ensure that the opportunities that the Future Internet can provide to a city region such as Manchester are fully exploited.

There are a number of specific lessons that can learnt from the Manchester's experience which will be used to inform future strategies and the proposed Local Digital Agenda for Manchester in particular:

- The need to develop digitally enabled services that are based on the social, cultural and economic needs of the neighbourhoods, requiring a combination of detailed local research and real efforts to consult with and engage local people as an essential prerequisite for capturing user needs and involving users in the design and delivery of new services, the start of the co-production process;
- That the stakeholders in the project, especially the public sector, need to demonstrate a long term commitment to community engagement and capacity building and invest as much in the development of people's skills, confidence and aspirations as in the technology being deployed;
- The need to have an ongoing evaluation strategy that not only has the ability to identify weaknesses, and even failures, but also has the role of communicating these results directly into the strategic decision making process so that the project can adapt and evolve as quickly and effectively as possible, backed up by effective project management resources;
- The importance of developing real exemplars that push the boundaries of what people know and their expectations, so that people's imaginations are

stimulated and horizons widened and that this is communicated with all the power that Future Internet enabled communications can bring, making use of all the capabilities that the most effective social media and social networking can offer;

- The potential for generating added value from innovation and new investment into the area while at the same time focusing existing investment within those locations and sectors which are most capable of delivering growth, in order to respond to the ongoing structural shifts in the economy towards knowledge industries, including Future Internet enabled services, particularly as this is accelerated by economic crisis.

This is the basis for the next stage of this work in Manchester:

- Using the Manchester Green Paper on 'Smart Cities: creating an inclusive and sustainable knowledge society' to stimulate further interest and involvement in the concept and future development through consultation and engagement;
- Developing the new 'Local Digital Agenda for Manchester' to support future work, coordinated by the MDDA and the Manchester Living Lab initiative with stakeholders and partners from across the city region;
- Continuing to build the trans-European 'Connected Smart Cities Network' to exchange experience and expertise on how to translate the concept of the 'smart city' into reality, working with networks including EUROCITIES and the European Network of Living Labs, and securing resources through EU collaborative projects and other initiatives.

References

Carter, D. (2013). Urban Regeneration, Digital Development Strategies and the Knowledge Economy: Manchester Case Study. Journal of the Knowledge Economy, 4(2), 169-189.

European Commission (2011). Digital Agenda for Europe. [Online]. Available at http://ec.europa.eu/information_society/digital-agenda/index_en.htm [accessed: 2011].

Manchester Digital Development Agency (2005). [Online]. Available at www. manchesterdda.com [accessed: 2011].

Manchester Digital (2011). [Online]. Available at http://www.manchesterdigital. com/ [accessed: 2011].

Open Living Labs (2011). [Online]. Available at http://www.openlivinglabs. eu/ [accessed: 2011].

Chapter 10
Rotterdam

Karima Azaoum and Chris de Lange

City Profile

Rotterdam's city profile is distinguished by the following: a large, young and diverse city that has experienced a great deal and has much to offer its residents. Through the ages the city has grown from a small fishing village into a world port. The devastation of the World War II bombardment has been overcome by rebuilding the city centre and redesigning it. The city is still always developing in this respect. Rotterdam is an enterprising city, where everyone has his place: a place to work, to learn, to relax. It is an attractive place for businesses, both on the national and international level. The advantageous location and easy accessibility also play a role. The issues that the city contends with are mostly of a social nature.

Spatial Features

Rotterdam and its conurbation together form the most densely populated area in the Netherlands. Other cities surrounding the Rotterdam region, like Delft, The Hague and Dordrecht, complement the strengths of the (greater) functional urban region. Together with Amsterdam, it is the most important urban engine of the Randstad.

Rotterdam is one of the major crossroads of world trade. Its strategic location in the delta of Rhine and Meuse give excellent access to the European market by road, rail, air and water. It is also connected to a vast network of fibre optic cables and pipelines. The open connection of the Port of Rotterdam to the North Sea, the busiest shipping route in the world, connects Europe to all the biggest western economies as well as the rising economies in Asia, the Middle East and South America. The port has become an international centre for trade and distribution, the city a home to a dynamic and diverse population.

Demographic and Social Structure and Change

Rotterdam is located in one of the most densely populated areas of the Netherlands. In terms of size, the city, with well over 610,000 inhabitants, is one of the largest in the Netherlands. Even though Rotterdam is one of the largest cities, it does have difficulty growing. At the moment, Rotterdam has lower population growth in comparison with the rest of the Netherlands. Forecasts predict that, up until 2025, the number of residents will increase by about 2 per cent. This is in sharp contrast to the national average increase, which is predicted to be around 4.5 per cent (Gemeente Rotterdam, 2011).

Statistics show that Rotterdam has a striking number of young residents. This makes it a young city, with the ambition to stay young. On 1 January 2011, Rotterdam had 101,479 residents between ages 20-29. Compared to the other age groups, this is by far the largest. Compared with the rest of the Netherlands, the number of young residents is noticeably large. One of the consequences of this is that the population is ageing slower in Rotterdam than it does in the rest of the country.

As all port cities, Rotterdam has attracted many people, seeking trade or work, sailing in and out, from all quarters of the compass. Industrialisation attracted many farmers from the southern provinces to the south bank, nicknamed the 'boerenzij' (farmers bank). Later immigrants from China, Southern Europe, the Mediterranean, the Netherlands Antilles and Surinam and more recently Eastern Europe, followed. Diversity is one of the stand-out characteristics of the Rotterdam scene. The city harbours a great variety of nationalities and their accompanying cultures. In 2011, Rotterdam was home to 166 different nationalities representing virtually every corner of the globe (Gemeente Rotterdam, 2011b).

In the course of a year, there is an influx of new city residents but also the departure of others. In general, the profile of the incoming resident can be typified as young, single, an immigrant and/or relatively poor. The departing 'Rotterdammer' is of a different 'stereotype': living together – with or without children – more well-to-do, higher educated and/or native Dutch. It appears that the residents of Rotterdam use the city to advance on the social ladder, also known as the 'lift function'. Once they have achieved a higher 'rung' they will be more inclined to leave the city. That said, this does not necessarily mean that Rotterdam does not attract the higher-educated and those holding higher-paying positions.

There are notable differences in the preferences people have as regards their choice of where to settle in. Poorer and lower-educated people gravitate toward Rotterdam Zuid (Rotterdam South), which is known as one of the most vulnerable areas in Rotterdam. In contrast, residents with better potential, such as students and those who are actively working, are more likely to locate to other parts of Rotterdam (Gemeente Rotterdam, 2010)

(Brief) History of Rotterdam

Rotterdam began as a 13th-century fishing village that lay on the banks of the river Rotte. The village people built a dam in this river to reduce flooding. The city transformed over the years into an urban settlement and starting in the 16th century, trade and industry began to develop (Gemeente Rotterdam, 2011c) The city expanded even further in the nineteenth century and advances in technology followed each other in rapid succession. A railway was built that significantly improved the connections with Amsterdam, Utrecht and Antwerp. Construction of the Nieuwe Waterweg canal provided better access to Rotterdam for shipping. As early as the 19th century, Rotterdam was one of the largest ports in the Netherlands. Completion of the Nieuwe Waterweg caused explosive growth of the port and local population. The increase in port activity attracted workers; residential areas were built on the South bank to house these new port workers. At the end of the nineteenth century many commercial buildings servicing the port and industry sectors were built. These developments, in combination with plans for improving the residential areas, continued up until World War II.

At the beginning of World War II a large part of the city centre was destroyed due to a bombardment. Initially, the rebuilding activities were focused on the recovery and expansion of the ports and wharves. During the 1950s however, large-scale residential building projects started as well. Some of the major projects from that period can still be seen in the streets. Examples include the Groothandelsgebouw and the Lijnbaan – the first car-free shopping zone in Europe. At the same time new living areas were developed around the old districts that surrounded the city centre. Citizens, especially young families, moved out to the outskirts, leaving the old districts to newcomers and students. Urban renewal of these districts started in the seventies.

Industrialization made the port and city jump across the river and develop the South bank at the end of the nineteenth century. Ports and industrial estates were developed further, growing bigger and bigger and moving out more and more away from the city centre, towards the coast. In the seventies new expansions of the port, the Maasvlakte, were built in reclaimed land and this process still goes on. The Port of Rotterdam has an open and fast connection to the North Sea and the rest of the world. Over the ages Rotterdam invested and continued to invest to deepen and restructure the port to become one of the most open and modern in the world. The Port of Rotterdam developed into the main port of Europe and connects Europe to the world (main port of call). One of the most important developments for the port was the construction and expansion of the Maasvlakte.

The move of the ports towards and into the North Sea left the city with old docklands and industrial estates. The city that first expanded into the region, has since the seventies been restructuring the old city (urban) districts as well as the old ports into new housing, tourism/leisure and business districts. The small old ports on the North bank have, from the seventies on, been turned into housing and leisure areas. The restructuring of the bigger ports on the South bank started in the eighties with the development of the Kop van Zuid, the area opposite to the city centre. A new iconic bridge was build to better connect the two sides of the city. During the last decade the redevelopment of Stadshavens Rotterdam was taken up, an enormous former port area close to the city, to be transformed into high quality living and working environments in the next decade.

Economic Structure and Economic Performance of the City

The port, industry and the care sector are all important to the Rotterdam economy. These sectors offer the most employment. The Rotterdam economic vitality web as outlined in the Economic Outlook 2011 (Ontwikkelingsbedrijf Rotterdam, 2011) shows which areas of the Rotterdam economy are doing well and which are doing less so. In the labour market, location and infrastructure areas, Rotterdam scores above the national average. In the latter two areas, the position of the city is also quite in line with the three other major cities. Rotterdam is less competitive in the knowledge and innovation areas. Businesses provide fewer positions to knowledge workers than they do in other cities. The number of knowledge workers in Rotterdam does lie around the national average. The level of industrial innovation is lower than that of the Dutch industry sector in general. By contrast, business services and the distribution sector have a level of innovation higher than the national average. Rotterdam's economically advantageous position is due to very high labour productivity (port and industrial complex) and the high number of beginning entrepreneurs.

A large part of the economy is driven by providing for the city's own residents. Around 186,000 jobs are directly linked to providing for the residents, the other 174,000 jobs are the result of the regional core function of the city and its advantageous location. Despite the economic contraction due to the recession, Rotterdam is performing better than the Dutch average. In 2009, this contraction amounted to 3.3 per cent. In addition, there was slight growth in employment during this period. The business services and care sector are responsible for this growth in employment. The sectors that the Rotterdam economy traditionally relies on, specifically the port, industry, transport and logistics, have been hit relatively hard by the crisis. Nevertheless, the port of Rotterdam is still doing well (Ontwikkelingsbedrijf Rotterdam, 2011).

The majority of the businesses in Rotterdam are small and medium-sized enterprises (SME). Although there are only 22 large businesses with more than 1,000 employees, together they account for a large share of employment. In 2010, these large companies employed 38,109 persons. The two largest employers in Rotterdam are the Erasmus MC (c.13,000 employees) and the Municipality of Rotterdam (c.12,000 employees). At the moment, the most important sectors to the Rotterdam economy are wholesale and retail trade, transport and storage and the care sector. For the coming two years, the number of jobs in Rotterdam is projected to increase by 0.8 per cent per year. Over the medium term (2013-2015), growth is expected to be slightly higher. This growth is roughly equal to the national average. Over the years the self-starters appear to have contributed positively to the growth in employment in Rotterdam. From 1991 till now, self-starters have provided the city with 55,000 jobs.

The economic recession has had repercussions for Rotterdam's real estate market. The recession was not wholly unwelcome as regards the commercial property market, as there is a structural shortage in this market. For specific sectors like logistics and wholesale trade, however, it remains difficult to find suitable space in the Rotterdam region. The office space market has been severely impacted by the recession. For a number of years, this market was already too large, in the sense that demand has long severely outstripped supply. The impact on the housing market is possibly more limited. This is due to the percentage of home owners in Rotterdam being relatively low (30 per cent of households). The care sector has greatly expanded in recent years and has provided for the largest employment growth, together with the government and education sectors (Gemeente Rotterdam, 2011d). Between 2011 and 2015, the net amount of job openings is expected to rise to 18,000, which is 5 per cent of the total number of jobs (Gemeente Rotterdam, 2011d). In the coming years, employers will be faced with an outflow of retirees. In the Rotterdam region, the educational sector, industry, construction and transport will have to contend the most with the ageing of the workforce (Gemeente Rotterdam, 2011d).

Although there are enough jobs in Rotterdam, the number of unemployed residents in the city itself is relatively high. Part of this can be explained by the fact that the workforce does not live in Rotterdam, but in the surrounding area (Ontwikkelingsbedrijf Rotterdam, 2011). In comparison with other cities and the national average, the gross labour market participation rate of the Rotterdam residents is low. Out of the four largest cities, Rotterdam has the highest number of unemployed as a percentage to the size of the working population: 12.8 per cent, compared to 9.6 per cent for Amsterdam, 8.7 per cent for The Hague and 5.3 per cent for Utrecht.

In comparison with other large cities, Rotterdam has fewer highly-educated people. This is concerning given the importance of the higher-educated for economical development. At the same time, Rotterdam has a good starting position. The presence of the Erasmus University, Rotterdam University, an INHolland University of Applied Sciences establishment and the close proximity of the Delft University of Technology attract many thousands of smart, young people to the region every year. These educational institutions ensure that there is a constant stream of fresh, highly-educated people entering Rotterdam (Ontwikkelingsbedrijf Rotterdam, 2011). The statistics moreover show that the higher the educational level, the more mobile the employee/resident. Being able to provide attractive housing and employment is therefore necessary to retain this group of highly-educated residents in the city. Another interesting detail is that is appears that with the rise of the educational level, there is a commensurate rise in the preference for urban living: more EUR graduates live in the city 1.5 years after graduation than work there.

This provides Rotterdam with opportunities. The bond with the city is the strongest when there is a connection built up with the city during the student years. This occurs most easily when the student lives in Rotterdam during their studies and builds up a social network here. In short, Rotterdam is successful in attracting students and also entices them to stay after graduation. However, they do not stay in Rotterdam for long: over time they leave again, causing Rotterdam to remain a city with a relatively low number of highly educated residents when compared to other large cities.

Rotterdam's weakest points are housing and the living environment and the standard of living of the residents. When it comes to housing and the living environment, Rotterdam performs strongly when it comes to education and medical care, but in comparison with other cities it does not score as highly in the cultural sector and the hotel and catering industry. Rotterdam averages under the Dutch standard for average standard of living, as it does average under that of the other three large cities.

Developments and Policy Changes since Early 1990s

Rotterdam strives to be an innovative and constantly evolving city. Over the last 30 years, this focus on innovation has become evident in the many developments that have taken place. There have been noticeable changes in both the economy and urban development. Economically, Rotterdam was stimulated to develop into a knowledge economy. The emergence of the service sector brought with it new expectations for the skill level of personnel: a higher level of education, or a completely different type of education. With extra attention paid to the services sector, this also brought with it improvements in the infrastructure in and around Rotterdam. The Municipality also began to place more importance on the quality of the living environment and housing conditions, both as regards housing and security. The disadvantaged neighbourhoods were given priority attention. Later on, the Municipality focused more on attracting middle-income residents to the city and on establishing large-scale projects, including in the city centre.

Knowledge Economy

The global economy faced a big downturn in the eighties. From 1985 onwards, the economy started growing again, both nationally and internationally, and the same applied to Rotterdam. Urban renewal became the ideal (van den Bent, 2010). There was less of a focus on the port (the 'wet') and more on the services sector (the 'dry'). In addition to being a world port, the city began to develop a distribution function, in order to position itself as a world trade centre. In order to reach this goal, it was necessary to develop the IT and services sectors, education and science, and small and medium-sized enterprises (SMEs). In addition, this focus shift called for large-scale investment in infrastructure. The Municipality of Rotterdam, the national Government and entrepreneurs collectively invested millions of guilders in new projects. Some of these projects were the expansion of the metro system, the doubling of the Van Brienenoord Bridge and the construction of the second Benelux tunnel.

Between 1993 and 2003, Rotterdam lost around 22,000 jobs in the industry, transport, wholesale trade and communication sectors. The direct causes were mainly the oil crisis, the competition from low-wage countries and technological advancements which reduced the need for labour. The labour-saving techniques in the nineties led to a rapid decline in employment in the transport sector and industry. However, at the same time, employment rose in the education, care, and business services sectors, with 60,000 new jobs being created in these sectors a clear shift between sectors thereby became visible.

The overall development of the 'knowledge economy' resulted in a rapid decline in jobs with lower educational requirements (van den Bent, 2010). This made it clear to the Municipality that Rotterdam needed to focus more on education, eliminating illiteracy, training for those with less education, and extra training for those with higher educations. This trend was also noticed in the Port of Rotterdam. Due to the continuing technological developments, the Port became a higher quality, knowledge-intensive operation with less need low-skilled workforce.

From Urban Renewal to Social Renewal to Urban Regeneration

The concept of urban renewal came into vogue at the beginning of the seventies. Central to urban renewal was careful renovation and improvement of the housing and living environment in older neighbourhoods. Improving accessibility and the functions of the city centre were a high priority as well. The urban renewal was mainly directed at residents with lower incomes and the development of housing was aligned to that target group. This focus resulted in the – inevitable – departure of the middle class from these areas (van den Bent, 2010).

Ten years from the introduction of the urban renewal drive there was a change in its perception. In this period, attention was mainly given to small-scale projects and social housing; this resulted in neglecting large-scale projects like creating a new use for the old port area. The City Centre Plan 1985 made connecting the city centre to the riverside into the central issue of the redevelopment of the city (van den Bent, 2010). The first development plans for the Kop van Zuid were also made in this time. A second change in perception involved the increased attention paid to the social problems of the neighbourhoods that had formed the target for urban renewal and in which low-income groups and immigrants were now concentrated. Urban renewal has become social renewal: not only are the structural quality of the housing and the environment improved, but social cohesion and management are being given attention as well. Quality, not quantity, of the living environment now is the goal. The idea was that, by improving the physical development of the city, the high and middle-income earners would once again choose to establish themselves in the city.

The latest trend is urban regeneration. This trend emphasizes social integration by building higher income housing on the left bank of the river Meuse. The goal is to achieve a less one-sided supply of housing and hence to maintain the higher-income earners in the city or entice them back to Rotterdam (van den Bent, 2010). In addition, attention is paid to security and retention. The latter means that, on the one hand, parts of the city are demolished and rebuilt, like the Nieuw-Crooswijk neighbourhood. Also, major projects are launched by the Municipality, such as the construction of the Beurstraverse ('Koopgoot') in the city centre. On the other hand, early twentieth-century housing complexes are being restored. This trend still continues.

Security Policy

From 1994 onwards, an 'explicit' security policy was employed in Rotterdam. This policy was maintained up until 2001 but ultimately it did not deliver many improvements. The policy had a number of disadvantages. It was said to be too project oriented and to be reactive rather than preventive or repressive. A third problem was that actions were often taken without there being sufficient proof.

In 2002, there was a change in thinking about the approach to security in Rotterdam. The direct cause of this was the emergence of the Leefbaar Rotterdam political party. The theme of the party's election campaign was 'Improve urban security'. The Municipal Executive that was formed in 2002 took over this party's ideas on security party and used them to develop a new policy. The goal was for there to be no more unsafe neighbourhoods in Rotterdam and for security to be maintained at a high level (van den Berg et al., 2005). On the basis of the so-called safety index, there has since been a look at the state of safety within the different neighbourhoods (Gemeente Rotterdam, 2011e).

Rotterdam Climate Initiative

The Rotterdam Climate Initiative started in 2008 with the aim of improving the climate for the benefit of people, the environment, and the economy. It was launched by the Port of Rotterdam, the City of Rotterdam, employers' organization Deltalinqs and DCMR Environmental Protection Agency Rijnmond. It created a movement in which government, organizations, companies, knowledge institutes, and citizens collaborate to achieve a 50 per cent reduction of CO_2 emissions, adapt to climate change, and promote the economy in the Rotterdam region.

The Rotterdam Municipal Executive works on with the new Rotterdam Sustainability Programme in order to reduce carbon emissions by half, preparing for the consequences of climate change, improving air quality and reducing noise. The Municipal Executive will invest €28 million in order to achieve the green ambitions.

City Governance and Regional Collaboration

After an amendment of the Municipalities Act (Gemeentewet) in 1964, it became possible for the municipalities to set up submunicipalities. The first submunicipalities were established in the seventies. At the beginning of 1990, the Municipal Executive issued a memorandum entitled 'Municipal Decentralisation and Submunicipalities in the 90s', which, for the first time, characterized the relationship between the municipal council and the submunicipalities as complementary. On the basis of this memorandum, the municipal council decided on 12 April 1990 to implement the submunicipality system throughout the entire city, with the exception of the centre. The submunicipalities became increasingly independent over time. They formed part of the municipality in the beginning, but over time have become their own bodies. They were assigned more duties and given more powers. Partly as a result of this, the central coordination of the submunicipalities has become a growing point of concern. The submunicipalities eventually became independent executive organisations with their own personnel. In the late nineties, the submunicipalities were furthermore allowed to have a say in improving governance in Rotterdam.

On a regional level, over the years, various bodies have attempted to connect the surrounding regions in order to implement a joint policy. Regional collaboration in the Rotterdam area began with the creation of the *Rijnmond public body*, in the sixties. This was an intermediate body between the province and the municipalities. It was a democratically elected body and it was especially significant in the field of spatial planning, the environment, outdoor recreation and ambulance transport. Rijnmond's policy was in jeopardy in the early eighties. Criticism was levelled against the organisation interfering too much with Rotterdam. A lobby was started to have the public body abolished. This was successful and by 1 February 1986 the Rijnmond public body was dissolved. The successor to Rijnmond are the city regions. The city regions should be seen as an extra layer of administration alongside the national government, the province, the municipalities and the water board. In contrast to the Rijnmond body, the city region's administrators are not directly elected by the citizen. Within the city regions the municipalities work together on the development and implementation of policy. Central policy themes are space, traffic, living, working the environment and youth care. In the meantime, the focus is being shifted to development of the The Hague-Rotterdam metropolitan region. The Rotterdam and Haaglanden city regions are to form a metropolitan region together.

Besides collaboration on the regional level, there is also collaboration between the four major cities referred to in the Revitalising policy for major cities ('Grotestedenbeleid'), the G4. The initiative for the establishment of the G4 came from the national government in 1994. The main goal of the policy was to improve housing, working, and living in the major cities. The G4 collectively determine which results should be achieved in these areas. It is up to the cities themselves to decide on how to achieve these results.

State of the City

This section discusses Rotterdam's strengths and points of improvement. The strengths are explained and there is also description of the ways in which the improvements are being worked on. The points for improvement in general all tie in with the theme of 'improving the lift function of the city' – and especially of Zuid. The strengths of the city are to be found in the port area, urban development and the business sector. Currently, the port is being expanded (Maasvlakte 2) and partially redeveloped (Stadshavens Rotterdam), and there is work being done on a new central station in the city centre to increase the accessibility to the city from other cities/countries. Rotterdam is not working on this alone. Help is being provided for various projects, mainly by means of subsidisation by the national government and the European Union.

Restoration of the 'Lift Function'

For years, the traditional logic of reconstruction was to solve problems by building, filling empty spots, starting projects – a physical effort with its own dynamics. Due to the stagnant market and the declining financial position of the Municipality, that approach was no longer useful and choices had to be made in the physical programme. A new, integrated way of thinking was required, the objective being to carry out those projects that would contribute most to the social and economic objectives of the city. The ambition to restore the lift function to the city brings all efforts in the physical, social and economic areas under one umbrella.

The current efforts are now focused on economic priorities, and the spatial-social approach through the focus on specific neighbourhoods and the South Pact investment programme are working in the right direction, but do not seem to be having enough impact to resolve the issues. Instead of this 'acupuncture approach', an integrated system approach is needed, an approach by means of which the existing problems are addressed and dealt with through coordinated action, both social and physical, in the field of education, economy and employment, market confidence is restored and the city will regain the strength and vitality to fulfil its lift function for the locals.

The restoration of the lift function is thus the key challenge for the coming years. By itself, the fact that social climbers depart is no cause for alarm, but an outflow that has become too large in relation to the inflow affects the lift capacity of the city. The consequence is that there are too few social climbers in the city to facilitate the rise of others. By now, Rotterdam has to contend with the situation that there are too many low-level entrants streaming in and too many upwardly mobile residents leaving the city. This is sometimes referred to as selective migration (Gemeente Rotterdam, 2010).

Obstacles to the Lift Function

One of the causes for the hampered lift function of the city has to do with the supply of housing. As a result of the cheap housing on offer, many people are attracted to the city. These are, in particular, people who generally connect to the bottom of the social ladder and who in the main should and need to develop further. Too many inhabitants, certainly from this group, have difficulty forming connections. In addition, there are other conditions which play a role. Part of the Rotterdam-based population is in many respects limited in being able to take part in social life: they are early school leavers, they do not practice sports, they may move too little or they do not speak the language that well (Gemeente Rotterdam, 2010). In particular, problems with integration, such as the language deficiency in both children and adults, are problematic. This group of citizens lacks a connection with

(Dutch-speaking) society. It is difficult to obtain an education and a degree, and it causes problems at a later stage when trying to find a job. In the area of health as well, there are striking differences. Research by the Erasmus MC has shown that Rotterdam locals – especially from Rotterdam Zuid – have poorer health and lower life expectancy than people in other (large) Dutch cities. An explanation can be found in unhealthy behaviour, such as inactivity and an unhealthy diet, but air pollution plays a role as well. Such poor health can be problematic for the economy, because sick people cannot work and leads to more people living on benefits. The Municipality of Rotterdam now aims to improve urban health. A first step towards improvement has been to have the Maasstad Hospital constructed in Rotterdam Zuid.

As a result of migration to the city in the past, partly inspired by the many manufacturing jobs to be had, a large group of low-skilled workers now live in Rotterdam. This group is increasingly less able to meet the growing demands of the modern labour market. Their children often do not obtain higher education, with the result that the disadvantage is passed on and the problem continues to develop.

Rotterdam South

Typically, someone moving into Rotterdam chooses to live in the pre-war neighbourhoods, which are in the main to be found in South. This is different in Amsterdam, for example, where new incoming migrants spread themselves throughout the city. Amsterdam also has a large influx of people with few prospects, but due to Amsterdam having a much stronger layer of advantaged people, these newcomers can more easily be taken in. The conclusion of the foregoing, roughly, is that the lift function is overloaded and stagnating in (chiefly) Rotterdam South. Having almost 200,000 residents, that concerns a large area. The majority of the 100,000 residences housing vulnerable families are located in this area. Unemployment here is noticeably higher than average. The new settlers in this area generally have low incomes, on average of €3,000 less than the rest of Rotterdam. The proportion of residents receiving benefits as their main income is also higher. In the field of education, South is lagging behind the rest of Rotterdam. Amongst other issues, the proportion of drop-outs is higher. The proportion of unemployed youth is higher as well. There is a positive net outflow of people with relatively higher purchasing power. This is because there is not enough suitable housing and jobs and also due to the poor accessibility of South: large parts of South are less attractive for the middle class as a residential environment, because the travel time to work locations in the Randstad is too long. Meanwhile, the large existing supply of housing for vulnerable groups ensures a continuing heavy influx of the disadvantaged.

The problems at play in Rotterdam are out-sized in comparison with those in other cities.[1] At this scale, they influence structure-enhancing investments,

---

1 The net migration of Rotterdam, being the number of residents minus the number of departing migrants, differs greatly from the other three major cities. Rotterdam has a negative balance, unlike the other cities.

including the realization of the housing programme, because they have a negative effect on the image and the residential and business climate of the entire city. The problems are mutually reinforcing: the bad housing supply comes with social and security issues, leading to the departure of social climbers, which in turn is at the expense of the lift function of the city. The city has a great capacity to offer its residents opportunities to advance but, owing to the accumulation of problems in a large part of South, there are seemingly no opportunities to stop this vicious circle. The municipality is therefore committed, through various projects, to break the southern part of the city out of this circle.

Influential New Policy Programmes and Projects

Below we describe the most influential new policy programmes and projects:

The *Rotterdam South Pact* (2006-2015) is a joint additional investment programme for Rotterdam South running until 2015 that has been drawn up by housing corporations, municipal authorities and submunicipalities in Rotterdam Zuid. The programme endorses the great importance of an additional strategy for Rotterdam Zuid and indicates which investments by the various parties are necessary. The Pact not only builds on existing initiatives, but also guarantees that measures are first and foremost intensified, adjusted and geared to one another.

The *Quality Leap South* (Kwaliteitssprong Zuid, 2011-2030) programme aims to tackle the disadvantaged position of South through talent development. A climate for learning and working needs to be formed, causing the social and educational level of its inhabitants to rise. The ambition is to bring South up to the same level as the rest of the Netherlands by 2030. The Municipality, the national government and other partners will cooperate towards this objective. The program is organized at a national level because the socio-economic problems concerned are 'in size and intensity, unprecedented in the Netherlands, while the young population in South is badly needed to foster further innovation and development of the major Dutch sectors such as the port, logistics and healthcare' (Gemeente Rotterdam, 2011f, p. 1.).

The development of both Maasvlakte areas caused available space to be created in *Stadshavens Rotterdam*, between the Erasmus Bridge and the Benelux Tunnel. An area of approximately 1600 hectares is available to be transformed and restructured (2007-2015). Stadshavens Rotterdam wants to develop into a quality port and an excellent location, not only for port and transport-related industry, but also for innovative businesses and knowledge institutes. Rotterdam is also creating an image of itself as a trendsetter in the fields of sustainable energy and climate adaptation, with the aim of attracting professionals and pioneers keen to try out these new trends. Stadshavens Rotterdam can provide them with everything they need for setting up their businesses, along with exceptional residential developments, cultural amenities and good educational facilities.

In the period up to 2025, an increase of 6,100 available jobs, 1,700 of which require highly educated and 4,400 require moderately and poorly educated personnel, is expected. The movement towards becoming a knowledge port and quality service city therefore benefits not only the educated but also the lower and middle classes, since activity in high-value sectors in the chain, through outsourcing certain services, also results in the creation of low-grade jobs. Furthermore, this connection runs through the expenditures (domestic services, personal services).

Clean Tech Delta

Clean Tech Delta is a partnership between companies, knowledge institutions and government (c. 40 parties) in the Rotterdam-Delft region, which invests in clean technologies. Its mission is 'to invest in clean tech in order to reinforce the economic competitive edge with a cluster of innovative, future-proof companies and knowledge institutes and a quality stimulus for sustainable area development in the Rotterdam-Delft corridor' (CleanTech Delta, 2011). The focus is on four strong sectors: bio-based economy, water and delta technology, infrastructure and mobility, and sustainable development/sustainable construction. The Stadshavens area of Rotterdam is an example of an area working with clean tech.

Maasvlakte 2

Maasvlakte 2 is the expansion of the Port of Rotterdam (2008-2013). A new top European location for port activities and industry is being created immediately to the west of the present port and industrial area. When the construction of Maasvlakte 2 began in 2008, the sea there was 17 metres deep. Maasvlakte 2 existed on no map, except for the design drawings. Maasvlakte 2 will soon encompass 1,000 hectares net of industrial ground, located directly on deep water. In the construction of Maasvlakte 2, sustainability is continuously taken into account. The idea being that current investments should not be at the expense of the quality of life of future generations. The most sustainable solutions are always being sought after.

Rotterdam Centraal Station

The largest project currently running within the *Central Business District* is the redevelopment of the *Rotterdam Centraal station* (2008-2014). The city will obtain an attractive, dynamic, well-functioning public transport terminal. The new Rotterdam Centraal will be a transportation hub of regional and international significance. Regional, due to the commissioning of RandstadRail, a metro service connecting The Hague and Rotterdam Zuid. Internationally, the high-speed rail line HSL will ensure that the travel times between Rotterdam and Schiphol, Brussels and Paris shrink. Amsterdam Airport Schiphol can be reached within 19 minutes by high-speed rail. Due to the commissioning of high-speed rail and RandstadRail, it is expected that the number of travellers at Rotterdam Centraal station will have increased to some 323,000 per day by 2025 (Gemeente Rotterdam, 2011c). The development of the station is fully underway. The goal is that the station area will become a pedestrian zone, which means that car traffic will take place underground. An underground parking garage and a large underground bicycle park that will garage more than 5,100 bicycles will also be constructed.

Main Opportunities

The city benefits from the port and the opportunities it brings. The port in turn benefits from the proximity of the city, its labour force and knowledge, the attractive living climate and the international connections to the European hinterland. The rapidly developing Rotterdam energy, water and climate cluster is the figurehead and carrier of this transition process and the Stadshavens Rotterdam area is the spatial focus. The movement toward sustainability and innovation within this cluster is typical of the transition process towards becoming a knowledge port city that Rotterdam is undergoing (World Port City). Rotterdam shows the world that this city and port are prepared for climate change and have an outstanding and sustainable business climate at their disposal.

The main port forms an important trump card for the region to overcome the setback following the economic crisis. The direct seaport-related added value in Rotterdam-Rijnmond amounts to 15.5 billion euros (Port of Rotterdam, 2012). The city aims to in the future benefit more from the port by pulling in a larger proportion of that added value, in the shape of advanced business services, knowledge and innovation in the field of water and energy, international trade, etc.

The Rotterdam Port Authority's ambitions for the coming years are big. The Port Vision 2030 states: In 2030, Rotterdam is Europe's most important port and industry complex. It is a strong combination of the Global Hub and Europe's Industrial Cluster, both leading in efficiency and sustainability. Rotterdam is closely connected with other North West European industrial and logistic areas Based on the vision, the success factors and the trends, developments and estimates for cargo throughput, it is analysed which actions need to be taken to realize the vision. These are crucial actions that need to be taken under any circumstance to realize the vision:

- Transition of the industrial sector;
- Efficient logistic chains in a European network;
- Improving accessibility;
- Improving the quality of life;
- Innovation and decisiveness.

The vision is already partially implemented with the construction of Maasvlakte 2. There is a response to the growth of international trade. Also, it stimulates the Rotterdam economy: 1,000 hectares of modern industrial area are available to three business sectors: container transhipment companies, the chemical industry and distribution companies. These sectors will have the most urgent need for space in the coming years and benefit the most from being located at a deep draught berth. In the context of preserving the environment, the Port of Rotterdam places strict demands on new customers. Customers who wish to establish themselves, must perform their activities while keeping the environment in mind.

The City of Rotterdam aims to be the most sustainable port city of its kind: clean, green and healthy. Rotterdam intends to achieve this using ecologically responsible solutions that also generate social and economic benefits. For this, Rotterdam is working together with all necessary partners to transform the city into a pleasant, safe and healthy place in which the economy can flourish. Building 'governance capacity' is an important task. The capacity of local stakeholders to search for joint accepted solutions and to really make it happen is central in ensuring that the large potential for investments in sustainable solutions is realized.

Responding to climate change will enable us to keep the city safe, accessible, and attractive, now as well as in the future. This will benefit both the people who live and work in Rotterdam, and the businesses and corporations established in the area. Trendsetting research, innovative knowledge development and a dynamic and decisive implementation of the suggested measures will result in strong economic incentives. Collaborating with prominent partners, Rotterdam will become the most important innovative water knowledge city in the world, and an inspiring example to other delta cities.

New developments and restructuring of the city provide good opportunities to make sustainability concrete and tangible. Stadshavens Rotterdam, Heijplaat, the Central District near Centraal station and the Heart of South are all obvious examples. The development of these areas creates opportunities that benefit the city and the relevant district as well as the people of Rotterdam and parties such as developers, housing corporations, building constructors and investors.

Influence of National and EU Policies

The Dutch government is currently focusing on spending cuts. In connection with the economic crisis, the effects of which are still being felt, cuts must be made in various arenas, including the municipalities. Not only do the cutbacks affect the subsidies Rotterdam receives from the national government for its operations, the reduced budget also impacts the way policy is formed by the Municipality. Another shift in thinking by the Municipality of Rotterdam is that it aims to co-create, with citizens and businesses involved in the development of policy. 'Work together' is the core idea. This involves eliciting and facilitating initiatives by companies and citizens. Increasingly, the Municipality is looking for this collaboration with corporations and industry.

EU legislation and regulations are closely monitored to ensure that Rotterdam can exert influence during the legislative process and be prepared for implementation. European specialists also keep the relevant subjects under review, endeavouring to secure subsidies and using their extensive European networks to represent Rotterdam's interests. An example of the influences of European regulatory policy is the manner in which procurement must be done by the municipality.

Europe is also a co-financier of local projects in Rotterdam. The city's services and institutions are grateful to benefit from European subsidy programmes. The city has a vast experience in applying for, spending of and accounting for European subsidies, especially in the field of urban development, urban policy. Rotterdam is the only local authority in Europe that has been given the responsibility as management authority for an Operational Programme of the ERDF, Kansen voor West. The Kansen voor Rotterdam [Opportunities for Rotterdam] component was given 46 million in European subsidies. In 2010, grants were awarded from this fund to the Floating Pavilion, De Hofbogen, the redesign of public space in Katendrecht and the revitalisation of the Oude Noorden shopping area, amongst others. The exchange of knowledge plays an important role in all European subsidies. Recruitment of European subsidies means not only extra money, but also the chance to acquire knowledge and to bring in personal experiences in further policy development.

References

Bent, E. van den (2010). *Proeftuin Rotterdam: droom en daad tussen 1975 en 2005.* Amsterdam: Uitgeverij Boom.

Berg, L. van den, Mingardo, G., Pol, P. and Speller, C. (2005). *The Safe City; Safety and Urban Development in European Cities.* Aldershot: Ashgate.

Clean Tech Delta (2011). [Online]. Available at: www.cleantechdelta.com/ resources/_files/clean_tech_flyer_a4.pdf [accessed: 2012]

Gemeente Rotterdam (2011). *Staat van Rotterdam 2011.* Rotterdam, Centrum voor Onderzoek en Statistiek, Gemeente Rotterdam.

Gemeente Rotterdam (2011b). *Bevolking van Rotterdam naar land van nationaliteit.* [Online]. Available at http://www.rotterdam.nl/COS [accessed: 2012].

Gemeente Rotterdam (2011c). [Online]. Available at www.rotterdam.nl [accessed: 2011].

Gemeente Rotterdam (2011d). *Werkgelegenheidsmonitor, winter 2011.* [Online]. Available at http://www.rotterdam.nl/COS/monitoren per cent20en per cent20indexen/Werkgelegenheidsmonitor per cent20Rotterdam per cent20winter per cent202011.pdf [accessed: 2012].

Gemeeente Rotterdam (2011e). *Veiligheidsindex.* [Online]. Available at http:// www.v-index.nl/ [accessed: 2012]

Gemeente Rotterdam, (2011f). *Zuid werkt! Nationaal Programma kwaliteitssprong Zuid, 2011.* [Online]. Available at http://www.rotterdam.nl/ BSD/Document/Perskamer/Zuid per cent20Werkt! per cent20nationaal per cent20programma per cent20Kwaliteitsprong per cent20Zuid per cent20met per cent20handtekening.pdf [accessed: 2012].

Gemeente Rotterdam (2010), Komen en gaan selectieve migratie in Rotterdam 2009. Centrum voor Onderzoek en Statistiek (COS). Rotterdam: Gemeente Rotterdam.

OntwikkelingsbedrijfRotterdam(2011).EconomischeVerkenningRotterdam2011. [Online]. Available at http://www.rotterdam.nl/OBR/Document/Economie/ EVR2011/EVR2011.pdf [accessed: 2012]

Port of Rotterdam (2012). *Havenvisie 2030*. Rotterdam: Port of Rotterdam.

Chapter 11
Looking Back and Forward

Leo van den Berg, Jan van der Meer and Luis Carvalho

Introduction

This chapter summarises the insights gained from the previous city reports, namely on how Cities and their officials have tried (and continue to try) to give substance to sustainable competitiveness. Competitive cities are cities with the *dynamic* capacity to grow and develop over time, nurturing and attracting jobs, people and skills. However, in order to do so effectively, in the medium- and long-term, competitiveness relies on social and environmental dimensions as well. Thus, for the purpose of this book, sustainable competitiveness is defined as the ability of cities to keep growing and developing over time while fostering social cohesion and environmental quality. Even in times of general economic recession and financial meltdown, social and environmental dimensions are not luxury alternatives and restrictions to growth – they are becoming increasingly integral parts of a full urban development "equation".

Part 2 of this chapter looks back and explores how Cities have viewed this relation over the past two decades and how they have given it substance in their local policies; it also points out some more recent, new generation policies and projects deployed by cities to improve their sustainable competitiveness. The third part fleshes out a number of challenges and opportunities open to cities in order to pave the way towards more sustainable competitive urban economies. It concludes with some reflections on the roles of cities supporting change at the National and European level and implications from the perspective of the EU Cohesion policy for the coming decade.

Two Decades of Competitiveness-Oriented Urban Policies

What did Cities do in order to attract and retain (more knowledge-intensive) jobs, people and skills? The analysed reports are illustrative of the experiences of eight European cities. The stories of their policies were told in the "first person", from experienced representatives in the Cities, complementing other studies and more analytical reviews on similar issues (see Chapter 1). This makes the story unique and insightful, but naturally does not rule out potential interpretation biases or guarantees that all or the most relevant policies and initiatives were assessed and described. In fact, some reports explicit focus on some concrete policy dimensions, leaving others untouched. Yet, the reports together provide a general picture on how European Cities and their representatives saw the link between urban policies and urban competitiveness, and what did they do to make it happen over the last two decades.

Attractiveness and Quality of the Living Environment

In order to attract and retain knowledge-intensive activities, people and skills, most Cities worked hard to improve the quality of the living environment. The most paradigmatic initiatives focused on the regeneration of old or deprived city districts (city centres, waterfronts, and industrial districts), enacting better accessibility and facilities, cleaning the physical environment and providing the conditions for private investments in new quality housing. Hence, the rationale has often been to tackle competitiveness in an indirect fashion, by providing better infrastructure, amenities and nudging image change. The overall social remits of such interventions have sometimes been questioned by the City representatives themselves, as in some cases they led to social gentrification and paid lip service to more demanding social inclusion targets (e.g. Porter and Barber, 2007). All in all, they are often more illustrative of the attention paid to the link between environmental quality, the living environment and the leverage effect on private investment.

Most of the reports in this book illustrate such type of initiatives in detail. Antwerp carried out different urban revitalization projects in order to increase the urban quality and appeal of many districts, specially combined with a number of community development programmes. An example is the Park Railway North project, grounded on the development of a new urban park and quality public space connecting formerly isolated deprived districts. In Dublin, the new Docklands area – currently an important location of finance and new media companies – became a flagship of comprehensive renewal plans in central Dublin. Rotterdam's Kop van Zuid district is representative of a whole generation of integrated urban redevelopment projects with an eye on the development of new quality housing in former waterfront and port locations. In Dortmund, the ambitious Phoenix project helped to clean many former steel plants towards the development of new amenities and knowledge locations, integrating them in the urban fabric.

Arts, Culture and Large Events

Apart from the physical-environmental requalification drive, many of the previous initiatives enlisted arts, cultural and consumption elements (e.g. Evans, 2009; Kunzmann, 2004) On the one hand, Cities recognized cultural and creative industries – e.g. media, design, audiovisual – as new growth spearheads (e.g. Helsinki; Dublin); on the other hand, cultural and arts venues have been perceived as amenities in their own right, namely as European cities struggled to increase their position as advanced cultural consumption centres. Moreover, despite the above mentioned limitations, culture was seen as a way to foster social cohesion in cities as well. For example, the Kop van Zuid redevelopment in Rotterdam was planned to combine new high-level housing with museums and galleries; in Dublin, the redevelopment of the Temple Bar district over the 1990s illustrates the close relations between physical development, social cohesion, culture, entertainment and consumption. In Antwerp, the opening of new libraries and landmark museums (e.g. MAS) were part of the redevelopment process of socially deprived quarters.

Another strategy widely deployed by European Cities to achieve sustainable competitiveness was to host large sports and cultural events, such as the European Cultural Capital, among others (Richards et al., 2013). Large events were seen as catalysts or "boosters" of broader physical, cultural and image change in cities; moreover, they became part and parcel of some of the abovementioned district's renovation and competitiveness ambitions. In Manchester, the staging of the Commonwealth Games in 2002 led to major investments in the city, both in the quality of the living environment and infrastructure, but also catalysed a number of initiatives towards new uses for ICTs in society at large. In Dortmund and Antwerp, staging the European Cultural Capital catalysed the development of new concert halls, museums and arts and culture centres. Currently, the City of Budapest considers the Csepel zone as a potential location if Budapest is to host the Olympics in the future.

During the last decades, policies to strengthen the link between culture, events and urban competitiveness had a strong orientation towards the infrastructural and image legacy dimensions. Presently, a new generation of year-long, "umbrella" events in cities are being designed with an eye to economic, social and broader city-wide legacies. Their objectives are shifting towards rather soft elements, such as the creation of new permanent and temporary networks of innovators and the diffusion of new behaviours in society. The city reports provide some interesting examples. One is the case of the 2012 World Design Capital in Helsinki, willing to embed design-thinking in the most diverse fields of urban life, while supporting the well-known design assets and innovation capacities of Helsinki. Other example is "Innovation Dublin", an umbrella event to showcase innovative solutions being developed by the city's organizations and citizens, taking place every year (started in 2009). The event has a very small budget. Its objective is to foster new unexpected combinations and "meetings" between Dublin's innovators, paving the way towards a more sustainable recovery of Dublin and the Irish Economy (see also Carvalho et al., 2012).

Integrated Urban Development and Planning

As suggested above, the deployment of competitiveness-oriented policies by Cities over the last two decades has been mostly linked with their urban and spatial planning responsibilities. Cities often have long established competences in physical planning, culture, education, mobility, environment, social domains, among others, and linked them with strategic objectives of quality of life, area-based regeneration, amenity provision and social cohesion. Also, beyond piecemeal and sector-based initiatives, Cities increasingly tried to pursue integrated approaches, using spatial planning tools to virtuously link physical/environmental, social and economic dimensions in their programmes – again, the redevelopment of deprived districts is the paradigmatic example. A challenge here has been to break local administration silos and departments, as well as to mobilize the right partnerships across local stakeholders (horizontal) and administration levels (vertical).

Most if not all cities analysed in this book recognized the potential that spatial planning competences can bring to strategic urban competitiveness objectives, even if in an indirect fashion. Planning can be a powerful public policy in its own right (Ferrão, 2011). For example, over the last decades, the City of Antwerp tried to improve and sustain the city's competitiveness by influencing the city's spatial structure, through different generations of Spatial Structure Plans. The redevelopment of a number of districts in Dublin over the 1990s and 2000s illustrate the same drive – currently, new planning guidelines have been introduced to consider all parts of planning and economic development together ("core strategies"). In Rotterdam, on-going and future spatial redevelopment projects that contribute most to socio-economic goals and change will get priority, like the project 'South Works' (aiming at empowering people in deprived areas). In Barcelona, the Metropolitan Territorial Plan already covers almost the entire functional metropolitan area and proposes structuring the area as an integrated, multi-nodal urban entity.

New Industries and Advanced Skills

Although many Cities mentioned their intentions to foster new knowledge-intensive activity and diversify economic structures, few of them reported initiatives directly tackling the cornerstone of their economies and thus of sustainable competitiveness: industries and skills. This is not surprising: contrarily to the renovation of old districts and improvements in the living environment, industries and skills are much less amenable to change, at least in the short-medium run. Moreover, Cities seldom have formal competences to (directly) intervene in such fields and a lot depends on other stakeholders such has the National Government, industry parties and universities.

However, there are still interesting initiatives to point out,[1] namely because they still reflect the DNA of the City's core competences (i.e. planning) while combining them with explicit economic-innovation dimensions. Out the initiatives described in this book, the Phoenix project in Dortmund is the most comprehensive one. It aimed at creating high quality living, working and leisure environment, while simultaneously supporting (through the Mayor's office) economic clustering

---

1   See also the new generation of innovation-oriented events in cities (as mentioned above, such as in Helsinki and Dublin).

initiatives, entrepreneurship, new firm creation and skill improvement. Manchester illustrates the integrated use of ICT policies as a way to regenerate the city's urban economy and create new knowledge-intensive industries; moreover, it shows the role of ICT improving the skills of a large fringe of the population, strongly affected by the economic re-structuring of the last decades.

In an indirect (yet intended) fashion, the involvement of the City of Dublin in the regeneration of the Liberties' area also supported new knowledge-intensive activities. The City has been involved since early 2000s in the development of the Digital Hub, a specific location for new media industries and the nurturing of new innovation ecosystems. Moreover, the project has a social and community remit: there is a large programme to train the inhabitants of the surrounding deprived neighbourhood on how to better use ICTs and work on digital media (e.g. designing software), tackling youth employment and skills enhancement (see also van Winden et al., 2012). Similar models are being tested out in Budapest. The City wants to support the reconversion of dilapidated neighbourhoods integrating them with new science and technology zones: by doing this, the City wants to build on Budapest's strong science base and prestigious universities.

The Unavoidable Relevance of the National Level

As said, although cities are unquestionably engines of development and competitiveness for their regions and countries, the competences of Cities/Local Authorities to intervene in such domains (e.g. economic and industrial policy, skills, R&D, labour laws) are overall rather limited. Moreover, policies deployed at higher levels tend to have profound impacts on a city's development and capacity to remain competitive over time (e.g. van den Berg et al., 2007).

The cases of Dublin and Budapest clearly show how national policies and regulations (e.g. incentives for foreign investment, tax cuts) drove the growth of both cities during the last decades, e.g. by attracting substantial investments, but also created latent problems currently jeopardizing the cities' sustainable competitiveness (e.g. urban sprawl). However, at the same time, National incentives in Ireland also contributed to regenerate the city centre and improve its vitality, encouraging market led development in inner city Dublin through rate rebates, capital allowances and income tax relief. In the case of Budapest, the scale challenges are even more complex, as also the city district bureaus have an important role and strong power in the definition of the overall city vision, in many respects.

In Europe, despite the relevance of local planning competences, interventions in environmental, transport and social domains also rely substantially at the National level. The reports of Antwerp, Budapest and Rotterdam refer to the relevance of national policies if the City is to tackle many of such challenges. This is very latent, for example, in the case of Rotterdam, in which on-going infrastructural developments to expand the port and its access are pivotal to the city's long term economic competitiveness, but also have profound environmental impacts.

New Alliances and Learning

In order to tackle some of the aforementioned blockages and limitations, many City Authorities engaged in formal and informal cooperation and alliances with other stakeholders, both vertically (across administrative levels) and horizontally (across urban stakeholders).

This book provides many examples of strategic partnerships between Cities and others administrative bodies, such as Ministries or other Municipalities in larger urban regions. Even if the situation is rarely considered optimal, Barcelona has largely improved cooperation with the surrounding Municipalities – a metropolitan transport authority was set in 1995, and the recent 2010 Metropolitan Plan promises to extend cooperation to other domains. For the design of knowledge-based strategies, Helsinki extended cooperation with other Municipalities in the region, as well as with different Ministries. Currently, many other cities (e.g. Rotterdam and The Hague) are pursuing better policy integration and coordination in different domains.

Simultaneously, many Cities entailed in formal and informal partnerships and alliances with other stakeholders, such as Universities and leading private companies. The examples in this book are manifold. In Dublin, the weak position of Cities/Local Governments vis-à-vis the National Government makes it difficult to coordinate meaningful economic development initiatives at the local level. Hence, the recent economic downturn in Ireland catalysed the formation of the Creative Dublin Alliance, a high-level platform between City representatives, Universities and other relevant local stakeholders (e.g. business sector) to discuss and initiate local economic development projects. Already since the 1990s, cooperation between the City of Helsinki and local universities intensified (resulting in the foundation in 1995 of Culminatum Ltd). Dortmund established a strong Economic Development Agency to guide economic reorientation to new knowledge-based sectors, stimulating networking and cross-clustering initiatives (e.g. "Efficiency", "Kreativ", "Innovationstandort"), in cooperation between business and academia. In Manchester, the implementation of different generations of a digital strategy required the participation of multiple stakeholders, including grassroots IT communities. In Rotterdam, the recent Clean Tech Delta initiative is a cooperative arrangement between authorities, businesses and knowledge institutions.

Over the last decades, the Cities in this book also report honest and considerable improvements in their capacity to organize large and complex projects across thematic domains. Some Cities explicitly report that City management became more strategic and professional over the last decade; the quality of the plans increased, became more integrated and community hearings became a standard and valued procedure. Antwerp reports that this has been one of the legacies of the EU URBAN initiative. Some cities also report how new generations of competitiveness-oriented urban interventions benefited from learning from past projects. This is for example the case with new urban redevelopment and campus development initiatives in Dublin (learning from Temple Bar and the Digital Hub), Dortmund (inspired by the Phoenix project) and Helsinki (design of new user-driven housing projects).

Perceptions on EU Structural Funding

Most cities are positive about the role of European subsidies and policies and about cooperation for exchange of experiences among Cities through EU-networks. Many of the initiatives described in this book have had explicit support from EU Structural Funding. Moreover, EU-driven urban initiatives such as URBAN have promoted an integrated approach to urban regeneration, also leading to changes and inspiration for other local policies (e.g. Barcelona's Act for Urban Neighbourhoods and Areas Requiring Special Attention). In Cities from newer EU member-states (Budapest), EU policy has come together with a new set of urban planning "orthodoxies" and "values" such as the need to foster "attractiveness" and "integration". All in all, EU orientations for urban, competitiveness-oriented investments seem to have made Cities increasingly aware of the need to combine investments in infrastructure and buildings with policies that stimulate entrepreneurship, innovation and citizen engagement.

Although some Cities have become very active and experienced in acquiring EU funds, they rarely led the whole process. More substantial EU contributions are coordinated by national governments (as in Ireland and Hungary) and many EU programmes target regions instead of cities. One exception is the case of Rotterdam, whose City has been given the responsibility as management authority for an Operational Programme ("Kansen voor West").

Summing Up: Policy Ambitions and Frustrations

Over the last two decades, Cities worked considerably to improve their competitiveness. They struggled to keep being attractive places for people and companies, while working on improving social cohesion and the living environment. With different degrees of success – whose explanation is beyond the objectives of this book –, many of the projects described tried to do this through integrated approaches, linking different sectoral fields and trying to tacking problems by linking them with latent opportunities. Many Cities made use of their planning competences and responsibilities to pursue competitiveness and economic development, e.g. integrating strategic socio-economic development ambitions in their spatial strategies. "Quality of life", "image change", "social cohesion" and overall "attractiveness" have been in the forefront of such strategies.

On a more indirect fashion, some Cities have also tried to intervene on the cornerstone of sustainable competitiveness, namely the capacity of city's economy to diversify over time, giving rise to new companies, activities and innovations (Storper and Scott, 2009). Some cities have progressively become more active in these domains, by supporting incubation and entrepreneurship programmes, cross clustering initiatives and other knowledge and industry-related platforms. The lack of formal responsibilities in these domains (vis-à-vis national governments and other stakeholders) has led Cities to entail in partnerships with universities and the private sector.

Despite the progress, the Cities in this book also reported – implicitly and explicitly – a number of limitations and frustrations in their policies and initiatives to improve their cities' sustainable competitiveness.

First, it is often recognized that "boosterism" is not enough. Many competitiveness-oriented initiatives, such as neighbourhood redevelopment or the hosting of large events had too much of a growth dimension – e.g. catalysing public and private investments – paying lip service to other environmental and social dimensions. In reality, despite some (anecdotal) evidence of image change and better infrastructural conditions, many Cities report that some key pressing problems in their Cities remain to be solved, and some of them increased over the decades, such as congestion, urban sprawl, selective migration, unemployment and social cohesion issues. On the one hand, even when the socio-economic conditions have improved at the district level, their diffusion towards the city level has been problematic. On the other hand, the proposed transformations had been often incremental, unfit to promote larger, more radical urban transformations and behavioural change on the social and environmental domains (see also McCormick et al., 2013).

Second, Cities report that it has been difficult to deal with industrial change, innovation and economic diversification: the cornerstone of competitiveness. Some Cities in this book have been doing substantial efforts, some of them with (at least some) success. However, Cities are still largely looking for the most effective ways to support such transformations, complementing actions of other stakeholders at the city, regional and national level. Examples of new ways of doing so have been through the support of new "knowledge locations" and the use of temporary events to support clustering and innovation. However, there is still considerable room for improvement and learning about the success of these and other associated initiatives.

Third, Cities report many frustrations associated with governance and the blockages imposed by complex administrative structures. Most Cities recognize that sustainable competitiveness challenges in cities cannot be tackled by them alone. Beyond industrial policy and innovation issues, mobility, transport and social integration issues rely on higher policy layers. In some cases, Cities believe that the lack of local autonomy and weak horizontal and vertical linkages between a multitude of boards and agencies undermine the effectiveness of service delivery, at least in a streamlined and cost-effective manner. Moreover, the issues of inter-municipal competition are still often mentioned as raising considerable challenges to implement meaningful competitiveness-oriented policies at the relevant spatial level.

Challenges Ahead

Which challenges lie ahead and what can Cities do to improve their economies over time? And how can EU cohesion policy better support the potential of cities in this fundamental effort? This is a critical issue, as the success of European cities in this respect will strongly influence the achievement of other, higher-level European objectives (economic, environmental, social and political). Indeed, many of the urban challenges pointed in this book are largely convergent with the EU challenges for the years to come. As described, they are giving rise to a new generation of policies and initiatives, combining economic, social and environmental objectives. Examples and on-going City actions are in the fields of:

- *Climate and energy.* Over the last decade, many cities started to pay more attention to the issues of climate and energy (see also Bulkeley et al., 2011). Key objectives are to mitigate the impact of climate change, develop and diffuse low carbon solutions and, if possible, monetize and export associated technologies. Some proposals and initiatives emerging in cities go beyond the air quality concerns of the 1990s and propose more encompassing transformations. In this vein, most cities analysed in this book are currently developing different sorts of energy efficiency action plans, new energy pilots and "green deals". Rotterdam's Stadshavens and the Climate Delta initiative are illustrative of the city's leading ambitions in this respect: to steer large climate-related social transformations while developing portfolios of exportable solutions.

- *Ecosystem formation* and user involvement in innovation. European sluggish growth and lower innovation rates vis-à-vis the United States (EC, 2013) makes the success of cities in this respect a central one for Europe. Hence, fostering knowledge exchange and new innovation networks has become a common objective of many Cities. Beyond traditional cluster initiatives and investments in general science and technology parks, Cities are experimenting new types of policies, complementing the actions of other government layers. For example, in this book, the City of Dublin and the Creative Dublin Alliance are developing new generation cluster policies for "cleantech" industries (Green Way) and doing a substantial effort in nurturing new networks of innovators through events and festivals (Innovation Dublin). Helsinki has been for some years now in the forefront when it comes to develop new ways of involving citizens and users in innovation platforms; more recently, leading initiatives focus on embedding design thinking in many realms of city life.

- *Skills and employment.* Skills enhancement, entrepreneurship promotion and the fight of youth unemployment are among the most acute European challenges, at the core of many cities' sustainable competitiveness. Despite the successful economic reconversion of some post-industrial cities over the last two decades, unemployment, lack of skills and dual labour markets are still pressing issues, and the situation is likely to persist even in contexts of economic recovery. They largely jeopardize a city's social cohesion over time. For example, despite recent growth and change, the economic reconversion in Dortmund still left a very high unemployment toll, reason why the City is currently working actively in this domain. In Manchester, among other initiatives, ICT policies have been playing an important role towards the reintegration of many inhabitants in the labour force, but a lot has still to be done.

- *Urban sprawl and mobility.* The growth of many cities over the last decades came closely associated with urban sprawl, and most of the city reports in this book put this issue at the core of sustainable competitiveness, namely for reasons of economic efficiency, social justice and environmental quality. Urban Sprawl is not an "ignored challenge" (EC, 2006) anymore. One new, important type of policies in this respect has to do with mobility management, namely demand-side actions in cities to reduce mobility while improving a city's internal accessibility and quality of life. Over the last years those become key challenges for some of the more sprawled metropolises (e.g. Barcelona, Budapest). The Territorial Metropolitan Plan of Barcelona is promising as an important platform to tackle this issue, but also smaller experiments of joint public-private planning of mobility issues, car-pooling, among others currently going on in many cities.

- *Social inclusion and integration.* Many cities in this book report that issues of social inclusion and integration of minorities have moved to the forefront of their policy agendas over the last decade. Weak integration of minorities and migrants is closely linked with safety issues and political tensions, but also means untapped economic and youth potential; both concerns are especially visible in times of general economic downturn in Europe. Rotterdam, Antwerp and Budapest point them as key challenges for the present and the future, calling for new integrated approaches that can effectively connect problems with latent opportunities in cities.

- *Government transparency, innovation and service provision.* Societal changes have been putting pressure on the emergence and development of new government models, more efficient and transparent, responding to enhanced concepts of democracy (e.g. from representative to participative democracy). Antwerp and Helsinki place citizen participation very high in the overall policy agenda, but it is an important trend in many places. Moreover, some cities have been championing new interaction modes with the citizen, while developing innovations out of it. One example is the release of data about urban services and provisions, "open data". In Helsinki, the City links this trend with their agendas of use involvement in innovation and design thinking, towards (even) higher transparency and accountability standards. In Dublin, and despite the severe economic crisis, the City has made a large effort in opening city data, in cooperation with universities and the private sector, with an eye to the innovation payoffs.

In Manchester, the open data movement is entering the local government sphere catalysed by grassroots IT communities in the city.

The answers and solutions to the above challenges will largely influence European cities' sustainable competitiveness over the next decade, as well as the one of Europe as a whole. The examples and cases reported in this book do suggest that the sustainable competitiveness of European cities tend to require more integrated approaches, in which social and environmental dimensions are paid more than just lip service. Today as in the past, many of the challenges of European cities can only be tackled from an integrative perspective, namely as the convergence and interconnections between the economy, society and the environment are clearer than ever. If this is true, it has implications on the increased need to break silos, share power and responsibilities in projects and policies – across government levels and stakeholders – as some of the abovementioned initiatives already illustrate.

Naturally, this is not to say that many of the (urban and European) challenges can be tackled exclusively at the city level, nor does it suggest that Cities and Local Governments can tackle those issues alone, or in the most effective and efficient way. First, the scale of the city per se is not always appropriate to tackle – at least exclusively – some important innovation-competitiveness issues. For example, the "proximity" needed for innovation in many industries in Europe – e.g. social, cultural and institutional (Boschma, 2005) – is often more consistently found at the level of larger regions, countries (Isaksen, 2010), cross-border regions (e.g. Lundquist and Trippl, 2009) or networks (e.g. Vale and Carvalho, 2012). Moreover, as seen, other critical sustainable competitiveness issues such as urban sprawl and mobility require regional and supra-regional approaches. Second, as analysed above, manifold policies and regulations at the European and National level have a strong impact on urban development, limiting the degrees of freedom of Cities to intervene in many critical domains of their sustainable competitiveness. Third, it is nowadays clear that many of the current European challenges are of a broader and systemic nature (e.g. the macroeconomic design of the single currency, the financial meltdown, political-cultural challenges). This has been imposing changes and uncertainty in the way national governments conduct economic policy and the fundamentals of their approach to support local growth (e.g. focus on endogenous growth *versus* place-neutral, supply-side structural reforms), having profound impacts in local development perspectives (Hildreth and Bailey, 2013).

Cities and Broader Societal Change

From a broader European perspective, it is important to recognize that many of the sustainable competitiveness challenges ahead (e.g. energy and environment, involvement of users, systemic innovation, mobility, integration, release of data, etc) require broader societal transformations and generalized behavioural change.

It is not a question of simply throwing money in, but of finding fertile ground for experimentation of new solutions and their diffusion in society. And in this case, there are strong arguments to consider cities as key places and agents in the process, beyond the rhetoric that "cities concentrate the problems and the opportunities".

First, larger transformations start and grow with experimentation (Kemp et al., 1998), and cities are places where such experimentation is feasible in the first place. The city and neighbourhood scale are usually appropriate to test and early implement new solutions, making it feasible to pursue integration between fields and domains. Moreover, the city scale is also adequate to monitor and evaluate the results and impacts of an intervention (e.g. Camagni et al., 1998). Importantly, it is out of such experiments and projects that new behaviour, culture and values start to be shaped and transformed (e.g. use of a new energy or mobility solution).

Second, cities often concentrate a number of key stakeholders to test new solutions and policies, such as leading firms, universities, associations, citizens, among others. Cities are places where it is easier to establish new networks, face-to-face contact and new tailor-made cooperative arrangements between actors in proximity (Storper and Venables, 2004). In this vein, cities often constitute favourable environments to test and explore new governance and planning models, which are essential to steer larger transformations (McCormick et al., 2013).

Third, cities provide differentiated contexts (e.g. institutional, cultural and social conditions, infrastructure) to adapt and fine-tune new solutions (Hodson and Marvin, 2010). Despite sharing common challenges, the socio-economic and political contexts of cities like Helsinki, Dublin or Budapest are very different. If such contexts make policy imitation very difficult and potentially ineffective, it also contributes to create a richer portfolio of solutions that can be more easily and effectively replicated in similar contexts. The early application of certain solution or initiative in cities also creates a number of images and imaginations, in which the solution (e.g. a new energy source, a new mobility solution, a new way of involving users in innovation) becomes intertwined with the image of the city itself.

Fourth, cities and local communities are still the scales that matter the most for people in general (Friedmann, 2011), and having their support is pivotal to tackle many of the abovementioned challenges. People live in concrete places; they test new solutions and adopt new behaviours in those places. It is also at that scale that users feel motivated to contribute to the development of new societal solutions, as they are closer to the "utility functions" of citizens rather than to "distant" actions at the national or European level.

Fifth, cities and Local Governments are political entities with lobbying power and influence at higher decision making echelons. Some mayors and elected representatives can exert considerable influence at a national and international scale, nudging new regulations and policy supports. Importantly, cities have key planning instruments and competences that can influence other key domains in a city's sustainable competitiveness (land use, accessibility, environmental and social domains). As seem in this book, Cities try to mobilize their power in this respect to the full.

From the previous and from the analyses in this book, it results clear that cities should be taken seriously in any European level policy targeting sustainable competitiveness – which is the naturally the case of the EU Cohesion policy. First, cities can "show the way" in many respects, by pioneering and experimenting new societal solutions for pressing societal problems. This is the case also concerning new governance solutions, which will tend to emerge first on cities. Second, cities are also poles of transnational connectivity, which should be also nurtured by EU level policies – many of the new solutions found in cities are co-developed in partnership with actors that cut across European regions and even outside Europe. Third, as new solutions are experimented and developed in cities, EU level policies should incentivize cities to keep developing knowledge on the evolution and success of new policies and initiatives, fostering the "contagion" to other spatial scales. Fourth, and even if the cities analysed in this book are all important metropolitan cities in the European urban systems, the challenges their face are not exactly the same, nor are their contexts and assets (demographics, environmental challenges, economic-industrial structures). This is a plea towards a more place-based approach to EU Cohesion policy as currently advocated in many policy and academic circles (Barca et al., 2012). Ideally, policy interventions should combine a mix of top-down (after all, there are important regularities among cities of similar types) and bottom-up elements (recognising different endogenous potentials of the cities and the need for local knowledge to better tailor the policies). Naturally, Cities and Local Governments have an increasingly essential role to play in this respect.

References

Barca, F., McCann, P., and Rodríguez-Pose, A. (2012). The case for regional development intervention: Place-based versus place-neutral approaches. *Journal of Regional Science*, 52(1), 134-152.

Boschma, R. (2005). Proximity and innovation: A critical assessment. *Regional Studies*, 39(1), 61-74.

Bulkeley, H., Castán Broto, V., Hodson, M., and Marvin, S. (2011). *Cities and low carbon transitions*. Abingdon and New York: Routledge.

Camagni, R., Capello, R., and Nijkamp, P. (1998). Towards sustainable city policy: An economy-environment technology nexus. *Ecological Economics*, 24(1), 103-118.

Carvalho, L., Berg, L. van den, and Tuijl, E. van (2012). *A world of events – how can cities anchor the advantage?* Erasmus University Rotterdam: Euricur.

EC-European Commission. (2006). *Urban sprawl in Europe: The ignored challenge*. Brussels: DG Joint Research Centre and European Environment Energy.

EU-European Union. (2013). *Innovation union scoreboard 2013*. Brussels: DG Enterprise and Industry.

Evans, G. (2009). From cultural quarters to creative clusters – creative spaces in the new city economy. In M. Legner (Ed.), *The sustainability and development of cultural quarters: International perspectives*. Stockholm: Institute of Urban History.

Ferrão, J. (2011). *O ordenamento do território como política pública*. Lisbon: Fundação Calouste Gulbenkian.

Friedmann, J. (2011). *Insurgencies: Essays in planning theory*. Abingdon: Routledge.

Hildreth, P., and Bailey, D. (2013). The economics behind the move to 'localism' in England. *Cambridge Journal of Regions, Economy and Society* [online first].

Hodson, M., and Marvin, S. (2010). Can cities shape socio-technical transitions and how would we know if they were? *Research Policy*, 39(4), 477-485.

Isaksen, A. (2009). Innovation dynamics of global competitive regional clusters: The case of the Norwegian centres of expertise. *Regional Studies*, 43(9), 1155-1166.

Kemp, R., Schot, J., and Hoogma, R. (1998). Regime shifts to sustainability through processes of niche formation: The approach of strategic niche management. *Technology Analysis and Strategic Management*, 10(2), 175-198.

Kunzmann, K. R. (2004). Culture, creativity and spatial planning. *Town Planning Review*, 75(4), 383-404.

Lundquist, K., and Trippl, M. (2009). Towards cross-border innovation spaces. A theoretical analysis and empirical comparison of the öresund region and the centrope area. *SRE – Discussion Papers, Institut für Regional und Umweltwirtschaft*, WU Vienna University of Economics and Business, Vienna.

McCormick, K., Anderberg, S., Coenen, L., and Neij, L. (2013). Advancing sustainable urban transformation. *Journal of Cleaner Production*, online first.

Porter, L., and Barber, A. (2007). Planning the cultural quarter in Birmingham's eastside. *European Planning Studies*, 15(10), 1327-1348.

Richards, G., De Brito, M., and Wilks, L. (2013). *Exploring the social impacts of events*. Abingdon: Routledge.

Storper, M., and Scott, A. J. (2009). Rethinking human capital, creativity and urban growth. *Journal of Economic Geography*, 9(2), 147-167.

Storper, M., and Venables, A. J. (2004). Buzz: Face-to-face contact and the urban economy. *Journal of Economic Geography*, 4(4), 351-370.

Vale, M., and Carvalho, L. (2012). Knowledge networks and processes of anchoring in Portuguese biotechnology. *Regional Studies*. DOI:10.1080/003 43404.2011.644237

Winden, W. van, Carvalho, L., Tuijl, E. van, Haaren, J. van, and Berg, L. van den (2012). *Creating knowledge locations in cities: Innovation and integration challenges*. Abingdon: Routledge.

Index